Across the Lines:
Travel, Language, Translation

Across the Lines
Travel, Language, Translation

Michael Cronin

CORK UNIVERSITY PRESS

First published in 2000 by
Cork University Press
University College
Cork
Ireland

British Library Cataloguing in Publication Data
A CIP catalogue record for this book is available from
the British Library

ISBN   1 85918 182 1   hardcover
       1 85918 183 X   paperback

Typeset by Tower Books, Ballincollig, Co. Cork
Printed by MPG Books Ltd, Cornwall

Dedicated to the Memory of
Timothy and Margaret Cronin

Contents

Acknowledgements   ix

Introduction: Floating Territories   1

1. THE RAMBLING HOUSE OF LANGUAGE   9
   Accent, translatability and lexical exoticism   11
   Fractal travel, polyidentity and sublanguages   16
   Touring cultures and rambling houses   21
   Minority languages, fragmented origins, names   26
   Home, purism and hospitality   32

2. THE CHANGELING   39
   Fantasy, paradox, infantilisation   39
   Intertextuality, informants and obstacles   50
   Triangulation, desire, transcendence   59
   Travel labour   65

3. MAKING SENSE   68
   Children and barbarians   68
   Passion, interpreters, autonomy   70
   Touch, taste, music, perfume   76
   The world as picture   81
   Guide books and complicated doubleness   85
   Critical universalism   89
   A prodigal art   92
   Resistance, power   94

4. BABEL EXPRESS   98
    The third world, origins, infidelities   99
    Drive, analog modes and forgery   101
    Trade, speed limits and machine translation   109
    Fast castes, kinetic resistance and the Grand Tour   114
    Risk and the nomadic dynamic   121

5. FINAL FRONTIERS   127
    Octospiders, Babel fish and the Holy Spirit   127
    Bodies, territoriality, metaphor   133
    Flâneur, flâneuse and taking a hint   141
    Reciprocity, the third culture and cybertravel   145

Notes and references   158
Bibliography   181
Index   191

ACKNOWLEDGEMENTS

In academic work in the humanities, signatures may be conspicuously individual but support is almost invariably collective. Mindful of this, I am deeply grateful to Professor Michael Townson and to all my colleagues in the School of Applied Language and Intercultural Studies at Dublin City University who allowed me to devote time and attention to researching and writing the present work. Their constant encouragement and genuine interest in the subject of my research made the hours in the study and library seem less solitary, illumined by their attentive curiosity. The Philosophy Reading Group organised by the DCU/St Patrick's College Drumcondra Joint Faculty of Humanities has been a delightful experience of stimulating, non-aggressive intellectual enquiry, and readings and comments by various members of the group have greatly helped me in exploring a number of issues addressed in the present study. In this context, I must particularly acknowledge enlightening discussions with David Denby, Barbara O'Connor, Joe Dunne, Martin Sauter, Tony Coulson, Máirín Nic Eoin and Patrick Burke. The undergraduate students in Applied Languages, International Marketing and Languages and Applied Computational Linguistics who have taken my special subject option in Travel Literature have taught me much about the experience of languages and cultures as they embark on their own journeys through literature and life.

Outside the academy, my fellow editors in *Graph* magazine, Peter Sirr, Evelyn Conlon and Barra Ó Séaghdha, have been a constant source of reference, constructive criticism and companionship. A special debt is owed to Barra Ó Séaghdha for his close and exacting reading of the chapters of the book in manuscript form. Stephanie McBride and Michael Cunningham are to be thanked for their own, wide-ranging intellectual journeying that I have found so stimulating down through the years. Sara Wilbourne of Cork University Press has been matchless in her understanding and support for the proposal that eventually resulted in the present work and her commitment and belief are deeply appreciated.

Juliette Péchenart and Máirtín Cronin are the best company one could possibly wish for on the long day's journey into writing. Their love, patience and robust good humour have sustained me in the brightness of day and in the midnight hour. For this, I am endlessly grateful.

Sections of Chapter 4 and Chapter 5 appeared in earlier versions in 'Shoring up the Fragments of the Translator's Discourse: Complexity, Incompleteness and Integration', *META*, vol. 40, no. 3, September 1995, pp. 359–66, and 'The Cracked Looking Glass of Servants: Translation and Minority Languages in a Global Age', *The Translator*, vol. 4, no. 2, 1998, pp. 145–62. All translations in *Across the Lines*, unless otherwise stated, are my own.

Michael Cronin
Dublin, November 1999

Introduction

Floating Territories

For Count Dracula, travel had its own terrors. His purpose in bringing Jonathan Harker to his castle in the Carpathians was not simply to sign documents relating to the estate Dracula had bought in London, but also to perfect his English. The count tells Harker that in Transylvania he is nobleman and master. However, in London he would be a nobody because:

> a stranger in a strange land, he is no one; men know him not – and to know not is not to care for. I am content if I am like the rest, so that no man stops if he sees me, or pause in his speaking if he hears my words, to say, 'Ha, ha! a stranger!'[1]

Harker who has gone to Transylvania as solicitor finds himself cast in the role of TEFL teacher, instructed to correct the smallest errors in the count's English and remove all trace of foreignness from his intonation. Dracula sees language difference as an unescapable consequence of travel and full translation into the language of the other ('I am content if I am like the rest') as the journey's end.

The count's fear of conspicuous otherness is the drama of travel in a multilingual world. Modernity is characterised by the exponential growth in travel and movement of people around the globe. Tourism is fast becoming the world's most important item of trade. The phenomenon of globalisation has become the focus of intense interest as commentators assess the impact of the increasingly rapid circulation of goods, signs and people on the self-perception, and the social, economic and cultural practices of human beings. Theories of travel have become increasingly popular in contemporary appraisals of the evolution of modernity. However, what Dracula reminds us of is what theorists often forget. All this movement is taking place between speaking subjects, on a planet that is currently home to approximately 6,500 languages. Critical writing on travel and tourism has, however, largely neglected this fundamental aspect of travelling – the relationship of the traveller to language. The neglect is all the more telling in that one of the most commonplace experiences of the traveller is the sudden humiliation of language loss as things go disastrously wrong and familiar words reveal themselves to be worse than useless. *Across the Lines* studies the role of language in the construction of identity of both the traveller and the other in a cross-section of late twentieth-century travel accounts. Indifference to the question of language in many of the key texts on writing and travel that have been published over the last two decades has led to a serious misrepresentation of both the experience of travel and the construction of narrative accounts of these experiences. In particular, the myth of language transparency, the relationship of language and power and the question of the possibility of representation on the basis of universals are highlighted as part of the investigation into the role of language in travel. Travel in a world of languages is fraught with difficulty. There are the innumerable pitfalls of translation: the potential for mistranslation; the loss of meaning; the dangers of approximation; the problematic political economy of translation in the Eurocentric appropriation of other peoples and places through ex-colonial languages; the misleading myth of transparent non-refractory translation. The relationship between travel and language is explored in the present work in the context of a nomadic theory of translation. The translating agent like the traveller straddles the borderline between the cultures. A nomadic theory of translation proposes the translator-nomad as an emblematic figure of (post)modernity by demonstrating what translation can tell us about nomadism and what nomadism can tell us about translation and how both impinge on contemporary concerns with identity.

The framework for the analysis of language in travel is Roman Jakobson's description of three different kinds of translation. *Intralingual translation* or translation within a language is the interpretation of verbal signs by means of other signs belonging to the same language. *Interlingual translation* or translation between languages is the interpretation of verbal signs by means of verbal signs from another language. Lastly, *intersemiotic translation* or translation into or from something other than language is the interpretation of verbal signs by means of signs belonging to non-verbal sign systems.[2] Chapter 1 begins by examining intralingual translation in travel, the language problems encountered by travel writers who travel within their own language. The apparent liberation from the problems of translation is illusory as the accounts soon reveal the intractable presence of language difference as the Anglophone travellers make their way through the English-speaking world. Different accents, lexical variations, dissimilar patterns of language usage and the multiple sublanguages of English reveal the daunting complexity of a language whose homogeneity the travellers can no longer take for granted. The detailed encounter with language difference points to the bankruptcy of the widespread rhetoric of exhaustion on the subject of travel. Intralingual travel accounts highlight not the limited repetitiveness of the travel experience but the endless series of finer discriminations that become apparent as the travellers chart the social, regional and national metamorphoses of the mother tongue. The language of home becomes stranger and more labyrinthine in the mouths and minds of others who ostensibly speak the same language. The language of origin becomes fragmented and plural and the potential for creative journeying in language gradually reveals itself to be inexhaustible.

Interlingual translation is what is most often thought of as translation in travel, in which travellers find themselves in a foreign country and in a foreign language and where they have some knowledge, however limited, of the foreign language. Although interlingual translation is a common feature of many travel texts, the fact of translation is often disguised by writers and critics to create the illusion of linguistic transparency. Chapter 2 examines interlingual translation in travel accounts and investigates the cultural, political and social motives for the translator's invisibility in certain travel contexts. Interlingual travel writing is examined in the light of the human desire to understand the world through language and the limits of human ability to learn, speak and understand languages. Speaking the language of others is enormously enriching but it can also be deeply humiliating. The necessary obstacles to language competence and the frequently troubled nature of the translation exchange in foreign-language travelling are analysed with a view to showing the hidden epistemic benefits of interlingual travelling. The uses of lexical exoticism and the featuring of translation as intertextual presence (phrase-books/dictionaries/tourist literature) in travel accounts are also explored. If travel, translation and language use are predicated on relationship and reciprocity, the question of gender in travel/translation contexts is discussed in the framework of a new understanding of desire in travel.

As people travel to more and more countries, they know proportionately fewer and fewer languages. Chapter 3 comments upon situations where the traveller has no knowledge whatsoever of the foreign language. The situation may be experienced as profoundly disabling – the traveller a mute presence in a world of foreign signs that is disorienting and threatening. Alternatively, the traveller may actively seek exile from language as a means of communicative rebirth. The conventional interpretive grid of language is abandoned for other ways of knowing, channelled through taste, touch, vision, smell and (non-verbal) sound. The primacy of the visual, often seen as a dominant feature of globalisation, is examined in its implications for intersemiotic travel experience and for the spread of one global language. Of course, in the absence of a common language, travellers can get other people like interpreters to do the translating and speaking for them. The indigenous status of the interpreter/informant would seem to confer a legitimacy on their narrative which adds to the verisimilitude of the travel account, but how representative their views are, what is their exact social position within their own communities, the extent to which their own familiarity with foreign languages sets them apart from the people whose world view they are seen to articulate are, of course, questions that are not often explicitly addressed in travel narratives. The doubleness and potential duplicity of the interpreter is examined both in relation to imperial suspicions of the native interpreter and the historical development of the guide book as a strategy to create a monolingual space for the travellers and remove their dependency on foreign guides/interpreters. In the traveller/interpreter relationship, issues of power constantly inform the relationship as do the relative prestige of languages spoken by travellers. Questions of resistance, the position of minority-language travellers and the possibility of critical universalism in travel encounters with others are addressed in the context of exoticism and the abusive shorthand of stereotype.

The classification of travel accounts into three different translation categories facilitates analysis but is, of course, at another level, an oversimplification. The experience of translation in travelling, and accounts of travelling, will often range from the intralingual to the interlingual to the intersemiotic. Travellers may meet fellow speakers of their language from a different country (intralingual), be able to communicate some ideas in the foreign language (interlingual) but, at other moments, be completely stymied and have to resort to gestures (intersemiotic). Jakobson's tripartite division does not represent an immutable delineation of travel experience but is a useful means of interpreting the otherwise confusing continuum of the language phenomenon in travel.

Translators have for centuries been on the move but what is the relationship between their wanderings and the profession they practise? In other words, if travellers are shown to be translators what conclusions are we to draw if translators are shown to be travellers? Chapters 4 and 5 explore the consequences for the representation of translation of seeing it as a nomadic practice and translators as key figures in a nomadic conception of late modernity. Chapter 4 situates the translator in a 'third world', an in-between space between languages and cultures that both enriches the language and culture of the translator's origin and makes any notion of (pure) origin and (unconditional) fidelity endlessly problematic. The translator ceaselessly moving between languages and cultures is reflected at another level in translation studies, a discipline that travels continuously between disciplines. The nomadic character of translation studies is its strength in terms of disciplinary openness but it is also a source of marginalisation, as evidenced in the recent work of James Clifford who managed to completely ignore the entire body of scholarly work on translation in a work allegedly discussing the question of translation and travel.[3] A feature of contemporary travel has been space–time compression. The twentieth century has seen people take less and less time to go further and further. The consequences of this increased mobility and compression for the translator are considered in the context of globalisation, the rise of English as a world language and the expanded use of machine translation. Modernity is not only characterised by speed, it is also synonymous with the desire to minimise risk as the infrastructure of modernity becomes more and more complex. Speaking foreign languages or reliance on translation is a risky business, so how are language difference and translation dealt with in a travel industry that seeks to minimise risk and the unforeseen for the traveller while promising the unexpected? Against more dystopian views of language homogeneity, the chapter points to the continued importance of local experience and languages for much of humanity and of the significance of translation centres and language departments as institutions that dwell-in-travelling and travel-in-dwelling, thus providing valuable sources of nomadic renewal for sedentary cultures. The renewal is based on a fundamentally dynamic conception of the translator as a subject who constantly approaches and moves away from the Other, who experiences neither absolute proximity nor absolute distance.

Chapter 4 focuses on the immediate present and near future, but Chapter 5 travels into a more distant future. If the historical novel is the account of travel into the past, then science fiction provides the travel narratives from the future. The novels of Samuel Delaney, Arthur C. Clarke and Douglas Adams provide insights into the textual representation of translators and translation in other worlds. A recurrent theme is the translator as hybrid, revered and feared, a principle of weakness and an agent of salvation. Machines are inevitable rivals to the human translators but their intervention does not always answer technocratic hopes, and universal equivalence does not equate with pan-galactic harmony. The pentecostal gift of tongues is used in this context as an example of an event that while appearing to facilitate communication with the Other may in fact lead simply to the expansion of the self and the obliteration of difference. Science fiction has famously anticipated a number of developments in computing so it is no surprise that the language of the Internet is saturated with the rhetoric of travel. Though the Web and the Internet have been primarily discussed by translators as reference tools or sources of work (translating web pages), cyberspace raises a number of interesting issues about translation and virtual travel or cybertravel. Translators may be recast as semi-autonomous software agents on the Web that will automatically collate and translate information, or, more prosaically, the new worldwide electronically mediated environment with networks everywhere will provide new settings for our translator-nomads, no longer constrained by physical geographical location. However, constraints of a different kind, political, economic, financial, are still likely to prevail and the argument is made for the continued

importance of the translator as an embodied subject, if only to prevent translators from being silenced once more, this time by the hierarchs of
relativism. This embodied subject is often a *flâneuse* rather than a *flâneur*,
occupies a floating territory between languages, cultures and disciplines,
and in pedagogic terms is more likely to take a hint than obey an order. To
view translators as nomadic subjects is to re-examine territorially based
national histories of translation and argue for a more diasporic perspective
on translation activity as translators working outside their native land are
integrated into translation accounts.

Adolf Hitler once remarked to Ariel Critall that he had only four words in a
foreign language – 'Vous êtes mon prisonnier.'[4] This idle boast is eloquent in
its poverty of enquiry. Babel is our benefactor in the richness of cultural
variety that is vouchsafed to us by the plurality of language. To minimise this
dimension to travel experience as has so often been done in critical writing
on travel is to do a grave disservice to the complexity of cultural experience
within and between languages. More importantly and perhaps more urgently,
on a planet that is suffering a constant erosion of its language base, there is
an important ethical imperative in considering how travelling practices might
highlight and enhance language awareness rather than systematically treat
language difference as an unacceptable risk to the increasingly monoglossic
bubble of global tourism. Translators as intercultural mediators have for
centuries experienced the creative tension between travel, language and
translation in the elaboration of culture and identity. Translators both
contribute to and will be affected by present and future forms of nomadism as
they impact on human cultures and languages. Their assistance, therefore, in
understanding what happens when we cross the lines of language and
culture on a multilingual planet is and will be invaluable.

The present study is part of a much wider enquiry that would see the
themes addressed in this book extended to many other cultures and
languages. Though historical issues are touched on, much more research is
needed to assess the specific impact of language on the travelling theories
and touring cultures of the past. Famine, war, genocide and exploitation
have meant the forced movement of millions of asylum seekers and political
and economic refugees who have found themselves coerced by circumstances into language shift and cultural displacement. The experience of
language and cultural contact in these conditions is obviously different from
the voluntary departure of the travel writer and the professional freedom of
the translator, and demands its own separate analysis.[5] There is nonetheless
for all human beings in late modernity the inescapable fact of language
diversity as, even within single languages, heteroglossic pressures make
travel a verbal event. In Barbara Wilson's novel, *Gaudí Afternoon*, the heroine
Cassandra Reilly emerges as the archetypal translator-nomad. She was
raised in Kalamazoo, Michigan, left when she was sixteen and holds an Irish

passport. She makes 'a sort of living as a translator', mainly of Latin American novels in Spanish.[6] Cassandra declares bluntly, 'I don't live anywhere' and that 'often as not I'm travelling'. When she is not translating, Cassandra works as a private detective, work that takes her to Gaudí's city, Barcelona. Like Jonathan Harker in the polyglot Carpathians, Cassandra Reilly finds that Barcelona is a liminal zone of cultural shift and polylingual nuance. She feels on familiar territory. It is the critical unfamiliarity of this territory we now wish to explore.

Chapter One

THE RAMBLING HOUSE OF LANGUAGE

John Gibbons bemoans his fate. In the late 1920s, the literary editor of the *Daily Express*, Nigel Pound, suggests to the author of a highly successful *Tramping to Lourdes* that he go to Ireland, but Gibbons is less than enthused:

> Why on earth for a really fair first chance could they not have made it somewhere foreign where something happens, instead of Ireland of all places, a sort of second-rate suburb of England![1]

A trawl through the dreariness of a Dublin weekday morning and an afternoon stroll around the capital city further confirm his anxious scepticism. The problem with Dublin is that it is too much like England and he confesses, 'Green pillar-boxes, Gaelic notices, even pipers in the Irish kilt, they all failed to give me that foreign feeling. I was disappointed.'[2] It is, indeed, only when he meets a lawyer who is a practising Catholic and who tells Gibbons about a place of pilgrimage, Lough Derg, that the Englishman gets his first 'glimpse into the island as a foreign country'.[3] Catholic piety is an obvious marker of difference for Gibbons, but as 'the foreign country feeling grows' language emerges as another faultline of distinctness:

> You are not of course in the Gaeltacht, where they really speak Gaelic; but even the English does not mean quite the same as it does at home. The chemist's shop somehow becomes a 'Medical Hall', and a 'Victualler' means a butcher. On the other hand, a public-house is generally a 'grocery' and it was with a little thrill of pleasure that I heard of a 'Grocer's Curate' as the most delightful of euphemisms for a bartender.[4]

Gibbon's anxieties are those of all travellers and travel writers who must signal a moment of departure from the familiar and the routine. The British sociologist John Urry sees the notion of departure as a defining moment of tourist practice where the mundane and the everyday are left behind for the unfamiliar.[5] Travelling to another country with a different language makes exoticism readily identifiable. Travel, in that case, appears to have an

9

obvious ally in translation. The departure is real because the linguistic arrival
is different. The transactions of translation must be immediately entered into
because the mother tongue is no longer the language of the surrounding
community but the idiolect of an isolated and fretful foreign-passport holder.
What of the traveller who travels within the same language? Does the fact of
departure have to be all the more emphatically established because there is
not the ready alibi of language difference? Do problems of translation exist,
and if so, are they core concerns or merely the stuff of anecdote? Does travel
in the same language liberate the writer from the approximations of translation? This is the view held by the American travel writer, Paul Theroux. In
The Kingdom by the Sea, Theroux presents his journey around the coast of
Britain and Northern Ireland as a welcome relief from the rigours of
language contact:

> Writing about a country in its own language was a great advantage,
> because in other places one was always interpreting and simplifying.
> Translation created a muffled obliqueness – one was always seeing the
> country sideways. But language grew out of the landscape – English out of
> England, and it seemed logical that the country could only be accurately
> portrayed in its own language.[6]

Theroux's geological vision of language as an inevitable outcrop of topo-
graphical difference can be categorised less exotically as thoroughgoing
linguistic relativism. The notion of language as both expressing and determining the quintessential genius of a people became, through the writings of
Herder and others, a central tenet of nineteenth-century nationalism. From
this perspective, translation is always something of a fallen condition, a poor
approximation. Only full possession of language guarantees that unmediated
communion with a culture and a people that is denied by the 'muffled
obliqueness' of translation. Hence, an English traveller in the United States
or an American traveller in England or an English traveller in English-speaking
Ireland or a French writer tramping through France would seem to have an
incomparable advantage over other travellers who do not have the language
of the country as their native tongue. They do not have to pick their way
through the codes of language transfer. Language can recede into the background (become 'landscape') while the travellers hold up a mirror to the
society through which they travel.

The difficulty, however, is in sustaining the fiction of one language.
Monoglossia fissures as soon as the travellers give their account of the
monoglossic elsewhere. If anything, indeed, translation is more explicitly
emphasised in intralingual travelling than in interlingual travelling. It is as if
intralingual accounts ward off the threat of (language) sameness through the
highlighting of (language) difference while interlingual accounts counter the
menace of irreducible (language) difference through the reiteration of

sameness (minimising or making invisible the transaction costs of translation). The obstacles to a unitary conception of language are many and a number are mentioned by Jacqueline Amati Mehler, Simona Argentieri and Jorge Canestri in their attempt to define a field of investigation for psychoanalysis in the area of language learning:

> En élargissant . . . le champ de notre pensée, en admettant qu'il soit possible de trouver un individu qui ne parle vraiment que sa langue maternelle, 'naturelle', à l'abri d'interférences de tout autre idiome, jargon ou dialecte, il nous faut nous demander si, à l'intérieur d'une même langue, dans le contexte identique, en apparence de mots, grammaire, syntaxe, tout événement de communication, qu'il soit interpersonnel ou intrapsychique, ne comporte pas toujours un acte inconscient de 'traduction' et d'interprétation.[7]

For Daniel Sibony, the situation of being between two languages is not confined to the child of the immigrant worker:

> C'est le cas d'à peu près tout le monde: le père s'escrime avec la langue ambiante – celle, multiple, du social. La mère a son origine regrettée (la maison de son père, son temps de petite fille, le temps de son fantasme). Et l'enfant est toujours entre deux langues, ne sachant laquelle parler car chacune est 'impossible'.[8]

The existence of parents, the practice of interpersonal communication, the encounter with dialect, jargon, sublanguages and register support a Bakhtinian, heteroglossic view of language that makes translation a recurrent presence in the field of same-language travel. One could argue that, because there is a lesser expectation of translation problems in intralingual travelling, when they do appear they are all the more significant for their unexpectedness, even though they may not always be explicitly signalled as problems of translation.

Accent, translatability and lexical exoticism

Classic representations of foreignness in sitcoms and serials from *Fawlty Towers* to *Allô! Allô!* revolve around accent. In programmes whose creators are unable or unwilling to have foreigners actually speaking foreign languages, heavily accented English is the sign of foreignness. In a sense, the accent becomes the foreign language. Similarly, voiceovers in advertisements for foreign produce are generally done by native speakers of the source not the target language. For scriptwriters and producers, the beauty of accent in these situations is that you have the exotic thrill of difference without (up to a certain point) the discomfort of incomprehension. Accent is not, however, the sole prerogative of interlingual contacts. The exoticising effect of accent is a constant in Jonathan Raban's *Old Glory*, an account of a trip down the Mississippi. Sitting in the bar of a motel in Hannibal, Missouri, Raban falls into conversation with the wife of the owner. She describes her husband's evangelical experiences:

> 'Then, one day he was watching Channel Six, and the *700 Club* came up. You know the *700 Club*? They have all these folks on who have had testy-moaney. Like celebs, and such. There was that guy, used to be on the *Today* show . . . what's-his-name? Tom Garraway, ain't it, Harry? He had testy-moaney. Anyway my husband was watching the *700 Club* and he heard these testy-moaneys, and he got to thinking . . .'[9]

Here the evidence of accent is in direct speech, with Raban as the external observer. In other instances, the accent is internalised, with the incorporation of accent and Americanisms into the narrative voice. Looking at his fellow drinkers in a bar in St Paul, Minnesota, and meditating on the decline of the American pioneer, Raban's narrative voice changes: 'If I had been great-great-granpappy, I would have wanted to whup them good, every one. Hell, those guys, they wouldn't have known one end of a five-dollar hog from the other.'[10] Raban's alertness to accent includes his own. In *Hunting Mister Heartbreak*, a further account of travels in the United States, the English writer is reading a local newspaper in the drugstore in Guntersville, Alabama, when he notes, 'I was deep in the *For Rent* ads when I was joined at the counter by the pharmacist, who'd heard my outlandish accent and wanted to give my voice a routine check-up.'[11] The difference between Raban and Theroux here is striking. Theroux continually reproduces accents that he hears on his journey around Britain and Northern Ireland as in the following excerpt from a conversation between Ernie Fudge and Harry Gummer in Blackpool about whether Harry had seen a man called Hodges:

> 'Aye,' Harry said. 'He waar at t'other end. I boomped into 'im. He waar wi' scroofy booger – a big thick bloke.' Harry showed with a gesture that the man had a big pot belly. 'Union bloke', 'odges says, and I says 'Oh, aye,' and he gives me 'is union bloody card. And then I says . . .'[12]

There is only one reference, however, to Theroux's own accent and this is in reference to benign smiles from English people in the aftermath of a visit by Ronald Reagan. Bill Bryson's account of his travels around Britain, *Notes from a Small Island*, is similarly unforthcoming about what might be the perceived difference of his own accent although he gives extended passages of direct speech in Devonshire and Glaswegian accents.[13]

Accents obviously serve a number of functions in travel accounts. They give credibility to the account through the reproduction of 'authentic' speech. They are often vehicles for comic condescension, setting up a distance between the standard English of the narrative (and implied reader) and the non-standard English of the speakers in the quoted dialogues. They are often, in addition, indices of cultural assimilation and tallymarks for cultural knowledge. Raban's fascination with the malleability of identity in the United States finds him repeatedly toying with various American personae so that his accent begins to change as he tries to merge with his linguistic surroundings. In Guntersville, he notes, 'I was pleased that my own voice was taking this southward turn; I was *getting assimilated*, to a degree that I had never felt assimilated in New York' (his emphasis).[14] Taking on the accent is a form of phonetic disguise, the intralingual equivalent of learning the foreign language and going native.

Theodore Roosevelt's expressed concern that immigration was turning the United States into a polyglot boarding house reveals the protectionist anxieties of language that views difference with mistrust. Accents become freighted with this linguistic/racial suspicion. In radio contact with a tow coming down the Mississippi, Raban is asked by the captain of the tow:

> 'Hey, if you don't mind me asking, where's that goddamn accent from?'
>
> 'England.'
>
> 'England? Shit, up here we had it figured for some kinda crazy coon-ass voice . . .'[15]

On the levee in Guntersville, Raban meets a woman out fishing. She asks him if he is Jewish:

> 'No – I'm English, from England. Why did you think I was Jewish?'
>
> ''Cause you speak funny. You speak real funny. I thought you musta been Jewish or somethin', speaking that way.'

Though comments on accent frequently centre on questions of social class, it is significant the extent to which, in intralingual travel writing, accent acts as a trigger for unseemly phobias that are less to do with class and more a question of racial and ethnic origin. In this respect, language contact in intralingual situations is every bit as fraught as the more obvious entanglements of foreign-language encounters. Tolerance of difference is intimately related to the question of *translatability*. The more opaque the accent is for the listener, the more negative the representation of the speakers. As other speakers of English, they gravitate towards the untranslatable and in their untranslatability become somehow less human. In his *Jaunting through Ireland*, Roy Kerridge descibes a taxi-driver taking him to the port of Dún Laoghaire:

> As he spoke, his language grew rougher and rougher, as if a Jekyll and Hyde transformation were taking effect. When he turned towards me at Dun Laoghaire, he looked the complete tearaway. I swear his nose hadn't been broken when I first stepped into the car.[16]

When Bill Bryson goes to Glasgow he finds himself in a pub where he cannot understand what anybody is saying and which he leaves because he finds the atmosphere threatening. The situation is presented as a site of translation, with Bryson claiming he indicated to one of the drinkers that he came from the 'English-speaking world' and notes that one of the customers 'saw himself as my interpreter'.[17] Paul Theroux in Northern Ireland similarly sees his position in translation terms: 'Each time I heard an Ulsterman open his mouth I reached for my pen, like a missionary learning a tribal language and imagining a vernacular language Bible or dictionary.'[18] Although Theroux himself found people in Northern Ireland relaxed and friendly, he notes that the 'Ulster accent is disliked in England' and 'the gabbling Ulster folk seem forever on the boil, trying to swallow and be cruel at the same time'.[19] Roy Kerridge's Victorian fantasy of his Irish angel mutating into a dangerous ape is paralleled by the ready association in other accounts of marked difference in accent with violence. The more the accent resists translation (Theroux describes the Glaswegian accent as 'untranslatable'), the more sinister its implications. The speakers must either be translated, as Theroux does in Ulster, and thus become hermeneutic subjects (people like us) or remain untranslated, positivist objects of speculation and dread.

If language from Descartes to Chomsky has been seen as the defining characteristic of *homo sapiens*, the interpretation of 'language' has narrowed to mean the language spoken by any one group. The inability to make articulate, understandable sounds, i.e. speak the language of the group, deprives speaking others of their humanity. They become dangerous animals. Edward Tylor in *Primitive Culture: Researches into the Development of Mythology, Philosophy, Religion, Language, Art and Customs* (1871) noted that the hunting down and killing of the indigenous peoples of Tasmania was possible because colonists heard the languages of the aboriginal peoples as grunts and squeals. Deprived of language and therefore of culture, the Tasmanians were dehumanised and treated as prey for imperial hunters.[20] For Theroux, 'the Ulster accent took a moment to turn from noise into meaning', but in Glasgow there is no meaning, only noise.[21] Thus, travelling in one's own language reveals itself to be a treacherous translation labryinth as the travellers begin to discover pockets of translation resistance and the seeming transparency promised by monoglossia turns out to be increasingly problematic.

It is not only *how* a language is spoken that announces its difference, it is also the words that it contains, the meanings they carry and the way they are assembled in sentences. If foreign-language travel accounts often aim for lexical exoticism, scattering foreign words through the text, intralingual accounts track their own exotica. In Charles Graves's *Ireland Revisited* he describes a scene in Dublin using a hibernicism and translates it for the implied British English reader, 'In Dame Street we saw the first of the innumerable ass-carts (donkey-carts to you).'[22] Words such as 'butt' (of the hill) and 'strand' (beach) are similarly translated. The wide vocabulary for various degrees of intoxication particularly excites Graves's fancy, 'Beginning with the delightful "Drink-taken", you have half-towed, sizzled, flukaw, flutered, spiflu, langers and stocious. The last word rhymes with atrocious and means thickly speaking drunk.'[23] For Graves, one of the charms of the Irish is that 'They have a wonderful vocabulary, a tremendous sense of imagery, and a wealth of delicious exaggerations.'[24] Bill Bryson is perplexed on his arrival in England as to the exact meaning of 'counterpane' and is astonished to find out what it is after spending three days fiddling with windows. England 'was full of words I'd never heard before – streaky bacon, short back and sides, Belisha beacon, serviettes, high tea, ice-cream cornet'.[25] For Theroux, the chief characteristic of British English is not lexical difference but a weakness for euphemism. When he tells a woman walker where he's going she says that it's a canny little step and Theroux comments, '*A canny little step* was similar to *a fair old trot*. Why didn't the English ever use the word "far"'(his emphasis).[26] Raban, for his part, frequently incorporates Americanisms into his texts and leaves them untranslated. The effect is often deliberate, as when he invents the persona of 'Trav, hauling ass down the Interstate', who 'would-n't *reach* places; he'd *hit* them'(his emphasis).[27] He contrasts the linguistic fate of two British women who live within a mile of one another near Louisiana, Missouri. Everett Asquith came to Missouri with her American husband in 1955 and her initial attempts at communication were met with baffled incomprehension. Nobody had heard of 'biscuits' or a 'chemist' and thought she was crazy to attempt to walk to the nearby store. She decided to effect a transformation in her lifestyle and overcome the barriers of culture and language:

> She was determined to turn herself into an American. She got a job as a night-nurse at the local hospital, she gave coffee-klatsches and learned to call biscuits cookies. She collected American words and wrote them down in a notebook. She dressed herself from the Sears catalogue and drove to the supermarket in the station wagon.[28]

'Jeannie' who lives in a squalid wooden mansion proves much more resistant to cultural assimilation: 'She spoke in the querulous, whiffly accent of suburban East Anglia; there wasn't a trace of American in it.'[29] Reminded of her former husband, she swears and wonders whether the word 'shoot' is English or American:

> 'Oh dear. I don't like to use American words. But I get them mixed up now, sometimes. I say things now, I know they're American, but I can't help it. Living here, you just hear that American talk. That's why I like listening to you; you don't talk American at all, you sound just like people did at home.'[30]

The different responses of 'Jeannie' and Everett to language change reveal the intense emotional investment in language difference. Travel writers who move in the space of their own language, like Georg Simmel's strangers, are noticeably preoccupied with notions of distance and proximity.[31] Due to their closeness to the language of the people that they visit, they must develop *strategies of estrangement*. This is Jeannie's dilemma, the fear that her strategy of estrangement will fail and that her identity will be silenced by 'American talk'. Retaining the sense of strangeness, the distance of observation in a language world that is your own, by virtue of the language being your mother tongue, means that the privilege of proximity must be tempered by the demands of translation. Lexical differences, figurative exuberance, word play, hyberbole, euphemism and accent are so many strategies of estrangement that make for a space of mediation and interpretation. These strategies are as much in evidence in accounts by travellers travelling around their own country, such as Jonathan Raban in *Coasting* or Rosita Boland in *Sea-Legs*, as they are in accounts where travellers travel to a different country with the same language.[32] This process of estrangement is equally a process of self-estrangement. Speaking in a foreign language in a foreign country can certainly make travellers aware of features of their own native language, but it is arguable that the encounter with different varieties of the traveller's own language creates an even sharper sense of specific linguistic identity. The experience has of course different possible outcomes. The fear of proximity can produce the distant condescension of satire, where the variety spoken by the traveller is deemed culturally superior or, alternatively, plurality can be a lesson in tolerance and the virtues of non-ethnocentric relativism. Part of the difficulty in intralingual travel is that writers encounter many of the difficulties of translation – linguistic misunderstanding, cultural difference, non-equivalence – but they are not generally described as such because translation problems are not supposed to be an issue.

Fractal travel, polyidentity and sublanguages

In a paper published in 1977, Benoît Mandelbrot asked the following question: 'How long is the coast of Britain?' The answer was that at one level the coast was infinitely long. An observer from a satellite would make one guess that would be shorter than a Paul Theroux negotiating every inlet, bay and cove on the coast and Theroux's guess would be shorter than that of a tiny insect having to negotiate every pebble.[33] In other words, as James Gleick notes, 'Mandelbrot found that as the scale of measurement becomes smaller, the measured length of a coastline rises without limit, bays and peninsulas revealing ever smaller subbays and subpeninsulas at least down to atomic scales.'[34] What Mandelbrot discovered was that the coastline had a characteristic degree of roughness or irregularity and that degree remained constant across different scales. Another illustration of this phenomenon was the Koch snowflake, where an infinitely long line surrounds a finite area. Mandelbrot named the new geometry that he had originated fractal geometry. The shapes or fractals in this new geometry allowed infinite length to be contained in finite space. The analogy with travel is compelling and worth exploring for a number of reasons. Firstly, a fractal conception of travel counters the discourse of exhaustion that has most notably been articulated by Paul Fussell.[35] According to this view, travel faded with inter-war privilege and all we have now are the exploitative simulacra of tourism.[36] In her own exploration of a coastline, Rosita Boland describes a scene on Sherkin Island, off the southern Irish coast, where she is looking for the whereabouts of an American friend, George Packer. She meets an elderly woman who tells her that Packer lives a long way past the church and that the woman herself has not been past the church in years. Sherkin Island is three miles wide:

> *Hadn't been further than the church for years? A house on the next hill was a long way away?* Continuing on towards the house, I thought again about distances and how, within the three-mile area of Sherkin, there was a space so open and densely-textured that two lives need never entangle and at the same time, a space so physically small that a couple of hours tramp and you could say you had 'seen' the island.[37] (her emphasis)

The shift in scale is a revelation for Boland. Small is not simple. The complexity of the open and 'densely-textured' space is the roughness or irregularity or complexity that carries across scales. A casual remark by an elderly islander uncovers the infinite possibility of travel in the finite space of an island. Tim Robinson's exploration of the fourteen thousand fields of Árainn, the largest of the three Aran Islands, is called, appropriately enough, *Labyrinth*.[38] The fractal dimension of travel leads Paul Theroux to the inescapable conclusion that 'every mile of England was different'.[39]

A second consequence that follows on from a fractal notion of travel bears directly on translation. The multiple instances of translation found in intralingual travel accounts, and highlighted by the strategies of estrangement mentioned above, point to the translation phenomenon being present across different scales of enquiry. Whether travel is examined across galaxies (see Chapter 5 and discussion of science fiction), continents, countries or regions, the complexity of the translation encounter remains constant. This is not to trivialise translation (if everything is translation, nothing is translation) by merely using it as a synonym for any kind of transformation but to argue that questions of mediation between and within languages that are properly the concern of translation studies are present at many different scales of enquiry. One of the difficulties to date in translation studies is that attention has been largely focused on interlingual translation, which has both restricted the remit of translation enquiry and also failed to alert scholars in other disciplines to the interpretive reach and relevance of translation scholarship. In *Routes*, the American anthropologist James Clifford argues that the concept of a contact zone first used in the context of travel writing by Mary Louise Pratt should have a broader application:

> The notion of a contact zone, articulated by Pratt in contexts of European expansion and transculturation, can be extended to include cultural relations within the same state, region, or city – in the centers rather than the frontiers of nations and empires. The distances at issue here are more social than geographic.[40]

A feature of the contact zone, the areas of encounter between the colonisers and the colonised, is the predicament of translation. What language to speak? Who to use as an interpreter? How to monitor meaning and intent? If we accept Clifford's extension of the notion to 'include cultural relations within the same state, region or city', then language and translation must also feature in this reconfiguration of the concept. Intralingual travellers can become highly sensitized to contact zones in both a geographical and social sense, a sensitivity that marks out contours of difference in their accounts. Sitting at the bar of the Rivertown Club in Vicksburg, Mississippi, Jonathan Raban hears the voices of the 'New South':

> Some did talk with the elastic, treacly vowels of Mississippi, as if the meandering style of the river had somehow worked its way inside their mouths; but I could hear Harvard Business School over in the corner, Brooklyn Irish on the sofa, the sand-and-snap of the urban Midwest in the armchair behind me.[41]

Here the accents reflect different trajectories of emigration, class and geographical origin, and the further, Theroux, Bryson, Graves, Boland, Kerridge, Raban travel into their respective territories, the more aware they become of the multiple contact zones of state, region, city and class. What they make apparent is a common experience of place, the seeming infinity of differences in finite spaces. Every county in Ireland, every shire in England, every state in America speaks differently. Within the county, shire and state, people from the town and country speak differently. People do not speak the same way in the east, west, north, south of the county, shire and state. Social class, gender and race spin further webs of difference.

Debates on identity can be something of a misnomer in that individuals have, to use Edgar Morin's term, a polyidentity. Thus, the writer of the current work has a regional identity as a Dubliner, a national identity as an Irishman, a continental identity as a European, a class identity as petty bourgeois, a gender identity as male and a racial identity as white.[42] The fractal experience of travel is a heightened sensitivity to polyidentity and to the infinite discriminations of language itself. The level of awareness of the finer detail of language use is related to the tension between what might be termed *horizontal travel* and *vertical travel*. Horizontal travel is the more conventional understanding of travel as a linear progression from place to place. Vertical travel is temporary dwelling in a location for a period of time where the traveller begins to travel down into the particulars of place either in space (botany, studies of micro-climate, exhaustive exploration of local landscape) or in time (local history, archaeology, folklore).[43] In travel accounts like *Notes from a Small Island* or *Sea Legs* the dominant travel paradigm is horizontal whereas in *Hunting Mr Heartbreak* vertical travel dominates, with prolonged sojourns in New York, Guntersville (Alabama) and Seattle. Although most horizontal travellers bemoan the hopelessness of their task, trying to give an account of Ireland or Britain after a few weeks in car, train or bus travelling around the island, there are always moments of dwelling-in-travelling where horizontal travel gives way to vertical. Literary travel involves these constant shifts between the macroscopic scale of the horizontal and the microscopic scale of the vertical. The sensitivity to language detail is partly then a function of the interaction between the two modes of travel. If translation is conceived of primarily as translation into the mother tongue (even if for practical reasons this is not always possible in reality), then the translator is, from the point of view of mother-tongue competence, first and foremost, an intralingual traveller. S/he must horizontally (going to different regions, countries where the mother tongue is spoken) and vertically (historical sense of language, awareness of detail of place) explore the complex spread of language. The dilemma for the translator is the eternal dilemma of the travel writer. Travel takes time. Theroux, Boland and Bryson compensate for time constraints on the horizontal journey by years of vertical travel through the cultures of the countries that have been home to them. Thorough knowledge of any language involves the complex and time-consuming pay-off between horizontal and vertical travel. Much bad translation comes from a failure to recognise this. The Cook's Tour of language ('he went to France on his holidays last year', 'she's been to Spain') results in the howlers that are the unexpected delights of hotel guests the world over. The increasingly common assumption that language-learning is a package holiday – buy the ticket, order the meal, book the hotel – rather than a lifelong journey leads to a serious underestimation of the difficulty of the translator's task. Intralingual travelling reveals how complex that task is.

One potential source of complexity that is related to social contact zones is the existence of sublanguages in language. Although sublanguages are generally understood in a more technical sense as the specialised languages of particular domains such as telecommunications or biotechnology, there are arguably sublanguages that have more to do with social distinctions and symbolic capital than technical competence. Raban eats at the Dock resturant in Davenport, Iowa, where he is bewildered by the sublanguage of service. He admits that he has never got used to restaurant English, an unsettling mixture of the ceremonial and the intimate. Raban is met at the door by the captain-waiter, a mournful figure in black:

> 'And is there just one in your party this evening, sir?'
>
> I admitted, a little shamefacedly, that there was only me; and I didn't feel at all like a party.
>
> The captain-waiter passed me into the hands of a girl usher in tights and frou-frou.
>
> 'Hi, my name is Julie! And I will show you to your table! Your waiter for this evening is Doug, and he'll be just right along. See you later!'
>
> Doug announced himself. 'Hi, my name is Doug and I am your waiter for this evening. I hope you enjoy your meal.'
>
> It was like dropping into the middle of a puppet show. Where did they learn this extraordinary style of speech? It must have been dreamed up in order to give waiting at table the impersonal professional status of gynaecology or the law, yet it succeeded in doing exactly the reverse. It made me feel like a customer at a brothel, all this false solicitude for my physical needs.[44]

Bill Bryson on the other side of the Atlantic ocean is similarly bamboozled by the sublanguage of restaurants. Studying the menu in a hotel in Dorset, he notes that it contains numerous 'ten-guinea' words such as *noisette*, *tartare*, *coulis* and *timbale* that ten years earlier were unknown to English menu-authors. Bryson comments on the 'curious inflated language with eccentric capitalizations' that produces 'Fanned Galia Melon and Cumbrian Air Dried Ham served with a Mixed Leaf Salad'.[45] The sublanguage translates the prosaic realities of flunkeydom and dismal food into the decorous language of the liberal professions and high life. A similar transmutation of the social self is tracked by Raban in his analysis of the changing language of Macy's department store in New York. The advertising copy is full of 'expensive golden words', 'little dabs of French, self-conscious archaisms, bursts of indulgent alliteration'.[46] Translating the hyperbole of the catering, retail and tourist industry into the mundane language of the everyday is often richly comic in its effects and is emblematic of the wry scepticism of Anglo-American travelling. The intralingual traveller as translator/interpreter emerges explicitly as social critic when Raban presents the language of Macy's advertising copy as symptomatic of a New York society where there are Air People and Street People and where those in between – the 'moderates', in Macy's security parlance – are condemned to disappear. In the analytic situation Amati Mehler, Argentieri and Canestri identify the multiple languages of experience as revealing the process of continuous translation in psychic and social life:

> Le langage privé, le langage infantile, le langage des idéologies – parfois explicites, mais le plus souvent cachées au sujet lui-même –, le langage

correspondant à l'âge et au sexe, doivent être considérés comme des variables, pas nécessairement partagées, même si on parle la même langue qu'un patient monolingue. Chaque analyste sait combien de 'traductions' requièrent ses propres paroles et celles du patient pour arriver à être des paroles semblables, pour parvenir à véhiculer un sens partagé.[47]

Social criticism and travel through different contact zones is often possible for travellers in a manner that is much more difficult for the natives of a particular place. Bryson and Theroux have the advantage of being American and thus outside the British class system. Raban is English and therefore a foreigner in the United States. Indeed, Raban is told in Lansing, Iowa, that while the townspeople hated 'strangers' (i.e. other Americans), they 'love foreigners'.[48] Rosita Boland is Irish and her range of social contact travelling around Ireland is noticeably more restricted. The relative social mobility of the 'stranger who moves on' had already been noted by Georg Simmel in his 1908 essay on the topic of the stranger, 'he often receives the most surprising revelations and confidences, at times reminiscent of a confessional, about matters which are kept carefully hidden from everybody with whom one is close'.[49] Though the objectivity that Simmel attributes to the strangers because they are not bound by group loyalties may be compromised by personal prejudice or attitudes linked to race, class and gender, the traveller has greater potential freedom to enter particular contact zones than natives who may be unwilling or unable to do so. Language alone is not sufficient. There must be a desirable element of 'strangeness' or 'foreignness' in order for the restrictions on social movement to be relaxed.

Touring cultures and rambling houses

In their introduction to *Touring Cultures: Transformations of Travel and Theory*, John Urry and Chris Rojek emphasise the centrality of travel in the construction of a culture. In the case of English culture, they argue, this can mean travelling to 'sacred sites' such as Buckingham Palace, the Albert Hall or Anfield. Other destinations might be Westminister Abbey, the Lake District or Stratford-upon-Avon or places where such key events took place as the Battle of Hastings, the Blitz or the Wars of the Roses. This process of cultural self-definition can involve crossing national boundaries, as in the case of England with its involvement in the British imperial project.[50] The thesis defended by Urry and Rojek, that cultures 'travel' and that tourism has played its own role in the construction of national cultures, is perfectly legitimate but they significantly fail to mention the role of language in the nomadic construction of national culture. The examples given, of seeing physical places and objects, tend to favour an overly visual reading of the travel phenomenon in cultural formation. It is, of course, possible to argue that all these places of tourist pilgrimage are made sense of through texts; that indeed without literary, historical or journalistic texts they would be meaningless as travel destinations. However, there is a more fundamental level at which travel and language are connected and this is to do with the nature of language itself. The linguist Charles Hockett has described 'displacement' as one of the features that distinguishes human speech from other forms of communication. 'Displacement' is the ability to talk about things that are distant in place or time.[51] This ability then allows us to travel to places and periods that we have never seen. Paul Theroux emphasises the power of linguistic displacement in deploring his own ignorance of the island he had inhabited for so many years:

> I knew a little about some parts [of Britain] because in Britain there was an oral tradition that took the place of travel, like the Bognor jokes and Scotland was breathtaking and Cornwall was creepy and South Wales was awful and Rye was ever so lovely.[52]

The Britain that Theroux travels around in language is implicitly contrasted with this oral tradition, a national British culture that has been constructed through language. In a sense, Urry and Rojek are right to insist on the nomadic elaboration of national culture but this elaboration has arguably been primarily linguistic rather than visual. Though people may visit 'sights', they have already 'seen' them in language. This is not to say that visitors will not be disappointed or excited by what they see or that real travel is a waste of time but that the places already feature in the prior 'oral tradition' of travel which has staked out the landmarks of cultural identity. In the America of airborne conventioneers described by Raban, each city strives for instant memorability, 'We went to sales conference there – that was the Alamo; *that* was the Paul Revere House; *that* was the Space Needle; *that* was the Grand Old Opry; *that* was Astroworld; *that* was Preservation Hall'(his emphasis).[53] However, this map of US cultural identity is as much a manifesto of anticipation as a record of experience. When the conventioneers go to certain cities, they expect to see certain things because they have already heard or read about them. One of the functions of in-flight magazines is precisely to establish a canonical set of expectations about 'things to see' in destinations served by the airline. Travel writers themselves contribute powerfully to the construction of national cultures through language. Their own travels in language allow readers to travel to parts of their country they would never and might never see. Anthony Burgess, quoted on the back cover of *The Kingdom by the Sea*, makes this candid admission: 'Few of us have seen the entirety of the coast and I for one am grateful to Mr Theroux for making my journey unnecessary.' Paul Theroux's account was a critical and commercial success and Bill Bryson's *Notes from a Small Island* was top of the bestseller lists for months in Britain. These accounts will in turn inform a new 'oral tradition' against which other travel writers will in their time react.

The shift in travel writing from travel log to travelogue is the shift from fact to impression, the movement from the bald description of physical phenomena to the interpretive luxuriance of emotion and opinion. Thus, the accounts themselves are active interpreters of the cultures through which they travel. They are in this respect *translations* of a culture into language and like all translations they are productions in time. Gibbons's Ireland is the austere Holy Land of the first Free State government, Theroux's Britain is strewn with the debris of the Thatcherite revolution, and Raban's America is buckling under the corporate greed of Reagan's Republicanism. Good translations can endure, of course, and travel accounts can be memorable additions to writing in a language but most translations, even the very best, have to be reworked and/or reinvented for a new generation of readers. Similarly, though travel writing aspires to something more than the anecdotal ephemerality of the weekend supplement holiday jaunt, the writing does bear the traces of history and places do change over time. This is why the discourse of exhaustion is misplaced. To say that there is no point in travelling to Ireland, Britain or the United States because it has been done so many times before is to proclaim that there is no point in new translations of Molière, Goethe or Cervantes, because they have already been translated. The open-endedness of history is the open-endedness of translation and travel and the need for new translations of time and place is ever present in cultures as they themselves change through time.

Stories are the gifts of travelling cultures. In rural Ireland, at the turn of the century, many districts had 'rambling houses'. These were houses where neighbours would come together and swap stories or retail the latest news. Travelling storytellers were also welcomed. The traveller was given a meal, drink and sometimes a bed for the night in exchange for stories told to the people of the house and neighbours. The travellers' tales were their passports to hospitality. The tales themselves would almost invariably be of events in other times or places.[54] This intimate connection between language and motion, the journey and the *journal* is still real for the people Rosita Boland meets on her journey around Ireland. She stays with an old friend outside Cork city who, after opening a bottle of wine and sitting Boland down by the fire, asks her to tell her about the journey so far: 'This ritual of story-telling went on in every house I stayed where I knew the people. As the weeks progressed, the story-telling sessions became longer from house to house.'[55] In Seattle, Jonathan Raban finds that the experience of travel and displacement 'had turned . . . immigrants into compulsive storytellers'.[56] In print culture, travel accounts have become the rambling houses of literature. The sedentary reader may read of wonders in foreign and not so foreign lands by a fireside but the voice is the disembodied narrative voice of the printed text. The relationship is, however, fundamentally the same, the traveller paying his/her dues to the community through narrative.

If bringing back souvenirs can be seen as an act of reparation for the act of betrayal in leaving your native family/community/environment, then the traveller's tale could be interpreted as a form of symbolic mediation that restitutes the gift of story for the temporary loss of the person gone travelling. The residual orality of the rambling house could be said to function at another level in travel writing, the level of plot. Walter J. Ong has contrasted the climactic linear plot of literate and typographic cultures with the absence of such plots in the epic literature of oral cultures. In a climactic plot, 'an ascending action builds tension, rising to a climactic point, which consists often of a recognition or other incident bringing about a *peripeteia* or reversal of action, and which is followed by a denouement or untying'.[57] This notion of tightly organised linear plot was foreign to the oral narrator whose primary concern was episodic structure and not the presentation of narrative incident in strict chronological sequence building up to a climax. Ong uses the image of the Freytag pyramid (an upward slope followed by a downward slope) to illustrate the climactic plot, arguing that the pyramidal plot involves ruthless selectivity. Its necessary artificiality explained the slow emergence of such plots in the West: 'We must not forget that episodic structure was the natural way to talk out a lengthy story line if only because the experience of real life is more like a string of episodes than it is like a Freytag pyramid.'[58] The famous public readings by Dickens and other nineteenth-century novelists are viewed by Ong as evidence of a 'lingering feeling for the old oral narrator's world'. He then observes:

> An especially persistent ghost from this world was the itinerant hero, whose travels served to string episodes together and who survived through medieval romances and even through Cervantes' otherwise unbelievably precocious *Don Quixote* into Defoe (Robinson Crusoe was a stranded itinerant) and into Fielding's *Tom Jones*, Smollett's episodic narratives, and even some of Dickens, such as *The Pickwick Papers.*[59]

Geography provides the structure for the episodic narrative of travel, closer to ancient epic than the modern detective novel. Writing a travel account of course involves a great deal of selectivity and the characterisation, introspection and avoidance of additive, aggregative and redundant prose that is said to characterise chirographic culture. Conversely, the accounts do not operate on the basis of extended linear climactic plot (there are, of course, mini-climaxes in different episodes). In this respect, they are indeed closer to people's lived experience and this may account for the continuing popularity of a genre that tells not only the stories of other lives but is nearer in form to the story of life itself.

It is a truism of translator training that translators must be initiated into the culture of the foreign language. Words have connotations and languages have contexts, so there must be due attentiveness to the cultural differences that feed languages. Common language on the other hand can produce a fiction of cultural immediacy. The German intellectual Wolf Lepenies noted that, in the case of the two Germanies, speaking the same language 'has nurtured the illusion that we understand each other'.[60] The illusion of understanding is all the greater because translation is not believed to be a problem. The traveller to another country with a different language anticipates translation difficulties and, because the language is different, it is assumed that naturally the culture is different. However, there can result a genuine sense of bewilderment if a seeming transparency of language gives way to cultural opacity. The labour of translation becomes slowly visible. John Gibbons is deeply affected by a scene he witnesses in Co. Sligo. Staring out at the Atlantic ocean, he is accosted by a young, poorly dressed man who invites him to his house. In the house, there are two other young men and an older man, the father. Gibbons accepts their offer of a meal but finds the atmosphere sombre. To his astonishment, at one point in the meal, the father suddenly bursts into tears, stands up and runs out of the house leaving one of his sons to explain that only that morning they had buried his mother and the old man's wife. Gibbons tries to analyse his own response to the scene:

> If my house in Hornsey was burned down with my wife and all my children in it I should of course be sorry. But my every instinct would be to try and look as unconcerned as though, on the whole, the matter rather bored me. And I should expect my friends to behave as though they were unaware that anything out of the ordinary had happened. The very height of impertinence, I think, would be any beyond the most perfunctory condolence. And I hope and pray that I might succeed in looking bored. For I am an Englishman, and that on the whole is the way that God has built us.[61]

Gibbons's conclusion to the chapter describing the scene is emphatic: 'Ireland is different . . . The place, if we are to own the truth, is a foreign country.'[62] Bryson contrasts the dry, ironic wit of the English with what he sees as American literalness. In Skipton, he had asked for a single ticket to Manchester with a receipt:

> When the man in the window passed them to me he said: 'The ticket's free . . . but it's £18.50 for the receipt.' If he had done that in America, the customer would have said: '*What*? What're ya saying? The ticket's *free*, but the receipt costs £18.50? What kind of cockamamy set-up is this?'[63]

Both Bryson and Theroux produce long lists of cultural differences between Britain and the United States, from putting knitted bobble-hats on soft-boiled eggs to keep them warm to drinking wine made out of something other than grapes. Theroux notes the potential for cultural misunderstanding in the different concepts of appropriate behaviour in both cultures:

> The English liked especially to mock the qualities in other people they admitted they didn't have themselves. And sometimes they found us

truly maddening. In America you were admired for getting ahead, elbow-
ing forward, rising, pushing in. In England this behaviour was hated – it
was the way wops acted, it was 'Chinese fire-drill', it was disorder. But
making a quick buck was also a form of queue-jumping, and getting
ahead was a form of rudeness – a 'bounder' was a person who had
moved out of his class.[64]

Less important than the actual truthfulness of the observations in each case
is the recognition of significant intercultural difference. It is these differences
that work in tandem with the linguistic strategies of estrangement described
above to make for the foreignness of cultures sharing a language. The differences are all the harder to track for being, in certain instances, quite subtle.
The traveller in revealing the codes, the behavioural logic of another culture
is, in a sense, underlining the *degree of translatability* of that culture, the
extent to which intralingual travel affirming a notion of departure/difference
must foreground rather than conceal translation.

Minority languages, fragmented origins, names

Daniel Sibony sees monolingualism as an unhappy ideal, 'Bien des Occiden-
taux "normosés" souffrent à leur insu de n'avoir qu'une seule langue . . . Une
seule "langue", une seule origine, et qui se veut telle; un seul territoire
symbolique dont l'unité les fixe.'[65] Polyidentity, the fractal dimension of travel,
strategies of estrangement and intercultural faultlines undermine notions of
fixity and unity. However, the nostalgia for wholeness can be strong and
breed its own instances of intolerance. As we noted earlier, language is not
an indifferent issue and the emotional commitment to it is often pronounced
and occasionally menacing. In *Hunting Mister Heartbreak* the slogan 'SPEAK
ENGLISH OR DIE, SQUINTY EYE' is seen spraygunned on the south wall of
the Central Community College in Seattle.[66] The desire to clear the space of
language of all other competing idioms is a standard trope of imperialism and
fear of the Other usually extends to a denigration of their language.[67] In this
context, the treatment of minority languages in intralingual narratives is
revealing. Charles Graves eyes the seagulls mournfully in Dún Laoghaire at
the beginning of his account and asks the rhetorical question, 'what intelligent creature, whether Gull or Gael, would talk Irish unless living in Dingle or
Galway or paid to do so?'[68] In *Round Ireland in Low Gear*, Eric Newby wonders
whether he and his wife could travel around Ireland by bus:

> Buses sounded a little more promising but a closer look at the *Amchlar Bus
> do na Cuigi agus Expressway* [sic], otherwise the *Provincial and Expressway
> Timetable* (not surprisingly there is no equivalent for 'Bus' and 'Express-
> way' in the Irish language) showed that some of the services were skeletal
> in the winter months.[69]

There is an Irish equivalent for 'Expressway' and the truncated Latinism 'bus' has made its way into many languages but it is the implied pre-modern backwardness of Irish that is important in Newby's remarks rather than their linguistic ineptness. Roy Kerridge, for his part, regrets giving money to two young girls for speaking Irish: 'I knew better than anyone of the dangers of Gaelic revivalism.'[70] What these dangers are and why Kerridge is more aware of them than anyone else is never explained. The hopeless inadequacy of minority languages is emphasised by Bryson when he presents the reader with a vignette of comic condescension in his description of a Welsh soap-opera:

> It was an odd experience watching people who existed in a recognizably British milieu – they drank tea and wore Marks and Spencer's cardigans – but talked in Martian. Occasionally, I was interested to note, they dropped in English words – 'hi ya', 'right then', 'OK' – presumably because a Welsh equivalent didn't exist, and in one memorable encounter a character said something like, 'Wlch ylch aargh ybsy cwm dirty weekend, look you,' which I just loved. How sweetly endearing of the Welsh not to have their own term for an illicit bonk between Friday and Monday.[71]

Johannes Fabian has used the term 'denial of coevalness' to describe the manner in which Western travellers have distanced themselves in time from the countries they visit.[72] The Western traveller represents the here and now, the trajectory of the modern while the country s/he visits is frozen in time. The response may either be to condemn this time-lag as further evidence of the feckless backwardness of the natives or to sentimentalise the glories of past greatness and adopt an elegiac salvage mode. Either way, the Western traveller is confirmed in his/her ready identification with modernity. The linguistic corollary of this temporal distancing is firmly situating other languages in the realm of the pre-modern. The minority-language speaker inhabits a pre-technical world of quaint moral propriety and irridentist crankiness. For Paul Theroux, 'Britain and the United States were the present', while in 'Third World countries I felt I had dropped into the past'.[73] When he arrives in Wales he is irritated by bilingual signs that he sees as an unnecessary sop to nationalists. At Llanelli station, Theroux notes that people are speaking Welsh but lapse into English when the train arrives, as if the great metaphor of modernity needed the appropriate idiom of English. Theroux sees bilingualism not as an asset but as a congenital problem:

> I wondered whether the Welsh could be explained in terms of being bilingual, which is so often a form of schizophrenia, allowing a person to hold two contradictory opinions in his head at once, because his opinions remain untranslated. The Welsh had that mildly stunned and slap-happy personality that I associated with people for whom speaking two languages was a serious handicap.[74]

In Theroux's view, this perpetual state of translation produces a nation of inexact and confused musicians. Again, the wholly unscientific nature of the analysis is less important than the implicit attitude to language difference. For the spraygun bigots of Seattle, being American means total translation. To be reborn as an American citizen is to be born again in the immersion course of language and to be translated linguistically and culturally into anglophone America. It is translation that will end all translation, that will return the United States to the mythical ground of originary, linguistic unity – one language, one origin.

The scandal of translation is to show that the origin is fragmented, that monoglossia is always provisional, that other languages precede, ghost or compete with the dominant idiom in any society. Translation is the metaphor of mainstream anxiety, as articulated by Dinesh D'Souza in his *The End of Racism* where he claims, 'We risk an American Babel, a breakdown of communication, if everyone does not speak a shared language. For reasons of practicality, this language must be English, which is rapidly becoming the global medium of intercultural communication.'[75] The existence of Welsh in Britain, Irish in Ireland and the International District in Seattle are reminders of the contested nature of language in different societies. If accents are the oral palimpsest of language, then living minority languages are a more vivid and often intolerable indication of the dynamic of translation that underlies all languages. This dynamic is revealed in the historical displacement of one language by the other, a displacement that is obliquely revealed by Bryson's comments on the Welsh soap-opera where the anglicisms point to the continuing pressure of a major language on a minor language rather than an imaginary lack of semantic resources. Translation is present at another level, however, in the continuous supply of words and expressions over the centuries to English from other languages. Language is always already translated, a polyglot boarding house that depends for growth on the news from elsewhere. Minority languages underscore the multiple origins and ultimately the potential of any language to be 'minoritised'.[76] Language dominance is contingent on historical, economic and political forces and there is no assured permanence to linguistic supremacy, as French has been finding to its cost in the twentieth century. If the prestige or power of a particular language demands that other people translate themselves into the language ('eat, dress, talk like an American'),[77] then the recurrent danger is that the language in turn may be translated. Translation is demanded of others but only in order to close off the infinity of translation, a closure frustrated endlessly by history.

Brian Friel has described the drama of language displacement in his play *Translations*. The translation polemic centres principally on the translation of placenames from Irish into English and the drama of loss that this transformation entails.[78] Placenames are a subset of the larger set of proper nouns, including names of people, that are an eternal challenge to the possibility of translation. Whereas common nouns classically have a signifier and a signified, proper nouns have a signifier and a referent but no signified. In an essay on translation, 'The Exact Art', George Steiner sees the separability of the *signifiant* and *signifié* as the very condition of translation itself:

> The translator proceeds as if, he *must* proceed as if, meaning was, to a large degree at least, a discrete product of the executive forms of expression. He must proceed as if the *signifié* can, to a greater or lesser extent, be extracted from the particular *signifiant* and 'taken away from it' via diverse operations of analogy, mirroring or parallelism.[79] (his emphasis)

If the signified, then, is the bedrock of translation – the promise of potential transfer – what is to be done when there is no signified, only the unique attribution of the referent, the reference to a specific person or place? Does the translator have resort to substitution, so that Dublin becomes Berlin in a production of an O'Casey play, or does the translator naturalise the names, so that Bertie Ahern becomes Beircheart Ó hEithírn for an Irish-language broadcast, or does the translator renounce all interference and leave the proper nouns untranslated, as Frank Sewell does with the Irish-language placenames in Cathal Ó Searcaigh's poetry?[80] Proper nouns test the limits of translation, and suggest a tension between uniqueness of reference and transferability of meaning that threatens the universalist aspirations of the translation process. It might be assumed in intralingual travelling that names of places and people could simply be recorded and not attract any particular attention as problematic sites of translation. However, this is not often the case, as if the fraught translatability of referents had its own fascination for travel writers.

Jonathan Raban describes the Atlantic passage to the New World as a place of fearful anticipation for generations of emigrants: '*Over there*, after the ocean had done its job, you'd have a different identity, and very probably a different name. You would not be *you*, at least not as you had known yourself to be up to this extraordinary moment'(his emphasis).[81] The immigrants from Europe shed families, occupations and languages, and 'you had a new name, assigned to you at Ellis Island by an immigration officer who was too busy to bother with the unpronouceable *z*'s and *x*'s of your old one.'[82] Although Raban claims elsewhere in *Hunting Mister Heartbreak* that a major difference between Europe and America is that Europeans cannot travel very far without travelling outside their own language, traces of translation are everywhere in the United States in the very names that people carry. Raban himself succumbs to the force of translation. In Guntersville, Alabama, he becomes 'John Rayburn' while in Seattle the name on his door reads 'John Rainbird'. In Raban's case, these name changes are a playful exploration of multiple identities, the dizzy possibility of reinvention through intralingual translation. In other instances, name change is infinitely more painful, as if the uniqueness of the referent is obliterated in the renaming and the loss of name becomes a metonym for the loss of language and personal identity.

Ewa Hoffman and her sister are taken by their guardian, Mr Rosenberg, to a school in Vancouver where they are to learn English. They have arrived as immigrants from Poland and Ewa is not too keen on speaking the harsh-sounding language of the children in the schoolyard. One morning, she and her sister are renamed. 'Ewa' becomes 'Eva' and her sister 'Alina' is rechristened 'Elaine':

> My sister and I hang our heads wordlessly under this careless baptism . . .
> We make our way back to a bench at the back of the room; nothing much
> has happened, except a small, seismic mental shift. The twist in our
> names takes them a tiny distance from us – but it's a gap which the infinite
> hobgoblin of abstraction enters. Our Polish names didn't refer to us; they
> were as surely us as our eyes or our hands. These new appelations, which
> we can't yet pronounce, are not us. They are identification tags, disem
> bodied signs pointing to objects that happen to be my sister and myself.
> We walk to our seats, into a roomful of unknown faces, with names that
> make us strangers to ourselves.[83]

The change from Ewa to Eva is the beginning of a long odyssey of translation for Hoffman, reconstructed as a new North American referent to match her new name. The gap persists, however imperceptible, and Hoffman struggles as she grows into adulthood with the trauma of a translated self. The declaration of allegiance in a name change (with its gender equivalent in marriage, women traditionally taking on their husband's name) is often sought as part of the cultural logic of *imperium*. In Edmund Spenser's dialogue on the state and proper government of Ireland, *A View of the Present State of Ireland* (1596), Irenius argues that the native Irishman should not be named after his family or tribe but after a trade, or some faculty or quality of his body or mind:

> whereby they shall not only not depend upon the head of their sept as they
> now do, but also shall in a short time learn quite to forget his Irish nation.
> And herewithal would I also wish all the Oes and the Macs which the
> heads of the septs have taken to their names to be utterly forbidden and
> extinguished.[84]

The power attributed by Spenser to naming is impressive. The extinction of the 'Oes and the Macs' (partially successful – in English, Ó Cróinín becomes Cronin) and family names will produce born-again Englishmen, loyal subjects in the new imperial order. This patriarchal concern with the symbolic force of the Name of the Imperial Fathers is centred around translation as a form of absolution. Whatever your previous condition or loyalties or state, you will emerge into the light of a new day through the good offices of translation. The fact that the translation is more often than not mistranslation – 'Alina' becomes 'Elaine', Ó Cróinín gets transliterated as 'Cronin' rather than being translated as 'small and swarthy', the busy immigration official awkwardly shears off *z*'s and *x*'s – points to the fatal weakness of power in assuming equivalence is possible. Indeed, it may be because equivalence is not so much possible as plainly not desirable that what happens is in effect often *pseudo-translation*. Names carry with them, then, the botched evidence of previous versions, a translation residue that has its own mischievous afterlife. Eric Newby's parenthetical comment on a piece of placename translation in Ireland is typical: 'After some miles I stopped at a pub at Cloonboo (what a name).'[85]

If names can get lost or distorted in translation, they can also be seen as 'typical' in their untranslatability, their referential uniqueness. Bill Bryson makes much of English proper nouns, the names of people, places and institutions. He finds the varied nomenclature of football results and weather forecasts deeply soothing. In his opinion, the British have a particular genius for placenames and he is fond of giving long lists of names that, among other things, 'summon forth an image of lazy summer afternoons and butterflies darting in meadows: Winterbourne Abbas, Weston Lullingfields, Theddlethorpe, All Saints, Little Missenden'.[86] On the most northerly point of Britain, Dunnet Head in Scotland, Paul Theroux finds 'only the place-names were exciting – not just Buldoo and John O'Groats, but Hunspow and Ham, and Thrumster, Scrabster, Shebster and Lybster'.[87] In the intralingual travel account, language must generate its own exoticism: it cannot rely on foreign loan-words, the italicised condiments of travel prose, to take the reader elsewhere. The strategies of estrangement discussed earlier are part of this process of exoticising the linguistically familiar, and for the two American travellers British place and family names are clear signals of being abroad in the same language. The exotic can of course be an occasion for rapt enthusiasm (*le japonisme* in late nineteenth-century England and France) or endless comic opportunity (funny foreigners). If Aristotle sees comedy as the art of distance, of a necessary emotional disengagement (too close to the consequences of an action and we are likely to be reduced to tears), then the exotic predicated on the view from afar has all the potential of the comic. Trawling through a gazetteer of Britain, Bryson provides an annotated guide: 'you can find fertilizers (Hastigrow), shoe deodorizers (Powfoot), breath fresheners (Minto), dog food (Whelpo) and even a Scottish spot remover (Sootywells)'.[88] In a guesthouse in Dover, one of the other guests introduces himself to Bryson but the writer confesses, 'I don't remember his name now, but it was one of those names that only English people have – Colin Crapspray or Bertram Pantyshield or something similarly improbable.'[89] Personal names are also an area of incontrovertible English/American difference for Theroux:

> They love candy and Lucozade and leftovers called bubble-and-squeak!
> They live in Barking and Dorking and Shellow Bowells! They have

amazing names, like Mr Eatwell, and Lady Inkpen, and Major Twaddle
and Miss Tosh! And they think *we're* funny.[90] (his emphasis)

Writing on authorial voice in V.S. Naipaul, John Thieme sees Naipaul as
deeply indebted to the 'habitual pose of detachment of the English ironic
tradition'.[91] It is this ironic tradition that is reversed in the accounts of Bryson
and Theroux. Affecting the burlesque distance of Oxbridge on Tour, the two
American writers practise 'the habitual pose of detachment' to make
England (and Britain) itself the object rather than the subject of ironic
comment. This comment, of course, often involves the verbal inflation of
satire. Although placenames generally correspond to real places on the map,
the personal names are frequently invented (particularly by Theroux) to
convey a sense of manifest absurdity. Travel becomes a form of Restoration
comedy where names ('Twaddle', 'Crapspray', 'Eatwell') define character
and establish an horizon of expectation. In a sense, the travel writers as
satirists have taken Spenser seriously and decided that names should indeed
reflect some faculty or quality of the body or mind. If colonialism and immigration have often involved the translation of names between languages,
caricature effects its own transformations of names within a language with
the highlighting of the signifier and the eclipse of the referent by the signified
where the name describes a quality or feature of the person.[92] If interlingual
translation produces opacity through phonetic literalism (Cloonboo) or
substitution (Elaine), then the intralingual versions of names in the accounts
of Bryson and Theroux generate their own opaqueness under cover of transparency. 'Pantyshield' and 'Inkwell' couple together common nouns in
limpid union. Cloonboo or Booterstown are meaningless to speakers of
standard English but 'Inkwell' readily suggests a meaning. Like the pseudo-
translation described above, the transparency implied by the caricature of
association is another fiction. Name is not destiny, though of course it can be
in the drama of satire. The common-noun connotations of component parts
of proper names fuel schoolyard ridicule but they ultimately make the referent as invisible as the Polish girls lost in translation.

Home, purism and hospitality

For travellers in foreign lands, writing in their native tongue can be a form
of homecoming. The letter, the postcard, the diary, or e-mail is a brief foray
into the home territory of language, a respite from the endless negotiation
of other people's language zones. Bringing it all back home to language, it
could be argued, is the implicit aim of the literary traveller. What is home
then for the travellers travelling through countries where most people speak
their language? If travel is construed as departure, it also implies return,
otherwise departure gives way to exile. So to what, linguistically, does the

intralingual traveller return? One of the questions that Rosita Boland is continually asked as she travels around Ireland is where she comes from, what is home for her. She finds the question difficult to answer:

> The truth was that I had not yet found a home that did not dissolve with restlessness, if a 'dwelling place' – the first definition of the ambiguous word 'home' in the dictionary – was what was meant by home. Yet I felt *at home* in many places . . . As I travelled around Ireland, I thought it was possible to have several homes and that the word 'home' was fluid; a word that I would continue to redefine for myself.[93] (her emphasis)

Born in Ireland, Boland has spent part of her life elsewhere. Theroux and Bryson, born in the United States, have spent many years in England. Jonathan Raban, born in England, has spent a number of years living in the United States. The different accounts all explore a notion of home. Theroux and Bryson set out to get to know the country that has been their home for many years but that still feels in many ways foreign and unknown to them. Jonathan Raban's *Coasting*, his account of travelling around the coast of Britain by boat, and Boland's coastal book are journeys around countries that are birthplaces to both of the writers. Raban's *Hunting Mister Heartbreak* is an experiment with a series of temporary homes in the United States. The travel accounts all share the conviction that what was, is or will be home is a strangely foreign place. The parallel with the anthropology of proximity is striking. Here anthropologists do not travel to distant islands to study indigenous tribes in exotic locations but stay at home and carry out fieldwork on their own tribe, making the familiar remote rather than the remote familiar.[94] This attentiveness to proximity raises questions about distinctions. How is *Home* to be distinguished from *Away*? James Clifford feels binary oppositions between home and abroad, staying and moving, need to be questioned:

> These oppositions have often been naturalized along lines of gender (female, domestic space versus male travel), class (the active, alienated bourgeoisie versus the stagnant, soulful poor), and race/culture (modern, rootless Westerners versus traditional, rooted 'natives'). The fieldwork injunction to go elsewhere construes 'home' as a site of origin, of sameness. Feminist theory and gay/lesbian studies have, perhaps most sharply, showed home to be a site of unrestful differences.[95]

Boland, Bryson, Theroux and Raban give us a picture of the place that they have been given or adopted as home as indeed a 'site of unrestful differences'. What is significant is that being a native does not appear to offer any decisive advantage of interpretation, the notion of 'home' is as fluid for Boland and Raban as it is for Theroux and Bryson. Part of the impulse of travel can be not so much to *leave* home as to *find* home. Bryson, on the eve of his departure from England, wants to find out what his home for many years looks like and ultimately why it is that he has felt at home in Britain.

When he and Theroux list the features of life in Britain that have made them feel comfortable in their adopted home, it is not similarities (with American culture) that they stress but differences. Theroux gives his own manifest of cultural preferences:

> the bread, the fish, the cheese, the flower gardens, the apples, the clouds, the newspapers, the beer, the woollen cloth, the radio programmes, the parks, the Indian restaurants and amateur dramatics, the postal service, the fresh vegetables, the trains, and the modesty and truthfulness of people.[96]

Thus, the exoticising effects of the travel accounts as the travellers make their way around Britain, Ireland or the United States often underline the alien nature of territory. However, it is this very *unheimlichkeit* that makes a concept of 'home' possible. Dwelling is made possible through the exploration or revelation of differences through travel. Home becomes at once a stranger and more complex place on the evidence of travel but it is that complexity, those 'unrestful differences', that make the concept of home in Ireland, Britain or the United States conceivable and desirable.

The differences itemised by Theroux do not explicitly include language, though products of language – newspapers, radio programmes, amateur dramatics – are mentioned. The evidence is in the accounts, however, of the journey through the English language undertaken by travellers to Britain, Ireland and the United States. The differences in words, accent, expression, syntax, connotation and usage that plot their movement through the language that is their mother tongue both highlight the foreignness of particular varieties of English for the traveller and emphasise the dynamism and the capaciousness of the language that is their home. Difficulties arise when eviction notices are served by purists who feel that they have prior claims to a language. Bill Bryson, who is the author of two books on the English language, is particularly sensitive to attempts to establish hierarchies of putative correctness based on a notion of originary primacy.[97] Bryson enters into conversation with an elderly couple in a hotel near the Lake District who begin to deride Americans for the 'things they do to language'. Bryson notes:

> One of the things you get used to hearing when you are an American living in Britain is that America will be the death of English. It is a sentiment expressed to me surprisingly often, usually at dinner parties, usually by someone who has too much to drink, but sometimes by a semi-demented, overpowdered old crone like this one. There comes a time when you lose patience with this sort of thing. So I told her . . . whether they appreciated it or not British speech has been enlivened beyond measure by words created in America, words that they could not do without, and that one of these words was moron.[98]

The proprietorial attitude to language could be seen at one level as the angry defensiveness of the owner-occupier of the ancestral house of language, suspicious of travellers from elsewhere with their new words and strange accents. At another level, the exchange with Bryson points to a lingering resentment that America politically will mean not the death but the survival of English.

Bruce Chatwin speaks of a basic human appetite for movement and suggests that much aggression is a violent response to the frustrations of confinement. Pilgrimage answers this deep-rooted therapeutic need for movement as an antidote to the quarrelsome vexatiousness of prolonged settlement.[99] In one sense, the petulant dismissal of other varieties of English can be seen as a refusal to acknowledge the dialogical nature of language itself. The notion of language as dialogue was most famously articulated by Bakhtin[100] and has been rearticulated, albeit somewhat differently, by Jacques Derrida in his *Le monolinguisme de l'autre*. Derrida advances two propositions that appear to be mutually contradictory: '1. *On ne parle jamais qu'une seule langue.* 2. *On ne parle jamais une seule langue.*'[101] The resolution of the paradox for Derrida lies in the recognition that 'Ma langue, la seule que je m'entende parler et m'entende à parler, c'est la langue de l'autre.'[102] Language comes from parents, siblings, friends, school, work, society in general, and outside the private languages of psychosis it is always used to communicate with another. Language develops through mediation with others and the absence of language produces the relational tragedy of autism. Acquiring a language involves moving outside the enclosure of self to engage with others. Intralingual travelling is the visible practice of this monolingualism of the other, underscored wittingly or unwittingly by the numerous instances of dialogue in the different travel accounts. Derrida employs the metaphor of journey to describe the personal odyssey of the speaker of the mother tongue:

> Je dis route et trace de retour, car ce qui distingue une route d'un frayage ou d'une *via rupta* (son *etymon*), comme *methodos* de *odos*, c'est la répétition, le retour, la réversibilité, l'itérabilité, l'itération possible de l'itinéraire. Comment est-il possible que, reçue ou apprise, cette langue soit ressentie, explorée, travaillée, à réinventer sans itinéraire et sans carte, comme la langue de l'autre?[103]

As we mentioned earlier, travel implies return and the accounts are the fruits of that return, the returned traveller returning in memory and prose to the places and experiences of travel. Thus, at the end of the journey, the traveller returns to language (writing up the account) and makes the journey once again in words, exemplifying the 'itération possible de l'itinéraire'. The coming home of composition is a *revisiting* of the mother tongue as the writer picks his/her way through the multiple traces of language difference from the journey. Through travel, the language has become unsettled. The 'home' of language becomes a halting site of difference. The accounts testify not only to individual encounters with language difference but that language itself travels.

Jonathan Raban details the changes in a language that has crossed the Atlantic ocean to the United States. Eric Newby, Roy Kerridge, John Gibbons and Charles Graves describe the transformation of a language brought across the Irish Sea to Ireland. For Rosita Boland and Paul Theroux, words, expressions, an accent in a particular region, are evidence of the passage of earlier travellers in the form of invaders or traders, the translated word or lingering accent bearing ample witness to the fundamental nomadism of language.

Language travels to the traveller too in the form of the language of other travellers. Jonathan Raban carefully assembles a library on his boat, the *Gosfield Maid*, before sailing around the coast of Britain. It is Mark Twain's text that sets Raban off on his journey down the Mississippi. Bill Bryson speaks admiringly of the travel writings of Jan Morris and Paul Theroux. Theroux quotes Sean O'Faoláin and Boland has the *Rough Guide to Ireland* in her rucksack. Intertextual travel takes various forms. The actual travel of the writers can be contrasted with the virtual experience of travel through the language of printed text. This involves splicing extracts from earlier accounts to the text or juxtaposing the solemn pronouncements of guide books with descriptions of the wayward reality of place. Frequently, the effect achieved is what Margaret Sabin has described as 'the conventional Romantic sequence of yearning departure followed by disappointed arrival'.[104] Intertextual pressure can also act as a shaper of itinerary through reaction. Dissecting the 'anti-tourist', Paul Fussell notes, 'Sedulously avoiding the standard sights is probably the best method of disguising your touristhood.'[105] Theroux refuses to visit castles and John Gibbons claims, 'I was deliberately giving a miss to all the famous places.' The latter does not bother going to the Aran Islands on the grounds that 'the thing must have been written up again and again'.[106] The particular anxiety of influence experienced by the traveller is not so much dictated by place as by how much and what has been said about the place. The difficulty for the literary traveller is in finding a new *language* within the already existing tradition of writing about a particular place or country that is felt to be adequate to their experience of the place and that commands attention. This task of endless reinvention may be even more problematic for writers describing a country that speaks the same language as their readers. The readier flow of information within the same language space can lead to assumptions of privileged knowledge. Watching American soap-operas or seeing British films without sub-titles can create delusions of understanding. Whereas an anglophone reading public might willingly acknowledge the necessary existence of intermediaries to translate for them the reality of life in Afghanistan or Greenland, there may be a greater resistance to the notion of the travel writer-as-translator within the English-speaking world. Indeed, as has become apparent in this chapter, one of the primary tasks of travel writers is to demonstrate how much translation has to be done, if only to justify their narrative role as interpreter of the scenes they witness.

Earning the complicity of the reader means that not only must the writers themselves travel through language but they must also make the readers undertake the same journey. This travelling by the reader can take two forms, the *ocular* and the *epistemic*. Ocular travelling involves being transported to a place and being made to imagine that one is eye-witness at the countless scenes described by travel writers. Great imaginative empathy is needed in these instances to sustain the multiple indiscretions of the travel narrative. Epistemic travelling can be expressed as the readers being persuaded to leave behind the safe berth of received opinion and to explore elements of their own or other cultures that they take for granted or of which they are ignorant. Whether operating in a descriptive or a rhetorical mode, the intralingual travel writer is not only dealing with myths of understanding but there is in addition the indifference of familiarity. Why read about Britain/Ireland/the United States? I live there. The reader must, in an almost Heideggerian sense, be un-housed. Language has to perform a function of defamiliarisation that is not the sole province of an esoteric avant-garde. To do this, the writer must decide how the travel experience is to be translated into a language. Amati Mehler, Agentieri and Canestri point out that, 'quiconque a traduit sait qu'à l'intérieur d'une langue il existe de multiples choix permis, théoriquement équivalents, mais personnellement privilégiés, ce qui caractérise, en définitive, un style'.[107] The perennial difficulty for translators is how to choose between competing alternatives, each occupying different parts of the semantic field; and the sum total of choices that the translators make constitute their specific style, making each translation of the same text different. Travel writers similarly may have the same source-place but the language choices, quite apart from the fractal dimension mentioned earlier, will generate a different target-text, a unique translation of place.

Emmanuel Lévinas has claimed that 'l'essence du langage est amitié et hospitalité'.[108] Travellers are dependent on hospitality as they journey on their way, hoping for the gift of a welcome, a conversation, an entry – however brief – into the lives of their hosts. Language can often indeed be a precondition of hospitality. As we shall see in succeeding chapters, failure to speak the language of the other can excite hostility and suspicion. There can be the potential awkwardness of silence or the tedium of explicit and continuous recourse to inadequate translation. Conversely, shared language is never enough to ensure the friendship promised by Lévinas. Theroux notes that 'Speaking to strangers was regarded as challenging in England; it meant entering a minefield of verbal and social distinctions.'[109] Eric Newby may dedicate his account to the Irish as the 'Eighth Walking (and Talking) Wonders of the World', but he oftens finds that language is more of a hindrance than a help as the directions offered by his good-natured hosts leave his wife and himself wandering aimlessly through the Irish countryside. The hospitality that the French linguist Émile Benveniste attributes to language is extended to readers of language in the presentation of travel narratives to a reading public. They are invited to share the journey and the experience of people, place and self with the writer. There is a further dimension to this practice of hospitality which lies in the critique of ethnocentrism that has inspired a certain tradition of comment on travel from Montaigne to Diderot, Montesquieu and D.H. Lawrence. Using the language of the travel encounter to comment on the shortcomings of one's own society is an incentive to a more generous, tolerant and hospitable humanity. The dilemma for the traveller and reader of travel literature is, however, the dilemma of translation itself. Derrida and Benveniste have commented on the semantic chain that links *hospes* (one who entertains a stranger) and *hostis* (a stranger, foreigner, enemy), the uneasy proximity that sees open welcome give way to nervous xenophobia.[110] Translation can be the ultimate expression of linguistic hospitality welcoming new languages, cultures and ideas into the mother tongue, or it can be a fortress of hegemonic difference translating people into the language of dominant cultures and annihilating difference. As in the accounts of writers who see certain things, offer their own interpretations of events, and make specific choices in language to describe or comment on those events, travel accounts have the understated power of the translation. Responses to the legitimate and illegitimate uses of this power will vary. One person's equivalence is another's mistranslation. Not everyone will agree as to the 'faithfulness' of the translation of a specific culture, more particularly when they can compare the translation with the source. The traveller and reader will compare translations. Any good translation will nonetheless involve scrupulous examination and close reading of the source text and it is in this discipline of attention that cultures and countries can be opened up. When the source language of experience and the target language of account are the same, translation does not seek invisibility. It becomes more urgent than ever.

Chapter Two

THE CHANGELING

Liam Ó Rinn feels sick. He has been walking Paris for three weeks and now his body and soul ache with the dis-ease of being elsewhere:

> Tar éis trí seachtaine do thabhairt ag rith trí shráideanna Phárais, fé bhrothall de ló is d'oíche, ag féachaint ar gach ní áluinn no iongantach no cuirialta do bhuaileadh umam, do bhí tinneas am chosaibh agus am shúilibh agus tuirse chuirp is aigne orm. Do ghoill sé orm, leis, gan a bheith ar mo chumas labhairt leis na daoine go réidh agus go héasca éasáideach, toisc gan mo dhóthain taithí do bheith agam ar theangain na tíre.[1]

Loneliness now darkens his vision of the city so he thinks only of home and the familiar. The experience of Ó Rinn is commonplace. Anyone who has travelled through a foreign country in a foreign language knows the exhaustion of evening, the headache of linguistic disparity as the brokerage of speech takes a physical toll. The somatic evidence of the intense labour of translation is the tired tourist looking for a compatriot in a late-night bar, the weary au-pair tuning in to news from home on a transistor, backpackers scouring a week-old newspaper in their mother tongue for pagefuls of familiar language. Translation is hard work but what are the traces of this labour in travel writing? Do writers draw readers' attention to the multiple transactions of language or is the process of translation artfully concealed as an indecent intrusion between the reader and the traveller's experiences? Does the Traveller feature also as Translator or does the Translator once again become invisible, overshadowed by the solar presence of the Traveller as Author?

Fantasy, paradox, infantilisation

A traditional problem for travellers in earlier centuries was convincing readers they were not making it all up. Travel was closely associated with the literature of fantasy and the claims of travellers were met with due scepticism.[2] The Renaissance travel writers began to freight their work with fact and erudition to allay doubt and guarantee authenticity. The subsequent shift to the tradition of the sentimental traveller was to produce a move away from the laconic verisimilitude of the log book towards a more speculative, inward response to phenomena, this response differentiating the travel account from the unadorned objectivity of the guide book. Detail still counts but the detail aims at recreating the experience of being a particular person in a particular place rather than acting as circumstantial evidence in the writer's case for being believed. Language is an important source of the detail that confers a plausibility on an account and makes the foreign textually apparent. Words become the souvenirs brought home to the expectant reader. These words often relate to culture-specific items that have no equivalent in the target language of the traveller. In *The Road to Oxiana*, Robert Byron meets an Indian merchant called Haji Lal Mohammad in Afghanistan who tells Byron and his companions that the place where their car has broken down is not a good place to be after dark. He tells them the 'robat is only one farsakh off'. The reader has already been told that the 'farsakh' is a Persian unit of measurement, but it is only on the next page that 'robat' is explained to the reader as 'the Afghan term for caravanserai'. Robat is also used 'as a measure of distance, since the main highways have these establishments every four farsakhs or sixteen miles'.[3] The word 'robat' refers to a specific Afghan reality, akin to the word 'caravanserai' that describes a similar establishment in Iran. Nicolas Bouvier, the Swiss travel writer, finds himself travelling twenty years later in the same region of the world as Byron and cites the names of a meat dish, '*kufté*', and breads, '*sandjak*' and '*lavash*', that are part of the culinary fare in the town of Tabriz in Northern Iran.[4] On the island of Madagascar, Dervla Murphy finds the untranslatable in the realm of sentiment. She points out that the Malagasy word '*Fihavanana*' has no exact English equivalent: 'It was translated by a Merina friend as "benevolence and friendship towards all one's fellow men" and it describes one of the most obvious Malagasy characteristics.'[5] Bruce Chatwin in Welsh Patagonia has an '*asado*' with the Powells. The reader is not told immediately what this is but Eddy Powell is described as cutting a side of mutton from a carcass. Then, 'he fixed the meat to an *asador*, which is an iron spit in the shape of a cross, and stuck it in the ground slanting over the fire. Later, we ate the *asado* with a sauce called *salmuera*, made of vinegar, garlic, chillies and oregano.'[6]

Culture-specific items are notoriously difficult to translate and indeed can be seen as indicating the limits of the translatable.[7] If items are specific to a particular culture, then their very specificity would seem to preclude translation into the languages of other cultures. Words in their untranslated state mark out cultural difference. The words occur, however, largely in isolation and one rarely gets extended speech in a language other than the dominant language of the narrative (though there are exceptions as we shall see later in the chapter). Thus, the words operate as signs of the untranslatable but in a *space of translation*. The reality that is happening in a foreign language is being conveyed to the reader in the language of the narrative; in other words, it is being continuously translated into that language but foreign words remain as witting or unwitting reminders of how fraught the process of translation is in the first place. Lexical exoticism is a palpable written trace of the foreign for the reader, a legible indication that, although the account has been written in English, French, Irish, Italian or Russian, the country is elsewhere, the language and mores different. Foreign-language terms can be italicised to draw attention to their conspicuous otherness in the text or they can be included in a more discreet manner as in Byron's account, the discretion adding to the seeming naturalness or casual inevitability of the incorporation of foreign words into the travel account. The reader is translated into a foreign climate through the untranslated. Though the words are almost invariably explained, their distinctness remains intact. If foreign-language words can refer to the culturally specific there are other instances where they are used in a more explicitly metonymic fashion, as general markers of foreignness.

Bruce Chatwin on his way south of Buenos Aires stops in a small town to meet a man named Bill Philips. He enters a small bar and asks about Philips's whereabouts:

> An old woman gave me a leathery sandwich and coffee. Naturally, she said, I could leave my bag while I tried to find Señor Philips.
> 'It is far to Señor Philips. He lives up in the sierra.'
> 'How far?'
> 'Eight leagues. But you may find him. Often he comes to town in the morning.'
> I asked around but no one had seen the gringo Philips that morning. I found a taxi and haggled over the price.[8]

Chatwin never tells the reader whether he speaks Spanish fluently or not. From the textual evidence that he can haggle over taxi fares and conduct conversations with people in a small Argentinian town, one can only assume that his Spanish is reasonable and that this was the language in which he conducted his business. Words like 'Señor' and 'gringo' could have been translated but they are retained, if only to create the impression of a conversation in Spanish – although the conversation is of course reported in English. The non-standard syntax of the old woman's 'English' also strengthens the sense of the language she is using as foreign and different. Chatwin's procedure is not unusual and is a more or less standard approach to foreign-language encounters in much of modern travel writing. No writer will include large sections of the foreign language in an account on the reasonable assumption that many readers will not know the foreign language and are not reading the travel account with language pedagogy in mind. The writer is expected to do the translation work for the reader. However, the status of the passages of language contact with native populations speaking languages other than the mother tongue of the narrator is markedly paradoxical. On the one hand, other languages disappear as all the direct and indirect speech is reported in the dominant narrative language. On the other, the passages of direct speech through the use of foreign-language terms, imperfect syntax and non-standard accent convey the impression of exchanges taking place in a foreign language. Thus, the act of translation at one level is concealed as if it was perfectly natural for Iranian police officials, Argentinian farm-hands or Italian television dealers to speak English, French, Irish or any language other than their own. At another level, however, the approximate, translated state of the conversation is inscribed in word, accent and word-order.

When the foreigner speaks, the report both is and is not a translation. In a sense, travel writing merely highlights the fundamental paradox of translation itself. A translation is paradoxical because it both is and is not the original. The translation only exists because of the original but the aim of translation as conventionally defined is that it should read like an original in the target language. The original is simultaneously present and absent. The translator is normally more aware of the paradoxical status of the translated text than the receiver, though it is likely that the paradoxical sensitivity on the part of the translation user/receiver is a function of the form of translation, i.e. the viewer of a sub-titled television programme is made more immediately aware of the presence/absence paradox of translation than the end-user of a software localisation product.[9] Travel writing where language difference is signalled contributes potentially to this heightened sensitivity to the paradoxes at work in translation. In a sense, the writers are using a non-fluent, exoticising strategy where the irreducible otherness of the foreign language and culture is indicated by the obviously *translated* nature of the text. The otherness is made less obvious in indirect speech, where the tendency can be to translate through paraphrase, and any traces of difference are excised from the narrative. Near Andkhoi in Afghanistan, Byron and his fellow travellers meet an Uzbek shepherd who will not speak to them at first, believing they are Russians. When the shepherd learns that they are not (though we are not told in what language he learns this – Persian? Uzbek?), the narrator continues, 'He excused his ill manners later by explaining that the Russians had stolen sixty thousand of the best sheep.'[10] He then explains to Byron the differences between the two breeds of sheep in his flock but only the words for the sheep breeds indicate the possible remoteness of the shepherd's language from the English of the narrative voice. These words, 'Karakulis' and 'Arabis', point to a dimension of language contact that subtly undermines the naturalness of the indirect paraphrase. Languages expand through contact with other languages. They need the words that other languages provide if they are to give an adequate picture of the world. Therefore, they must translate but what they translate lexically is frequently that which is the least translatable, the culture-specific item. In this respect, translation is like the 'esperantosamizdat' described by Claudio Magris in *Danubio*. The term was coined by a Romanian writer of German, Nikolaus Berwanger, and Magris defines it as the belief that, 'True poetry ought to be secret and clandestine, concealed like a prohibited voice of dissent, while at the same time it should speak to everyone.'[11] Smuggling is intimately bound up with the history of travel and the travel account in a sense brings in the private, clandestine words of other cultures either through the open secret of italics or the normative disguise of standard type-face. The hope is that in this way the other culture should 'speak to everyone' in the target language.

Speaking not just to everyone but to anyone in a foreign language can be difficult, embarrassing, even humiliating. The fear of ridicule, vulnerability and helplessness that comes from the inability to express oneself in another language is a key element in the language infrastructure of the tourist indus-try. Ferried from coach to museum to hotel, the tourist is insulated from the shock of language contact by the omnipresent guide/interpreter, speaking the mother tongue of the group. Language familiarity breeds content. Erwing Stengel, a German psychoanalyst forced to flee Nazi persecution, noted in a 1939 article the particular difficulties adults have in learning foreign languages. Stengel believed that the super-ego had a decisive role to play in success or failure in acquiring a foreign language. The super-ego, more to the fore in the adult psyche, polices the exact appellation of objects and the relationship between words and things. For children, the super-ego is less active, so that they are more spontaneous and less concerned about making mistakes.[12] Amati Mehler, Argentieri and Canestri sum up adult resistance to language learning:

> d'un côté la difficulté à renoncer à l'illusion narcissique universelle selon laquelle sa propre langue est la meilleure, la seule en mesure d'exprimer la complexité de la vie et de réfléter la vérité: de l'autre côté, les sentiments de honte, de culpabilité, de peur du ridicule et de blessure narcissique liés à la régression vers les processus primaires nécessitée par l'apprentissage de la compréhension et de l'utilisation d'un idiome étranger.[13]

The adult fear is one of infantilisation, of desperately trying to make sense of what mother is saying. The parental function of many tour guides/interpreters as they usher their charges on and off coaches is not an accident but a logical consequence of the tourist fear of being suddenly orphaned in a strange house of language where the parents are not around to hear the cries for help.

Jonathan Raban noted in Seattle how for Koreans adult/children hierar-chies were inverted in the language learning situation. From an early age, the children are pressed into service as translators, to deal on their parents' behalf with landlords, business clients or the Inland Revenue Service. The children have an adult's grasp of the language (through dealing with many 'adult' situations) while many of the adults continue to have a child's grasp of the language. Joining an English-language class for immigrants in Seattle, Raban comments on how the husbands, wives and breadwinners entered a second childhood through language:

> The students clapped, giggled, shot their hands up (*'Me!' 'Me!' 'Me!'*). Failures were met with *oohs* and *ahs*, success with whistles and applause. The students, infants in the language, had reverted to the social behaviour of a happy, squealing infant school. They were six years old again.[14]

The classroom situation in Seattle is a haven for the immigrants where they can safely make mistakes, but the streets outside Central Community College offer the more brutal censure of impatient incomprehension. Immigrants differ from modern literary travellers in that the stakes are much higher in their language contact and the outcome can be tragic rather than comic. However, the force of alienation that language distance implies is expressed by Lisa St Aubin de Terán in *Off the Rails* when she describes her train journey to Sestri Levante, in Italy, where she intended to live for a while. She remembers the noise of Italy, the colour and a sense of belonging, but has forgotten the primary fact of language:

> Every time the train emerged from the tunnel, the sight of the sea filled me with a vague irrational hope, but every time it blacked into a tunnel, I brooded in the ensuing darkness on a life of monosyllables and slow dictionary phrases.[15]

The difficulty for travellers is trying to establish purposeful and meaningful contact with people as adult human beings, but their knowledge of language may mean that the only communication possible in language is a maddening simplification of their personality and ideas. Hence, the stereotype of the dumb tourist in many cultures, a grinning child bullied by adults who shout at him/her in loud, staccato speech. Language in one's own culture, as we saw in Chapter 1, is complex and is not a simple given, but the centrality of language to cultural contact becomes immediately apparent once the traveller crosses the language divide into a foreign culture. Here, the simplest transactions become nightmares of complication. The sociologist H. Schutz has described the type of knowledge that people typically have about their own culture:

> It is a knowledge of trustworthy *recipes* for interpreting the social world and for handling things and men in order to obtain the best results in every situation with a minimum of effort by avoiding undesirable consequences.[16] (his emphasis)

This taken-for-granted thinking as usual about the world sustains a social group and gives it a certain coherence. The problem for strangers is that they do not share the basic assumptions of the group that govern in an unspoken way the group's interaction with the everyday lifeworld:

> He [the stranger] becomes essentially the man who has to place in ques-
> tion nearly everything that seems to be unquestionable to the members of
> the approached group. To him the cultural pattern of the approached
> group does not have the authority of a tested system of recipes, and this, if
> for no other reason, because he does not partake in the vivid historical
> tradition by which it has been formed.[17]

Cultural patterns are not a refuge or a haven for strangers but a labyrinth in which they have lost all their bearings. Eva Hoffman articulates a similar idea in *Lost in Translation* when she concludes that 'Pattern is the soil of significance and it is surely one of the hazards of emigration, of exile, and extreme mobility, that one is uprooted from that soil.'[18] This sense of loss and dislocation is amplified by language that infiltrates all areas of social exchange. Lisa St Aubin de Terán, when she finally arrives at the station in Sestri Levante, is reluctant to ask the ticket man if her trunks have arrived from London: 'I didn't dare stumble with misremembered words and risk being laughed at.'[19] Úna Ní Mhaoileoin, on her way to Tunisia, finds that Italian is not much use in looking for toilets on a Spanish train:

> An focal céanna acu is atá ag na hIodáiligh ar theach agus ar bhó agus ar
> rudaí eile nach mbeifeá á n-iarraidh ar aon nós, ach níl a fhios agam cén
> focal atá acu ar leithreas. Ní thuigeann siad gabinetto agus nuair a d'iarr
> mé áit da lavarsi le mani thug siad ansin go díreach dom, gan faic le chois!
> Caithfidh mé spás a dhéanamh sa mháilín d'fhoclóirín, tá faitíos orm.[20]

Though his knowledge of Persian improves, Robert Byron makes the kitchen staff laugh in his hotel in Herat, Afghanistan, by asking for a 'lady'(khanum) instead of a hot-water bottle. The translation predicament can be a source of tragic self-awareness or a licence for self-mockery. Literary travellers often exploit mistranslation for its comedy of inappropriateness. If speaking through another language and negotiating a different culture engenders an inevitable distance – although you are trying to get close to the culture, you are still at a remove from it – then the foreign reality can appear theatrical. Indeed, Henry James in his *Italian Hours* suggested that to travel anywhere is, 'as it were, to go to the play, to attend the spectacle'.[21] The translation mistakes, the misunderstandings, the rough approximations provide the dialogue for the mock-sentimental drama of intercultural encounter. The comic *verfremdung* of translation has two modes of operation in modern literary travel accounts. The first is self-directed and the second is other-directed. In the first mode, the traveller-narrator is a picaresque hero or heroine whose cultural knowledge and linguistic assuredness are undermined or relativised by interlingual travelling. The sovereign ego is humbled by the intractable detail of foreign language and the traveller is no longer at the centre of his/her own language world but on the margins of another. Culture and language become cultures and languages and the onset of relativism in a world turned upside down provides endless scope for farce. In the other-directed mode, it is the speaker of the foreign language rather than the traveller who emerges as the figure of translation fun. In the space of language contact it is the foreigners who translate themselves into the language of the narrator. The procedure is extremely common in literary travel narratives as it has the signal advantage of offering the reader native material in the language of the narrative. A famous example is Byron's transcription of his conversational exchanges with the Afghan ambassador to Iran, Shir Ahmad. Ahmad compliments Byron on being an honest man and Byron replies:

> R.B. 'Your Excellency is too good.'
> Shir Ahmad (*mf*): 'I am good, ha, ha. All Afghans good peoples. They have good lives. (*pp*) No wines, (*f*) no other men's wives. (*mf*) They believe God, and religion. All Afghans good peoples, all fiddles.'
> R.B.: 'Fiddles?'
> Shir Ahmad (*mp*): 'Fiddles, no? Is it French? Faithfuls, yes?'[22]

Byron has inserted musical notation in brackets to convey a more vivid impression of the ambassador's speech. Byron's laconic questions and statements are juxtaposed to the effusive musings of the Afghan diplomat. The expansive, unidiomatic pronouncements of Shir Ahmad are undoubtedly intended to be comic, even to the extent of using theatrical conventions to indicate different speakers. However, the other-directed comedy of language in this instance tends not to subvert but to confirm the linguistic superiority of the traveller. It is the foreign speaker that bears the taint of ridicule and grapples with the intricacies of syntax and the treacheries of *faux-amis*. The convention of the 'funny foreigner' in English almost invariably relies on the prop of language, and the power of the convention is apparent even in the Irish-language account of Úna Ní Mhaoileoin where she offers extended passages of a Dutchman speaking heavily accented pidgin English. Since as a minority-language speaker she is unlikely to meet many foreigners speaking Irish Gaelic, she looks to her other language, English, for the opportunity of easy comedy.

We have already discussed the question of accent in intralingual settings but, of course, it is a fundamental aspect of language contact in interlingual situations. Alexandra David-Neel is continuously worried that it is her accent in Tibetan that will give her away as a foreigner and lead to her expulsion from the country. Accent is the final frontier of assimilation, the ultimate disguise. In his autobiographical account, *Adieu, vive clarté*, Jorge Semprun describes a public humiliation in a baker's shop in the Latin quarter in Paris where the *boulangère* ridicules him because she is unable to understand what he is saying in French. She cites Hugo, and his reference from another era to the Spanish 'armée en déroute'. The year is 1936 and Semprun, the son of a Spanish Republican minister, is a political refugee in France. His reaction is immediate:

> J'ai pris la décision d'effacer au plus vite toute trace d'accent de ma pronon-
> ciation française: personne ne me traitera plus jamais d'*Espagnol de l'armée
> en déroute*, rien qu'à m'entendre. Pour préserver mon identité d'étranger,
> pour faire de celle-ci une vertu intérieure, secrète, fondatrice et confon-
> dante, je vais me fondre dans l'anonymat d'une prononciation correcte.[23]

Jacques Derrida, French speaking, Jewish, born in Algeria, notes that 'On n'entrait dans la littérature française qu'en perdant son accent.' This acqui-sition of another, 'foreign' accent is a struggle, 'L'accent signale un corps à corps avec la langue en général, il dit plus que l'accentuation. Sa sympto-matologie envahit l'écriture.'[24] The difficulty lies at one level in the anxiety of disguise, the recurrent fear of being unmasked, of being troubled in the anonymity of accentual equivalance. Julia Kristeva, Bulgarian in origin, writes in French of the precariousness of the illusion of acceptance. You learn the other language and become proficient in it as you would with a musical instrument or algebra:

> Vous pouvez devenir virtuose avec ce nouvel artifice qui vous procure
> d'ailleurs un nouveau corps, tout aussi artificiel, sublimé – certains disent
> sublime. Vous avez le sentiment que la nouvelle langue est votre
> résurrection: nouvelle peau, nouveau sexe. Mais l'illusion se déchire
> lorsque vous entendez, à l'occasion d'un enregistrement par exemple, et
> que la mélodie de votre voix vous revient bizarre, de nulle part, plus proche
> du bredouillis d'antan que du code d'aujourd'hui.[25]

The experience of Semprun, Derrida and Kristeva indicates that there is more at stake in accent in a foreign language than effective masquerade. Physical danger, political or religious persecution and cultural or economic discrimination can be sufficiently persuasive reasons for perfecting an accent in a foreign language and concealing the traces of origin. This ideal, as borne out by the reported speech in travel accounts and Kristeva's dark caveat, is not always achieved. Intelligent, knowledgeable speakers of a foreign language can still speak with a distinct accent that is not simply the acoustic pains of the struggling beginner in another language. Daniel Sibony sees in foreign-language accent the mark of inhibited origin: 'on parle avec un accent la langue d'accueil, la seconde; l'accent venu de la première, sa musique modulée, la trace d'une gêne: amour malheureux de l'origine, ni voulue, ni quittée'.[26] The unconscious fear of being unfaithful to the mother tongue prevents the accent of the mother tongue from receding. The sounds of the mother's language are perceived at an early stage in the infant's devel-opment so that these sounds come to be viscerally identified with personal identity as elaborated through language.[27] Not to betray one's origins (perfect accent) is to betray one's origins. The jaded adage about poetry being what gets lost in translation hints obliquely at this prosodic dilemma of accent. If translation is criticised for failing to render the original sounds, the prosodic pattern of the original, then the fluent translation is, in a sense, accentless, or rather, there is no 'foreign' accent in the target poem, only the accent of the native speaker (we can use the term 'accent' for music, poetry and language). When a speaker does make the transition to the other language in a successful translation of the language self, what is the relationship between distance and assimilation? If the speaker of a foreign language is taken to be a native speaker of that language, after the initial feeling of self-congratulation, is there a sense of acting under false pretences, of pretending to be another and so losing one's identity? An inner distance of separateness can be camouflaged by the perfect accent, as Semprun has shown to be the case for him, but the tension may be debilitating. As Eva Hoffman remarks:

> The soul can shrivel from an excess of critical distance, and if I don't want to remain in arid, internal exile for the rest of my life, I have to find a way to lose my alienation without losing my self. But how does one bend towards another culture without falling over, how does one strike an elastic balance between rigidity and self-effacement?[28]

Self-effacement is generally a function of time. Passing travellers can long for the anonymity of the long-time dweller if only to pass unobserved as they observe or to have access to less public, more intimate rituals of the lives of others. Úna Ní Mhaoileoin regrets that in Tunisia she is so obviously a foreigner, 'chomh soiléir sin im eachtrannach'.[29] In the oral encounters of travel, languages or accents in languages rapidly flag difference. The ready equation of language and nationality has other unforeseen consequences. Liam Ó Rinn meets a Dutchman outside the ticket office of the *Folies Bergères* in Paris and they converse in English, 'Am thaobh-sa dhe, toisc an Béarla bheith agam ba dheacair dom a chur ina luighe air nár Shasanach mé. D'ain-neoin mé a shéana san do lean sé de bheith ag labhairt fé is da mbá Shasanach mé.'[30] The Dutchman is extremely irate at what he perceives to be English reluctance to learn foreign languages and berates Ó Rinn for this national failing. The latter tries to point out that he is not in fact English because he speaks Irish but his Dutch interlocutor believes the '*Irish language*' to be a simple dialect of English. In an intralingual situation, the confusion of Ó Rinn with an Englishman would have been much less likely as his accent would have signalled his origins. However, accent has markedly less currency as a means of identification in an interlingual context. So the Austrians are mistaken for Germans, the Belgian Walloons for the French, the Irish for the English, Canadian anglophones for Americans, to name but a few examples.[31] The enamel flag on the lapel and the cloth ensigns on rucksacks are identificatory responses to this confusion. The success of cultural nationalism in making nation synonymous with language results in cultural misunderstandings, often paradoxically at the expense of smaller nations. Linguistically, speakers of a language will tend to be identified with the larger, more powerful nations speaking these languages. Ní Mhaoileoin is habitually taken to be English because she is seen reading English newspapers and books on her travels.

One language, one nation, one origin is the initial essentialist response to difference and it is only gradually that the notion of multiple origins and cultural differences not only between but within languages become apparent to those who meet with the traveller. Conversely, if differences are jealously and stridently fetishised, the traveller from the less powerful community in a language area can become unduly fixated on glorying in the signs of divine election. Claudio Magris, on his journey through Slovakia, points up the difficulties of groups who need to shake off the disdain or the indifference of the great:

> Those who have long been forced to put all their efforts into the determination and defence of their own identity tend to prolong this attitude even when it is no longer necessary. Turned inwards on themselves, absorbed in the assertion of their own identity and intent on making sure that others give it due recognition, they run the risk of devoting all their energies to this defence, thereby shrinking the horizons of their experience, or lacking magnanimity in their dealings with the world.[32]

The emergence of English as a world language in the twentieth century has made the experience of non-native speakers of English using the language as a means of communication increasingly commonplace.[33] The instances of translation are greatly multiplied. The more speakers that do translate themselves into English, the easier it is for English speakers to remain in their own language space and see the planet as a space of intralingual as opposed to interlingual translation. The danger, of course, is that non-English speakers only feature in travel narratives as improperly translated beings, losing their depth and complexity in the crude literalism of Survival English.

Dervla Murphy is alive to this dilemma as she describes her empathy with a Malagasy schoolboy who is forced by his mother to recite his English reader so that Murphy and her daughter Rachel might correct him:

> He did quite well in his struggle with the crazed illogic of the English language, once described to me by an Amhara student as a 'crime against humanity'. We may laugh at a people with kings called Andria-mandi-soarivo, Andrianamboa-satismarofy, Andriant-simitovia-minandrian-ehibe – and so on. But the Malagasy can laugh louder at people who think about what they have thought but do not brink what they have brought.[34]

The empathy is arguably more difficult in the light of the translation predicaments that result from time–space compression, namely the ability of goods, people, currencies and bits of information to circulate at ever greater speeds in a global age.[35] As travellers move with greater speed between different locations on the planet, they range far beyond the pale of their own language to radically different language zones. Travellers have of course done so in the past but a feature of the modern age is the acceleration of this mobility and the relative democratisation of access. Temporal compression in the area of travel generates temporal discrepancy in the domain of language. The proper acquisition of a language is the labour of a life. Even a modest ability to function effectively as a comprehending and receiving subject in a language, contrary to the belief of university administrators and government funders, necessitates a considerable investment of time. There is no evidence to suggest that people learn languages any faster than they did two centuries ago but all the evidence is there to show that they travel faster (and more of them further) than they did two hundred years earlier. The time of language acquisition cannot cope with the velocity of displacement. There have been two responses to this phenomenon. The first has been technological, with the production of language gadgets, the pocket translators that generate equivalent commonplace words or phrases in major (i.e. mainly Western) languages. The pocket translator with the portable PC/modem and mobile phone become the accoutrements of the modern traveller/communicator. Miniaturisation greatly enhances the nomadic potential of objects and the pocket translator promises the abolition of the time-lag of language discrepancy for the contemporary nomad. The second response to the linguistic consequences of time–space compression is less utopian in its promise of instant communication but is the most widely practised, namely the acquisition of a world language. In the case of English, for example, the difficulty for the English-language traveller is that travel can become increasingly a question of *secondary translation*, translating the already-translated-into-English, rather than *primary translation*, directly translating from the foreign language into English. For the native speaker of a world language the temptation is to see a heteroglossic not a polyglossic world where travel even outside the area where that language is spoken as a first language becomes a journey through varieties of Language not languages.

Intertextuality, informants and obstacles

Translation is not merely figured as an oral activity in travel accounts, however, but also features as an intertextual presence. The literature that informs travellers' itineraries and responses in foreign countries must draw, at least in part, on literature produced in the languages of these countries. The echo of translation is heard in the texts that accompany the traveller.

Robert Byron's specific interest in the Timurid Renaissance is increased by his enjoyment of the sixteenth-century Memoirs of Babur. He has the English translation of the memoirs with him in Afghanistan and in Herat he seeks out the buildings that Babur looked at. Babur originally wrote in Turki and Byron relies on an available printed translation for knowledge of Babur's observations. In the case of Ernest Diez, however, who writes in German, it is Byron who is the translator. He brings Diez's *Churasanische Baudenkmäler* on his journey in addition to a collection of Oskar von Niedermeyer's photographs of Afghanistan, prefaced in German by Diez. Byron foregrounds this translation activity when describing the minarets of the Musalla in Herat:

> Diez, who knows the subject as well as anyone, and is not the slave of his journey's emotions like me, says these minarets are adorned with such 'fabulous richness and subtle taste' ('märchenhafter Pracht und subtilem Geschmack') that no others in Islam can equal them.[36]

Another strategy is to simply make this intertextual translation invisible. In Bruce Chatwin's *In Patagonia*, the reader is given an extract from Ercilla's epic in English with no indication of the source or who did the translation. The barber Señor Macías who commits suicide facing the mirror in his own barber's chair leaves a testament. Chatwin turns over a colour print of a long-haired dachshund and notes, 'I read the following: True missionaries assume the authority and concentration of the apostle Paul.'[37] There is no reason to believe that Señor Macías would have written his testament in a language other than Spanish. The translator becomes truly invisible here as Chatwin lists the items in the testament as if they had been originally composed in English. The status of translation is repeatedly uncertain as no indication is given of whether a text was in fact provided in English or whether what we have is a *post hoc* translation by Chatwin himself as the anonymous translator. The description of the murder of Fr Pistone in the museum of the Salesian Fathers in Punta Arenas is reproduced in English but the text may well be a translation from the Spanish. The text bears the traces of translation but we have no information on who the translator might be. In facilitating the English-language reader, Chatwin in a sense diminishes the otherness of a Spanish-speaking Argentina and minimises his own role as translator in a classic act of self-abnegation.

A less exalted form of translation is the example of the literature of the hospitality industry. The irony is that here as elsewhere translation is visible in failure and invisible in success. When Úna Ní Mhaoileoin visits Djerba in Tunisia she quotes the English-language guide book on fishing in the area: 'The high tide she washes in to shore the fish in a net of palm trees.' In her hotel in Tunis, a bilingual French–English sign on the wall reads in English: '*Not to throw flowers in the lavabo, neither the window. And please do keep the cocks in.*'[38] Dervla Murphy delights in quoting passages from the Air

Madagascar guide book which describes in one instance a hotel in Moro-Moro as having comfortable bungalows with the 'possibilities of two superposed extra beds' and where the diving school allows 'submarine exploration with autonomous diving suit'.[39] Similar translation howlers feed the dinner-party anecdotes of returned holidaymakers and are stock fillers for the journals of professional translators. They make evident, if only by default, the presence of translation in the travel experience. Only when the process of translation breaks down or ends up in the humorous cul-de-sac of the howler is the 'naturalness' of translation exposed as artifice. The concealed laboriousness of the process becomes evident. In the case of Nicolas Bouvier it is the translator's aids that become conspicuous in their oddness. Travelling through Yugoslovia, he has in his possession a *Manuel de conversation franco-serbe* produced by a Professor Magnasco in Genoa in 1907. Leafing through the phrase book in a barber shop in Belgrade, Bouvier finds the phrases hopelessly anachronistic:

> *Imam, li vam navoštiti brk?* – dois je cirer vos moustaches? – question à laquelle il convenait de répondre aussitôt:
> *Za volju Bozyu nemojte puštam tu modu kikošima* – à Dieu ne plaise! je laisse cette mode aux demoiseaux.[40]

In another of Bouvier's translation tools, Colonel C.D. Philott's English–Persian dictionary, definitions are often the occasion for idiosyncratic comment. The word *shahrah* is defined as a 'highway', but the colonel adds testily that 'there are no ways in Iran, high or otherwise'.[41] The purpose of the tools is of course to allow a passage into the other language, to allow for communication to happen. It is also an act of courtesy. The traveller returns the hospitality of welcome with the tentative gift of the language of the host. Furthermore, it is a recognition by writers, who of all people profess the sanctity of language, that language is a fundamental constituent part of a people's culture. To understand a people's culture would logically seem to demand a knowledge of their language as a first step towards translating the experience of elsewhere into the cultural universe of the mother tongue. Lastly, language learning may be viewed as a possible strategy of differentiation. One of the techniques Fussell sees as part of the arsenal of the anti-tourist is 'speaking the language, even badly'.[42] The serious traveller differs from the casual tourist in his or her commitment to learning the language and merging into the surroundings. The degrees of language knowledge that travellers do in fact possess vary of course, from the limited vocabulary of Lisa St Aubin de Terán in French Guyana to the years of study of Tibetan that precede the voyage described by Alexandra David-Neel in her *Voyage d'une parisienne à Lhassa*.

David-Neel disguises herself as a pilgrim in order to go to Lhassa and language is part of the disguise. Speaking a new language is to assume a new identity. The conflation of language with persona is noted by Lisa St Aubin de Terán on Corfu where she meets a local man whose monosyllabic grunts in Greek to the other women in the house contrast with his elaborate Florentine voice in Italian: 'When first I tried him with English and French and German, he had stared at me with sullen incomprehension that robbed his face of his smile, yet at the cue of "Italiano" he had seemed physically to ease himself into another persona.'[43] St Aubin de Terán, for whom the metamorphosis of language is as desirable as travel itself, argues elsewhere in her account that there is a vast amount of pleasure to be had from adapting to an alien society and being accepted by it. Thus, 'to pass undetected in a foreign country is an honour'.[44] The aspiration St Aubin de Terán describes is the hope of every language-learner who longs one day to hear the formula of consecration, 'but I thought you were French/German/Chinese!' Like Raban accelerating on the freeway and adopting the terse Americanisms of 'Trav', foreign language provides a stage, a space for the exploration of another self or of another element of self, depending on whether the writer has a unitary or fragmentary notion of self.[45] If travel means uprooting oneself from the familiar, embracing the anonymity of flight, then language difference can further accelerate the move away from the known world of mother-tongue utterance. This has arguably been one of the functions of modern language departments since their inception, to prepare students not only for travel to foreign lands but also for travel-by-proxy through the reading of the foreign language, thus in some way complicating the sense of monoglot belonging to one language alone. Playing at being another person, disguising yourself as a native (Byron as native Persian, David-Neel as native Tibetan) offers the promise of liberation from an older self or former selves through the good offices of language. When such a transition to full mastery of language occurs it is usually the result of extensive vertical travel, that dwelling-in-travelling which allows time to expand and space to contract. The perennial tension in the interlingual travel account is the conflict between knowledge-through-immersion and knowledge-through-observation. If the reader is to be told about a particular place then the people who would appear to be best informed are those who actually live there. If they are to emerge as fully articulate subjects rather than indifferent objects of observation, then the traveller has to immerse himself/herself in the language and culture of a community in order to give a full account of the places s/he travels through. Lisa St Aubin de Terán expresses this viewpoint ironically. When visited by the 'gift of tongues', she is able to tell a television dealer that she wants to rent not buy a television set. St Aubin de Terán felt that she had finally succeeded in 'luring the locals out of their monastic cult. I had proved myself to be human and no known relation of the she devil.'[46] As we shall see in the next chapter, non-linguistic forms of knowledge are possible for travellers but if we remain with language we can ask the question as to how travel writers negotiate a compromise between competence and insight. How, in other words, does the traveller in the onward march of horizontal travel deal with the pressures of translation?

One solution is to have others do the work. Here we do not mean so much interpreters as encounters with compatriots or others speaking one's native language and who are more in the nature of informants in the anthropological sense. Bruce Chatwin meets Bill Philips, Sonny Urquhart, Mrs Ivor Davies, Archie Tuffnall and many other British people on his travels through Argentina but surprisingly few named Argentinians who are not of British descent. Nicolas Bouvier spends time in the Franco-Iranian Institute in Teheran and the French Club in Kabul. Robert Byron uses a network of British institutions to sustain him on his journey through Iran and Afghanistan, from the English Club and British Legation in Teheran to the British Consulate in Meshed to the English Mission in Shiraz and the British Legation in Kabul. Speaking with compatriots who have spent many years in the country and who speak your language produces a certain economy of translation. This economy comes at a price, however, in that relying on others to translate a culture raises the inevitable spectre of infidelity. Stereotypes can be good travellers and expatriate communities are often remarkably resilient in resisting attempts to understand the host community, a community that may earn their contempt more readily than their admiration. On the other hand meetings with compatriots and with others speaking the language of the narrator has the added advantage of conferring linguistic credibility on the account. Too much foreign language or endless translation might exhaust readers reminded of their own linguistic inadequacies and increase scepticism, well founded or not, as to the language skills of the travel writer. The manner of travelling, as much as the origins of the people the traveller encounters, will also determine the exposure to translation. Robert Byron spends much of his journey in the company of Christopher Sykes. Nicolas Bouvier travels with his friend, the Swiss artist Thierry Vernet. Dervla Murphy tours Madagascar in the company of her daughter. These travellers, therefore, always have another speaker of their native language to hand. The potential disadvantage is that of the honeymoon couple or the school group who remain indifferent to the outside world, numbed by the familiarity of companionship and a shared language. It is striking in the case of Úna Ní Mhaoileoin, who travels alone, that language is constantly an issue and that she is repeatedly drawn into conversations with others in other languages. It is worth remembering here, however, the loneliness of Liam Ó Rinn at the beginning of the chapter. The interlingual world has a potential for great solitude. Lisa St Aubin de Terán entitles one of her chapters in *Off the Rails* 'The Absence of the World', and notes that, while she worked on improving her Italian in Sestri Levante, she was marooned in a Bay of Silence. Travel has all the predictable exhilaration of escape but it also has the anxious despondency of what am I doing here? The solitariness of being away from familiar faces can be compounded by the absence of language so that the traveller feels only the hard labour of translation in any communication with the world, his/her inner self immured in silence for the lack of ready equivalence in the language of others. Even if travellers can readily translate their thoughts and feelings into the foreign language, there is the tedium of the cultural footnote, explaining references to people, places or events. A longing can build up for the casual conversational shorthand of a compatriot speaking the same language.

Translators are not only the travellers themselves, picking their way past language obstacles; translators can also feature as an intra-textual persona in travel literature itself. Robert Byron recounts a meeting with the governor of Shiraz, whom he describes as a man of wide interests: 'Translation, he said, was an art, as he had learnt from rendering Plato and Oscar Wilde into Persian.'[47] At a display of feats of physical prowess in a 'Zur Khana', Byron meets a scholar who was translating the *Encyclopedia Britannica* into Persian with the help of four assistants. In Tunis, Úna Ní Mhaoileoin meets an interpreter who is eager to practise his English on her and she gives extended passages of his somewhat parodic public-school English. Bruce Chatwin devotes a chapter in his account to the work of a missionary-translator, Thomas Bridges, who compiled a dictionary of the Yaghan language, the language used by the *Yámana* people in Patagonia. Chatwin pays particular attention to the extreme difficulty of equivalence in the process of translation which often led to a tragic misrepresentation of non-Western peoples. Abstract concepts such as 'good' or 'beautiful' did not exist in isolation in the Yaghan language but were always related to things. The figurative inventiveness of the language and the carefully circumscribed semantic fields of Yaghan verbs meant that Bridges's translation task of not only preparing the dictionary as a translation tool but also translating the message of Christian scripture into the Yaghan language would prove endlessly complicated. This was the language that Charles Darwin had derided as 'barely articulate'.[48] Chatwin's parable of linguistic sensitivity and cultural curiosity in his brief life of Thomas Bridges reveals the immense potential for misunderstanding in cultural contact when the relevance of language to the framing of human experience is ignored. Bridges found not only that it was difficult to express specific concepts of the Gospel in the 'labyrinth of the particular' that was the Yaghan language but that the *Yámana* had seemingly unlimited reserves of expression. The translator-figures that appear in travel accounts are curious echoes of the travellers themselves. Travellers are similarly engaged in different interlingual settings in the task of translation. The more linguistically sensitive travellers make the 'barely articulate' objects of Darwin's jibe expressive and inventive subjects of their own lives. The trust that is confided in the translator is the credence given to the traveller-linguist and in both

cases there are inevitably concerns with loss, infidelity and misrepresentation. The capacity for manipulation in translation situations is highlighted in
The Road to Oxiana, where a translation stratagem is conceived of by an
Indian doctor so that Byron could get permission to see the Oxus. The doctor
advises writing a letter to the local 'Vazir', Mohammed Gul, in an English
style so elaborate it could not be translated by the telegraph office employee.
In that case, 'one of the resident Indian merchants will be summoned, who
may put in a good word for us'.[49] The delicious ambiguity of the modal verb
'may' shows the full scope for intervention. What Byron is banking on is that
the obstacles to understanding will be so great that the Afghan officials will
call on the help of more malleable, less neutral translators. The stratagem
fails but the connection here between translation and obstacle is crucial in
the context of travel.

Happy holidays make for poor reading. Postcards are the ideal medium for
the morse prose of delight – 'Having a wonderful time! Wish you were here!'
Travellers' tales gain in interest as they tell not of what went right but of what
went terribly wrong. Narrative is sustained by the peripeteia. There is no story
if Aeneas takes a direct flight to Rome or Ulysses is whisked away by waiting
jet to Ithaca. The hero myth as described by Joseph Campbell involves the
hero setting out from home, going through various trials, tribulations and
rites of initiation, before finally returning home as hero.[50] Without the obstacles, there is no consecration. It is the obstructions that give meaning to the
journey and ensure that there is a story to tell at the journey's end. Travel
writing not only describes obstacles but it also creates them in the endlessly
digressive structure of its narrative. The digression is an obstacle to linear
closure. In her two travel accounts, *My Ireland* and *Farewell Spain*, Kate
O'Brien offers the reader reflections on travel, personal and political opinions,
autobiographical anecdote and short historical essays that resist the serial
discipline of the calendar.[51] She makes the digressive postponement of arrival
an explicit principle of composition in *Farewell Spain*:

> But my journey will be a composite one, made up of many, and without
> unnecessary chronological reference. The route will be a plaiting together
> of many routes; seasons and cities will succeed each other in reminis-
> cence as almost certainly they did not in fact; companions or chance
> acquaintances of travel will crop up, interrupt, disappear and return
> without sequential accuracy, and with no justification from all those useful
> diaries which I never keep.[52]

In an essay on obstacles, the British psychoanalyst Adam Phillips asks the
rhetorical question, 'Why would we need to wish if nothing were in the
way?' He explains the necessity of obstacles in the construction of desire: 'If
I know what I want by coming up against what prevents me from having it,
then there must anyway be a wish for obstacles as unconscious mnemonics
of desire.'[53] Not only desire but our understanding of what or who something

or someone is relies on the existence of obstacles: 'The search for obstacles – the need to impose them in their familiar guise of time and space – is part of the endless, baffled inquiry into the nature of the object. I know what something or someone is by finding out what comes between us.'[54]

If the object of the traveller's desire is a country – Argentina, Iran, Afghanistan, Tunisia, Italy, Serbia, Macedonia – then the various obstacles – accommodation, transport, political circumstance – that frustrate the traveller's progress are part of the 'baffled inquiry' into the nature of a country and a people. One of the things that can come between the traveller and a people is, of course, language, and the attempts to overcome that obstacle are as instructive as the other impediments that transform royal roads into labyrinths. Henry David Thoreau found time between the construction of his house and the hoeing of his beans by Walden Pond to 'read one or two shallow books of travel'.[55] Thoreau felt the books were unworthy of his august solitude and he soon abandoned travel literature. After his prompt dismissal of 'shallow books', Thoreau praises the labour of the classics: 'The student may read Homer or Aeschylus in the Greek without danger of dissipation or luxuriousness, for it implies that he in some measure emulate their heroes, and consecrate morning hours to their pages.'[56]

Learning even a few words of an ancient language is worth the expense of youthful days and costly hours because these words become 'perpetual suggestions and provocations'.[57] The industry of translation makes the Latin and Ancient Greek text memorable. The obstacles to understanding that require spending many youthful mornings in close exegesis make us more sensitive to the suggestions and provocations of ancient authors. If we let others do the work for us – 'the modern cheap and fertile press, with all its translations' – the risk is amnesia.[58] In the absence of the obstacle of language, we may find that we remember less as we move from being the producer to being the recipient of translated material. Of course, Thoreau's argument has an inherent weakness which even he admits, namely that even 'in the character of our mother tongue' classical texts have an interpretive burden that demands close, difficult reading. However, the connection between obstacle, the agency of translation and knowledge/memory is a real one for many interlingual travellers. In an essay on travel, writing and otherness, Nicolas Bouvier argues that the incomprehensible or the unintelligible have their value in travel. To illustrate his argument, he offers the reader a Hassidic version of the Babel story. In this version, everybody spoke the same language and everybody complained. Men complained about the weather, women complained about their husbands and everybody complained about their health. People became so used to the monotonous litany of each other's complaints that they no longer listened to each other:

> C'est donc pour échapper à l'indifférence et à l'ennui que nous nous serions lancés dans cette construction inepte. À en croire certains auteurs,

même ce défi n'aurait pas suffi à tirer l'humanité de son laconisme et de sa torpeur. En regardant attentivement la toile de Brueghel l'Ancien, il m'a bien semblé entendre chanter quelques coqs, et le fouet des charretiers claquer dans le froid, mais aucune voix humaine. La tour se serait édifiée dans un silence de mort. Dieu qui contemplait ce gâchis avec un sourire navré aurait alors, dans son infinie miséricorde, créé toutes ces langues, dialectes ou patois différents pour réveiller une curiosité qui s'était éteinte.

Notre esprit étant plus occupé de ce qu'il ne saisit pas que de ce qu'il a déjà compris, l'Autre qu'on ignorait la veille était d'un seul coup devenu personnage énigmatique, objet d'hypothèses, d'étude et d'intérêt.[59]

The foreignness of the language of others generates its own enigmas, speculation, its own desire to know. We can produce that sense of mystery through experiencing our own language as *foreign*, as we saw in the last chapter, or we may find that the very opacity of a language in intersemiotic translation – where we have no notion whatsoever of the other language – has its own specific cognitive or affective charge. In all three cases – intralingual, interlingual and intersemiotic – it is the perception of others, at some level, as linguistically estranged from us that creates the exciting momentum of inquiry.

The reactions to language difference are not, however, uniformly positive. Obstacles may lead as much to irritation as insight. The unknown can engender interest but it may also spawn fear and paranoia. Languages exist too in relations of power, and travel may indeed sharpen linguistic tensions as travellers are thrown together in the time capsule of the railway carriage or the floating village of the ship. A young Lisa St Aubin de Terán is eager to try out her newly acquired Russian on the train passengers on the return trip from Leningrad to London. As she notes, 'A lot of the newly arrived Polish passengers in the second- and third-class wagons wanted to talk, but they weren't as keen as they were principled and wouldn't sink a lifelong policy of not understanding Russian.'[60] The train journey takes place during the Cold War and Polish resistance to translating themselves into Russian is strong. Úna Ní Mhaoileoin occasionally pretends not to understand English and replies to questions in Irish. Identity is generally a question of differentiation, the figure of identity emerging against the ground of difference. Travelling through differences makes a sense of difference more keenly felt. It is a common experience for travellers abroad not so much to be aware of the cultural identity of others as to feel a strong and growing sense of their own specific cultural difference. Hence James Joyce's quip that the shortest road to Tara was through Holyhead. The situation is highlighted by Ní Mhaoileoin when she describes the fierce patriotism of the Italian immigrants from Brazil and Argentina who are with her on the boat to Naples. She had previously spent a year in Italy and believed that the Italians were completely indifferent to any notion of *la patria*. It is significant that the most visible expression for Ní Mhaoileoin of the immigrant's nationalism was language, 'tá an grá céanna acu don tír agus don teanga agus atá acu do na bambini'.[61] The emergent awareness of separateness is constantly stalked by the bogey of stereotype. Almost all of the English speakers that Ní Mhaoileoin meets are immersed in the idiom of a Bertie Wooster, whether the speakers come from Tunisia, South Africa or Ireland. On the boat train to London from Paris, she meets a group of South African schoolgirls, one of whom breezily declares, 'I'll just go and have a sniff to see if my jolly old suitcase is in.'[62] Lisa St Aubin de Terán's Germans are forever shouting. Ní Mhaoileoin, who baldly states that the only problem with Marseilles is the French, represents them as snobbish, condescending and engaged in suspiciously high-brow conversation – 'is iontach dáiríre atá siad'.[63] For Robert Byron, arriving in India over the Khyber Pass is to contemplate the wonders of British industry and organisation:

> if the English must be bothered to defend India, it shall be with the minimum of personal inconvenience. This was our feeling. It was the spectacle of common sense that thrilled us amid the evil heat, the eyries of the tribesmen, and the immemorial associations of pilgrims and conquerors, a spectacle for complacent, boasting patriotism.[64]

Byron, a witty and acerbic critic of nationalist excess, practises his own version of 'complacent, boasting patriotism' in this paean to English common sense. His reaction, however, is not entirely unexpected, coming as it does after a long period spent travelling, so that familiarity of a kind brings its own rewards.

Triangulation, desire, transcendence

What becomes increasingly odd, particularly but not only for the solitary traveller, is the sound of one's own voice, the sounds of one's own language. Language has a less self-evident quality in the company of speakers of another language. The intonation that falls on deaf ears in the everyday lifeworld of the language becomes amplified by distance and displacement. The effort at translation makes us conscious of the words we use, the idioms that we employ. One of the first casualties of foreign-language contact is idiomatic expression. Using an international language to communicate means the deft elimination of idiom, so that there is no figurative peculiarity, with its specificity of reference, to trouble conversational exchanges. On the other hand, to become conscious of idiom, of language difference, is to become more aware of the conventions and range of expression of the mother tongue. As Stéphane Mallarmé argued: 'On ne voit presque jamais si sûrement un mot que du dehors, où nous sommes; c'est-à-dire à l'étranger.'[65] Mallarmé's interest in English and what happens to French and English words in translation is a part of this creative and poetic defamiliarisation of language. Interlingual travellers are dislodged from the centre of the linguistic universe. Their language no longer corresponds with the world in which they (temporarily) live. Like translators, however, they must eventually return to their home language and express foreign-language experience in mother-tongue prose. This is the process of 'inaudible, perpetual triangulation' that is described by Eva Hoffman. From two points drawn in the sand, the ancient Greeks try to extrapolate the moon's distance from the earth. From two languages, the writer/translator extrapolates his/her distance from language, culture, experience. This triangulation can create a weightlessness where in any given situation, 'nothing here has to be the way it is; people could behave in a different manner ... I could be having entirely different conversations.'[66] Any experience is relative to the point chosen at the base of the triangle. The liberation and drama of travel is this relativity. A travel account is an existentialist summing-up of choices made, of roads taken, and there are always all the other paths, all the other points on the base that would have triangulated differently. The weightlessness that Hoffman details is the frugal reduction that moves Bouvier as he evokes the experience of travel:

> Le voyage fournit des occasions de s'ébrouer mais pas – comme on le croyait – la liberté. Il fait plutôt éprouver une sorte de réduction; privé de son cadre habituel, dépouillé de ses habitudes comme d'un volumineux emballage, le voyageur se trouve ramené à de plus humbles proportions. Plus ouvert aussi à la curiosité, à l'intuition, au coup de foudre.[67]

At the age of sixteen, Lisa St Aubin de Terán experiences her own 'coup de foudre'. She is approached on the street in London and a man proposes marriage to her. She does not understand his language, Spanish, but two words, Italy and Venezuela, 'needed no translation' and she agreed to go to these places with him and be his wife. St Aubin de Terán had found with her new Venezuelan husband that her lack of Spanish meant that the marriage began in a communion of silence alleviated only by the consultation of the atlas and the recitation of placenames. In Brian Friel's *Translations,* placenames are again the currency of desire, as the English soldier Yolland and the young Irish woman, Máire, lovingly repeat English and Irish placenames to each other in a toponymical duet. In both cases, the language for the young women promises liberation, escape from the grey familiarity of their surroundings. There is a long history of women travelling and recently anthologies and scholarly works have celebrated the particular achievements of women travellers faced with scepticism, prejudice and hostility.[68] As numerous as women travellers have been women translators, and they too have had to contend with the screens of invisibility.[69]

What then, if any, is the connection between interlingual women travellers and the overwhelmingly female membership of the translation and modern language professions? To explore this question, it is worth speculating on the strong female presence in these professions. The conventional explanation is the most obvious, sexism. Parents and educational systems make gender assumptions about 'suitable' professions for boys and girls and the boys get to be engineers and the girls linguists. This is undoubtedly an important factor in explaining the striking gender imbalance across different faculties in universities throughout the world. However, for the purposes of our discussion, it may be useful to examine other elements in vocational choice that have a direct bearing on the relationship between women and foreign-language acquisition. Amati Mehler, Argentieri and Canestri speak about sexual differentiation in the development process of human beings:

> si pour un garçon la conscience de sa différence anatomique d'avec sa mère peut constituer une poussée physiologique vers la différenciation psychologique, nous pensons, à l'inverse, que, pour la fille, la ressemblance morphologique à la mère peut prendre un sens anti-évolutif, puisque la croissance et le processus de séparation et d'individuation conduisent vers la différenciation psychologique de la mère, mais que l'acquisition de l'identité féminine prévoit de devenir comme elle, corporellement, d'être enfermée, à nouveau, pour toujours, par cette mère de laquelle on tente désespérément de se détacher.[70]

Leaving the mother tongue is a way of finding another space that is not occupied by the mother, by her language, thus finding an identity that is not that of the mother. Learning a foreign language, travelling in a foreign language, offers the liberatory possibility of an exploration of identity that is not uniquely beholden to the tongue of the mother. Alice Kaplan captures the excitement of the opening-out to new worlds through language in *French Lessons: A Memoir*. Here she describes the effects of learning French in a Swiss-French boarding school:

> Learning French and learning to think, learning to desire, is all mixed up in my head, until I can't tell the difference ... French got me away from my family and taught me how to talk. Made me an adult.[71]

Translation involves, however, a serious commitment to working with the mother tongue and the travel accounts we are considering in this work are all written in the mother tongue of the travellers. How then can the desire for escape be related to the necessity, indeed the desirability, of return in travel and translation? To examine this relation, it is worth considering the differences the British psychoanalyst, Darian Leader, sees as operative between male and female versions of desire. He begins by citing the work of Deborah Tannen on children's games. She observed a group of children playing in the kitchen of a day-care centre. When Sue wanted a toy that Mary had, she told Mary not that she wanted it but that she had come to collect the toy for Lisa, another little girl. Later, three boys are playing in the same area when Nick sees that Kevin has the toy and demands it for himself. When this fails, Nick then tries to recruit another little boy, Joe, to forcibly remove the toy from Kevin. Sue is effectively saying that her desire is the desire of an other, she has appropriated someone else's desire. Nick's satisfaction is in obliterating the desire of another through coerced cooperation. Leader sees this episode as illustrative of the difference between male and female relationships to desire. The little boy wants to destroy his rival so that he can take the coveted object but what the little girl aims at is less the object than the desire of the other girl.

> What a woman searches for in the world around her is not an object –
> female collectors, after all, are extremely rare – but another desire. Hence
> the interest not in one man or woman but in the relation, the desire,
> between them: it is no accident that women are often exceedingly inter-
> ested in the romantic entanglements of their friends. Their radar is tuned to
> desires rather than to objects as such, and this is also perhaps the reason
> why women often make excellent psychotherapists or analysts: it is not
> that they simply evoke the figure of the mother, as some commentators
> have argued, but because the wavelength of desire is closer to them.[72]

To the professional roll-call of desire, Leader might have added travellers and translators. In this context, it is interesting to note that in her analysis of women's travel writing and colonialism Sara Mills claims that 'women travel writers tended to concentrate on descriptions of peoples as individuals, rather than on statements about the race as a whole'.[73] Defending her writing of *Farewell Spain* in grim, political circumstances, Kate O'Brien proclaims, 'Let us praise personal memory, personal love.'[74] Generalisations about gender differences in modern travel writing are extremely problematic but it is nonetheless important to examine the manner in which the question of interlingual travelling is bound up with gender and translation. The rela-tionship between mother-tongue distance and identity-formation, and an interest in the relations between objects as opposed to the objects them-selves, imply at the very least a potential aptitude among women for the transactions of translation in the world of travel.

Jacques Lacarrière, the French travel writer, talks of his feeling of dissatis-faction every time he leaves a café or a village. He is walking down through France but despite the fact that he has deliberately chosen the slowest means of going from the north to the south, he feels he passes through everywhere too quickly and that he does not really see or share in anything:

> Ces conversations, ces regards échangés avec les inconnus, pendant
> quelques instants, je voudrais qu'ils m'entraînent plus loin, qu'ils me lient
> à eux autrement, que je ne sois pas seulement celui qui passe. Mais cette
> seule idée est absurde ou démente. Comment pourrais-je vivre à moi seul
> la vie de tous, suivre le temps nécessaire l'existence de chacun d'eux, être
> moi-même et tous les autres en même temps? Il me faudrait plusieurs vies
> ou plusieurs corps pour cela.[75]

This is Baudelaire's 'amer savoir', the bitter truth that we glean from our travels – the villages we have not visited, the people we have only glimpsed, the bar that we had to leave, the minor perforations of dawn departures, all the heartache of movement. The threnody of loss is a familiar tune for translators. The inadequacy of the translation to the original is one of the most formidable truisms that translators have to contend with in any discussion of their practice. Losses can be profitable, however. There may be a sense in which the traveller and translator in their failure to reproduce the original in its totality are not dark angels of privation but guarantors of the essential humanity of their undertaking. In an essay entitled 'Transcending Humanity', Martha Nussbaum opposes a theory of internal, human transcendence to religious, otherwordly transcendence. She takes as her starting point the decision of Odysseus to forsake the immortal lovemaking of Calypso for the mortal embrace of Penelope. Nussbaum argues that the human reader applauds Odysseus's decision because it is only within the limits of human fragility and boundedness in time that we can conceive of the truly good life. There can be little passion in the eternal couplings of the gods, only playful and ultimately monotonous variations on a theme. Divine parenthood breeds only indifference as immortal charges are, by definition, beyond harm. Love's intensity feeds off the anxious sense of possible ending. We can only admire, therefore, actions that seem in some sense to transcend normal human limits. Our dismay at athletes found guilty of taking performance-enhancing drugs is based on a sense of the violation of that internal, human transcendence. As Nussbaum remarks: 'Human limits structure the human excellences, and give excellent action its significance. The preservation of the limits in some form . . . is a necessary condition of excellent activity's excellence.'[76] The transcendent impulse is to try to surpass the current limits of our human condition, but if these limits were to be abolished, we would no longer be human. Nussbaum sees the athlete as the literal *embodiment* of this creative contradiction:

> She wouldn't wish to be without the human body and its limits altogether, since then there is no athletic achievement and no goal; but it seems perfectly reasonable, in any particular case, to want, always, to be better, stronger, faster, to push against those limits more successfully. It is the paradox of a struggle for victory in which *complete* 'victory' would be disaster and emptiness – or, at any rate, a life so different from our own that we could no longer find ourselves and our valued activities in it.[77]

The pilgrims to Rome, Mecca or Jerusalem are the expression of an ancient link between travel and transcendence. Spiritual quest like the metamorphosis of the hero is the pilgrim's progress from the familiar to the promised land of redemption, illumination, rebirth. There is an epistemic necessity in journey in that you can only understand what something is if you stand outside it, if you move away from it. For the pilgrims, their former life stands out more clearly from the remove of Santiago or on the island sanctuary of Lough Derg as intimated by the narrative voice of Seamus Heaney's *Station Island*.[78] The necessity of distance for intellection is insisted upon by George Steiner in *Real Presences*, where he argues that 'theory' not only tells of concentrated insight but that it 'pertains also to the deed of witness performed by legates sent, in solemn embassy, to observe the oracles spoken or the rites performed at the sacred Attic games'.[79] Steiner stresses observance here, the distance of the observer, but he neglects to mention movement. Yet, it is surely the journey undergone by the legates, the leaving home, the encounter with the unfamiliar that lends acuity to the observation and intensity to the insight. Travellers in going beyond their normal human limits of time and space – going away from home, abandoning the routine of their everyday lifeworld – are engaging in their own particular form of internal, human transcendence. There are limits to what they can see and whom they can meet, the limits detailed so poignantly by Lacarrière. Yet, it is these limits that we will use to judge their excellence, that make their accounts of travel so movingly human. Limits, too, make the work of the translator the activity of mortals rather than a hobby for the gods. The excellence of translation is judged within the limits of equivalence. If there is perfect equivalence, there is no more translation. Indeed, a certain measure of condescension towards commercial and technical translation is often based on the mistaken belief that because perfect equivalence is always and everywhere possible it is not genuine translation. There is no complete 'victory' in translation. Translators can always in each age produce a more effective, appropriate or convincing translation, but the movement is always transcendent, it is never final. Loss is not the perennial admission of defeat but the very precondition of the activity of the translator. As Adam Phillips notes: 'Wishing is the sign of loss; wanting things to be otherwise because they are not as they are supposed to be. For the child to live his curiosity is itself an acknowledgement of loss; of wanting as a sign of life.'[80] The desire to do a translation is a desire for things to be otherwise, either for the translation to exist if there is none or to improve it if it is felt in some way to be deficient.

In the process of translation, the translator engages in a form of dual transcendence. On the one hand, there is the journey out into the source language. On the other, there is the return to the target language. In the first instance, there is the discovery of another world, another way of saying and viewing things, and in the second, there is the knowledge of distance, of having considered, as we saw earlier with Mallarmé, our language from a remove. Translators have been justly celebrated over the centuries for the journeyings to other cultures and the manner in which they have broadened the horizons of their own. Conversely, translators have also been ignored, disregarded and viewed with deep suspicion.[81] The suspicion stems less from the outward than the return journey. The return of the native is an ambiguous offering in literature and scripture. Odysseus's return to Ithaca is immediately followed by a bloodbath. The Prodigal Son may be fêted by his father but other family members feel only resentment. The promise of closure, of synthesis in return, becomes an open or festering wound. The traveller who has been to foreign parts is not only *unsettled* but s/he becomes on return an *unsettling* figure for the settled community. In Teheran, Robert Byron is taken in evening suit to the New Year's Eve ball at the Anglo-Persian mess. He notes, 'Expecting only that casual politeness which seeks to prevent the returned traveller's reminiscences, I was touched at people's interest in my excursion.'[82] The tales of the traveller may be welcomed in the rambling house but the 'returned traveller's reminiscences' may also be shunned as too foreign, remote or different. The community is wary of these changelings. Translators are a disruptive presence in that their return to their native language has the capacity to *unsettle* that language. The purpose of the naturalising, fluent strategy is to efface the traces of travel, to make the text appear, in effect, as if it had never left home. The central paradox is that home, in this instance, is the target not the source language. The fluent translation becomes home from home.

Travel labour

Interlingual travelling is both travel in translation and travel as translation, translation as travel. The translation labour of the travellers in the different accounts highlights the no less important travel labour of translators. The vast majority of translators – there are exceptions – acquire or perfect their foreign language through periods of residence in a foreign country. It is a requirement in many translation schools that students spend anything from a semester to a year in the country of their chosen language. Translation students will often state in interview that they wish to be translators because 'they want to travel'. Travel as an experience involves the repeated dyad of arrival and departure, settling in and moving out. The effect of displacement can be salutary: 'l'homme dépaysé', to employ Tzvetan Todorov's term, learns not to confuse nature with culture, the real with the ideal. It is not because people behave differently from us that they are less human. Alternatively, resentment grows at a sense of impossible difference, of being trapped on the margins of the exotic. However, if the positive effects of displacement predominate, then tolerance and curiosity are emergent virtues. Todorov argues that it is not only the individual who is displaced but also the host community:

> Sa présence parmi les 'autochtones' exerce à son tour un effet dépaysant: en troublant leurs habitudes, en déconcertant par son comportement et ses jugements, il peut aider certains d'entre eux à s'engager dans cette même voie de détachement par rapport à ce qui va de soi, voie d'interrogation et d'étonnement.[83]

Host communities are differently defined in translation. They are the communities that welcome texts in translation produced by the displaced persons that are translators themselves. Translators have an impact on the source culture of their translations in that translation is a common arbiter of literary fame; the more translations of a work, the greater its prestige. The impact of translation is, however, primarily on the language in which it is produced and the 'autochtones' to whom it is addressed are the other speakers that share the language of the translator. The 'effet dépaysant' mentioned by Todorov has its correlative in translation practice. Edwin Gentzler describes one such case in his discussion of the American poet and translator Robert Bly, whose translation work would profoundly affect political and aesthetic practice in the United States in the 1960s. Gentzler claims that Bly '*used* translations to change the system, to break down dangerously metaphysical thinking and moralizing attitudes, in order to create cultural conditions to let his verse appear' (his emphasis).[84] The translator can unsettle a culture either through the nature of material translated or the way in which it is translated or both. Much debate in recent decades has centred on the translator's signature, on the visibility of the translator in the process of translation. Historical work has centred on the making visible of translators' contribution to the development of languages, the emergence of cultures and the dissemination of ideas. The risk in practice is that the more visible the translator, the less visible the text. It is in this context that a conception of travel advanced by Nicolas Bouvier allows for the formulation of a notion of translation that is enabling for both translators and texts. Bouvier speaks of the multiplicity of elements that make up the world that has been the stage for his travelling. Our senses are generally dulled by routine to the motley variety of experience: 'Le monde est constamment polyphonique alors que nous n'en avons, par carence ou paresse, qu'une lecture monodique.'[85] The polyphony of the world emerges in extreme states of fatigue, the vertigo of love, close encounters with death. It also occurs in prized moments of illumination for the traveller where s/he is suddenly present to the exhilarating diversity of the lifeworld. Here, the traveller finds that there is not one way but several ways of reading the world and that worlds are always ghosted by other, parallel worlds of meaning and interpretation. Alberto Manguel, the Argentinian writer, critic and translator, sees the task of the translator as the revelation of the implicit polyphony of text: 'Translation proposes a sort of parallel universe, another space and time in which the text reveals other, extraordinary possible meanings.'[86] In order for the harmonic richness of experience to become apparent, Bouvier advocates an ethics of frugality:

> Je trouve qu'entre le voyage et l'écriture il y a un point commun, pour moi très important. Dans les deux cas, il s'agit d'un exercice de disparition, d'escamotage. Parce que quand vous n'y êtes plus, les choses viennent.

Quand vous y êtes trop, vous bouffez le paysage par une sorte de corpulence morale qui fait qu'on ne peut pas voir [. . .] Et du fait que l'existence
entière est un exercice de disparition, je trouve que tant le voyage que
l'écriture sont de très bonnes écoles.[87]

The more discreet the writer is, the more present the world. The trav-
eller/narrator has to strive for a limpidity that reveals rather than conceals
what s/he has seen. Bouvier's vision might appear retrograde to the modern
translator, an invitation to submission, the craven self-abnegation of earlier
periods. However, the central paradox of Bouvier's argument is that the travel
account is pre-eminently sentimental; it is the willed creation of an individual
human subject, working of course within the discursive conventions of the
genre. Yet, he calls for attentive transparency, the gradual evacuation of the
cumbersome subject as a nomadic ideal. It is in the tension between these
two positions that the work of the translator can be articulated. Each translation is a *translation account*, the record of a translator's interpretive
journeying through a text that is authored by the translator. The sentimental
dimension to translation is the subjective activity of interpretation and
authorship. As we noted earlier, no translator embarks on exactly the same
path through a text. The 'exercice de disparition' that is also translation is the
making visible of the radical heterogeneity of the foreign text without undue,
explicit translatorly intrusion that obscures the aesthetic, moral or political
landscape of the text. The absence is of course artifice, in that the translator
is present in every translated word or sentence. However, the discipline of
selflessness that underlies Bouvier's ideology of travel implies duty and
promise for the translator. The duty is maximum openness to the parallel
universes of the text to be translated, and the promise is the bringing of a
bracing otherness to the host language. The translator is not unlike the poet
described by the traveller Magris when he speaks of the poet who is different
from Achilles or Diomedes ranting on a chariot but is more like Ulysses, who
knows he is no one. The poet 'manifests himself in this revelation of imper-
sonality that conceals him in the prolixity of things, as travelling erases the
traveller in the confused murmur of the street'.[88]

Chapter Three

MAKING SENSE

Dervla Murphy is in trouble. On a bus to Tulear in Madagascar, she finds herself beside a young mother feeding her baby. Each time the baby is fed, it vomits over Murphy's rucksack and wails pitifully:

> Obviously the real problem was a stuffed nose, leading to too much air being sucked in. I tried to console the mother by explaining this: she looked about Rachel's [Murphy's daughter] age and was almost in tears of anxiety. But she spoke no French and my attempts to deliver a Dr Spock lecture in sign-language merely provoked gales of laughter among our fellow-passengers.[1]

The lecture fails to elicit the appropriate response and relief only comes when the exhausted mother has no more milk to give the infant. Murphy notes elsewhere that 'pure farce' is 'something easily achieved when sign-language is the main means of communication'.[2] It goes without saying here that what Murphy has in mind is the amateur use of gesture and not the strictly codified languages of the deaf community. Murphy's predicament is that of any traveller who finds himself or herself without a common language of communication and who must use other forms of non-linguistic communication. The implications of this common dilemma are many.

Children and barbarians

The arrival scene in the foreign city has a well-rehearsed cast of horrors: aggressive taxi-drivers, importunate beggars, dead heat, driving rain, exorbitantly priced rooms found after sundown that turn out to be the entomological showcases of domestic natural history museums. The common denominator of the traveller's misery is language. The language is incomprehensible, nobody makes any sense and the traveller feels lonely and vulnerable. In *Exit into History*, her account of a journey through Eastern

68

Europe at the beginning of the 1990s, Eva Hoffman describes the vague fear that has accompanied her on her travels: 'It's been a low-level, discomfiting anxiety that this business of trekking on the Eastern European road will get to be too much: that I can't manage my luggage, can't find my food or drink, that I'll get lost on dark roads in a godforsaken town, with no language to explain myself to unfriendly strangers.'[3] The absence of a language to explain yourself to unfriendly strangers means a temporary loss of control over circumstances, the terror of helplessness. The traveller in this situation is both *child* and *barbarian*. The infantilisation of the traveller is the assumption that failure to understand the language is a correlative of intellectual immaturity and that if words are repeated slowly and often and loudly enough, the obdurate child-(wo)man will eventually get the message. The same process obtains in colonial encounters where the epithet 'boy' captures the infantilisation of native peoples through language disparity – in this case, differing competence in the master's language. Barbarism too is rooted in the multiplicity of mutually unintelligible languages. For the Greeks *barbaros* is literally the stammering sound that they associated with speech in foreign languages. In his preface to the 1611 Authorized Version of the Bible, Miles Smith remarks that 'Nature taught a natural man to confess that all of us in those tongues which we do not understand are plainly deaf; we may turn the deaf ear unto them.'[4] History shows, he argues, that among others the Scythian counted the Athenian, the Roman and the Syrian as barbarous because their respective languages fell on deaf ears. The traveller arriving in a foreign place speaking a foreign tongue is seen as a barbarian and inspires fear and hostility. Dervla Murphy in Southern Tanzania loses her way and arrives on a farm where 'a small boy became hysterical with terror on seeing me. His father spoke no English and seemed almost equally scared, though in a more restrained way.'[5] Earlier, Murphy had remarked that, 'Faced with a language barrier, Kenyans tended to be aloof, almost hostile.'[6] A reason for Kenyan or Tanzanian unease might well be the disastrous experience of encounters with white travellers who considered the indigenous peoples of Africa to be barbarians, speaking incomprehensible languages. The more recent dehumanisation of Kenyans as speaking subjects is described to Murphy by a teacher she meets in a lodging house in Katika: '"Ordinary Kenyans meet few *mzungus* [foreigners]. We only *see* them, millions of tourists staring at us as if we were part of the wildlife."'[7] Here there is no language exchange, the Kenyans are stripped of language and become objects of curiosity, losing their humanity as they merge with the 'wildlife'.

The disorientation produced by language loss does not, however, have only undesirable consequences. The infantilisation may be embarrassing or disabling but it may also be openly embraced. The Romantic association of freshness of vision and spontaneity of response with the untutored perceptions of the child can transfer to the traveller arriving in a foreign land without the language. In the absence of language, the traveller's other senses come more strongly into play. Thus, sights, sounds, smells, tastes, sensations, are more keenly perceived because they rather than language become the primary vectors of communication. The vividness of these sensory experiences suggests parallels with early childhood where the child is not fully implicated in the language of the adult world and is more sensitive to information from the senses that bypass speech. If, as Hoffman notes, we need 'the tint of difference, of contrast, for perception to arise', then consciously alienating ourselves from language, one of our most fundamental means of acquiring knowledge about the world, generates a marked sense of difference leading to heightened perceptions.[8] This aspect of intersemiotic travel may explain in part the large claims made for travel from the scallop shells of Santiago to the anarchic promise of Rimbaud's drunken boats. The traveller is desensitised by the habitual use of language, so that removal to another place and culture and language is tantamount to a rebirth, a second childhood of sensory wakefulness. Whereas a traveller's place of birth can be primarily a locus of history, story, anecdote, verbalised project, in another place there are no longer the familiar coordinate systems of native language. So the traveller begins to look at the buildings above ground level, pays attention to the smells in the market, tastes the food on his/her plate, notices the fire hydrants. This is not to say that these experiences are denied to a person in their own language and place of birth but that the communicative resourcefulness demanded of the traveller in situations of total linguistic incomprehension makes a scrupulous attention to the multi-sensory detail of the everyday lifeworld much more likely. In the oneiric city of Joseph Brodsky's essay, 'A Place as Good as Any', the traveller does not know the language of the city. This is why a 'a stroll in an amusement park, half an hour in a shooting gallery, or a video game' is preferable to curling up in your hotel room with Flaubert, 'something that boosts the ego and doesn't require knowledge of the local tongue'. Brodsky notes the emptiness of the composite city of his dreams and claims, 'It is empty because for an imagination it is easier to conjure architecture than human beings.'[9] The absence of inhabitants Brodsky attributes to a failure of the imagination could also be traced to the tongue-tied state of his dream traveller. An exhaustive attentiveness to the material infrastructure of a city compensates for exclusion from the narrative networks sustained by the language of a place.

Passion, interpreters, autonomy

Dervla Murphy has not been the first traveller to use signs or gestures to communicate in difficult situations. In a letter from 1500, Pedro Vaz de

Caminha, one of the early Portugese explorers, describing the discovery of Brazil, devotes much space at the beginning of his account to describing the encounter of the Portugese with the Tupi Indians. Following physical descriptions of the men and women, he observes: 'It was not possible to speak to these people or understand them. There was such a chattering in uncouth speech that no one could be heard or understood. We made signs to them to go away.'[10] When Redmond O'Hanlon and James Fenton travel to the tropical jungle of Borneo in 1983, it is not they but one of the indigenous peoples that make the most extensive use of gesture in an effort to get O'Hanlon and Fenton to minister to their various ailments:

> A queue of mothers and children formed; we dressed hundreds of cuts that had gone septic, small ulcers, patches of skin fungus, rashes. And then the men began to trickle in. They mimed with a suppleness, a balletic grace that would have impressed Nijinsky, excruciating, disabling back pain; with eyes as big and bright as those of a fox hunting in the dusk they indicated that they were suffering from the kind of headaches that amount to concussion; with contortions that would have torn Houdini into spare ribs they demonstrated that their stomachs had ceased to function, that they were debilitated almost beyond assistance.[11]

The use of mime is a standard set-piece in travel writing where the possibility of language contact is remote. However, gestures are more than a simple cue for comic exaggeration: they raise questions that are fundamental to the practice of travel. David Denby in his examination of eighteenth-century sentimentalism speaks of a general distrust of linguistic expression.[12] Passion as a primary touchstone of authenticity is externalised in cries, inarticulate sounds and gestures. The nephew in Denis Diderot's *Le Neveu de Rameau* gives exuberant expression to the pantomime of his own emotions. Both Jean-Jacques Rousseau in his *Essai sur l'origine des langues* and Étienne Bonnot de Condillac in his *Essai sur l'origine des connaissances humaines* link the history of gesture to the history of language. For Condillac, the archetypal origin myth of language is two children lost in the desert with no language (two early intersemiotic travellers). One of the children sees the other child suffering, a suffering made audible by cries and visible by gestures. The child is suffering because it is deprived of an object. The child who is not suffering begins to look at the object and without fully understanding what's happening makes a connection between the cries and gestures and the child's needs.[13] Denby remarks:

> The origins of language lie in natural cries and gestures, not forming part of any structure of intention but, on the contrary, involuntary: it is the observer who, almost without knowing it, attaches a meaning to these mysterious signs emanating from the other, and who thus participates in the construction of a code.[14]

The gesture which is there at the inception of language is in a sense part of a pre-Babelian code of universality. The universality of gesture is prior to the differentiated codes of separate, human languages. The suggestion by travel writers of an understanding that is arrived at through gesture and that obviates the need for language points to the birth of a commonality of human experience and understanding that Condillac sees as concomitant with the gestural emergence of language. However, translation appears inscribed even in this moment if we examine Marshall Sahlin's *Islands of History* where he describes how Cook's final, fatal encounter with the Hawaiians was fraught with tensions resulting from the mismatch between gestures and cultural systems.[15] As Gillian Beer, in fact, argues,

> Language, though limited is less volatile. With our current emphasis on
> the indeterminacies of language it is striking to realize the degree to which
> in travel narrative gesture is treacherous, language (even a few words) a
> blessedly stable resource and coin.[16]

The language of gesture can quickly lose the fraternal innocence of human empathy and become itself an instrument of manipulation and control. This becomes apparent in Pedro Vaz de Caminha's narrative: 'If we signed to them asking them if they wanted to come to our ships they at once came forward ready to come. So that, if we had invited them all, they would have all come. We did not, however, take more than four or five with us that night.'[17] Gesture as code enters the realm of translation so that the intersemiotic moments are not so much outside as within the problematic of translation. The putative universality of the gestural systems of the body has relatively benign consequences in modern travel accounts but travellers rapidly yearn for the stable coin of language. Here, interpreters enter as the indispensable intermediaries in the transactions of language, interlingual agents in what for the travel writer was formerly an intersemiotic context.

The interpreters are often recruited as 'guides' so that the act of travelling is explicitly bound up with the act of translation. Not only the traveller but the translator is *translated* – in the physical, geometrical sense of the term – in the travel account. Interpreters are valuable not only because of what they do but because of who they are. They are generally part of the host community and as such are conduits for privileged 'inside' information on the society and culture. They confer authenticity and verisimilitude on the account. For this reason, the interpreter may become as much an object as an instrument of inquiry in travel writing. When V.S. Naipaul went to visit Iran in 1997, he employed a university student, Mehrdad, to be his 'guide and interpreter'.[18] The initial section of his Iranian account is devoted to a discussion with Mehrdad himself about the war with Iraq, a description of the circumstances of Mehrdad's sister and a thumbnail sketch of the fortunes of Mehrdad's father. Mehrdad remains strikingly present throughout the account, not simply as Naipaul's interpreter but as his interlocutor. For Eva Hoffman, her Czech interpreter, Wendy, is also more than a hired language functionary. Hoffman visits Wendy's friends in the Bohemian countryside, meets her husband, eats with her parents and plays with Wendy's child. Leon, the Iban interpreter and guide in Borneo, is one of the main figures in *Into the Heart of Borneo* and is present on almost every page. The narrative focus on the interpreter is not only because they convey information but because, as their name wittingly or unwittingly suggests, they *interpret* it. Although the interpreters spend part of their time translating what is being said, a considerable amount of time is devoted to intepreting cultural context, generally implicit in the source language but which must be rendered explicit in the target language. When Naipaul and Mehrdad go to see Khalkhali, the infamous 'hanging judge' of the Iranian revolution, their departure is delayed because their car will not start. After forty-five minutes, Khalkhali appears again and asks them if they would like some bread and cheese. Mehrdad's intepretation of the meaning of the request differs radically from that of Naipaul:

> This seemed to me a good idea; it might give me a chance to talk in another way to the Ayatollah. But Mehrdad said with some firmness that the offer of bread and cheese was just a form of words, a courtesy, that the Ayatollah was asking us to leave.
> We stood up to say goodbye.[19]

It is not only the implicit meaning of speech acts that must be teased out for the traveller but the words themselves can appear to elude the embrace of equivalence. These moments of hesitation or doubt are revealing of the potential for misunderstanding and misinformation in the translation transaction. The American sociologist R. Bruce W. Anderson comments on the particular authority of the interpreter: 'his position in the middle has the advantage of power inherent in all positions which control scarce resources'.[20] When Hoffman meets a Hungarian entrepreneur, Eva Jeles, it is Jeles's husband, András Török, who acts as interpreter. Jeles explains what she finds so compelling about business: 'What fascinates her is not so much making money as "venturing" – a word her husband translates after a careful pause.'[21] The interpreter here is concerned about exactness of rendition, a word in English that will capture the specific nature of Jeles's entrepreneurial passion. The interpreter can agonise over the fidelity to a source-language concept but there is also the concern for target-language impact. Naipaul and Mehrdad visit Abbas, a veteran of the Iran-Iraq war. At the end of a long conversation, Abbas is reported as saying, '"I have said more than I should. I have talked like a drunk man."' Naipaul then comments parenthetically on the interpreter's translation revisions:

> (That was Mehrdad's first translation when we were back at the hotel. But then right away he said, 'No, that's too strong. It wouldn't be good for

> Abbas.' He thought and said, 'A drunken man doesn't know what he says, and I feel I have been like that. That would be better.' I didn't see the difference, but Mehrdad said, 'The second one is softer.')[22]

The intervention can be more forceful. Hoffman is provided with a Roumanian interpreter when she asks to see some video documentaries of the miners' attack on the student demonstration in the Piata Universitate, Bucharest. The interpreter tells Hoffman that the students didn't behave as well as they should, singing and playing late into the night, and that is why people were glad the miners came.[23] When the French travel writer, Jean-Claude Guillebaud, decides to retrace the route of the first crusade, he employs Ayberk as his interpreter in Turkey. Guillebaud notes that certain questions, such as queries about alleged massacres, are taboo: 'Il arrive qu'Ayberk refuse de traduire une question que j'aimerais poser à des notables villageois.'[24] The position of intermediary makes the interpreter both powerful and vulnerable. Naipaul's interpreter is extremely reluctant to go and interpret at a suggested meeting with the Ayatollah Montazeri, a close ally of the Ayatollah Khomeini who had fallen out of favour with Khomeini's successors. He says simply, 'That is the way of death.'[25] The Roumanian interpreter is operating in a context where Iliescu is still in power and extreme nervousness continues to prevail over the operations of the Roumanian secret police, the Securitate. There are situations and contexts where interpreters can become dangerously visible, exposed to the rancour of regimes who want obedient rather than faithful translations. However, the difficulties experienced in the interpreting situation are not only to do with the politics.

Interpreters are not diaphonous creatures of passage. They embody cultures. Messages do not flow through them in a frictionless world of zero-resistance. Hoffman realises that there are limits to cultural understanding when she expresses her dismay to her Czech interpreter at a display of brassieres on a clothesline in a pub. Wendy, the interpreter, is annoyed at Hoffman's reaction and tells her that it is a specific kind of humour that offends no-one in Czechoslovakia. The difficulty for Hoffman and for any reader not familiar with Czech culture is distinguishing idiosyncratic preference from cultural difference. When a cultural reality is interpreted by the interpeter, is the traveller getting the benefit of measured judgement with general applicability or personal opinions disguised as cultural generalities? Göran Aijmer, the Swedish anthropologist, describes the political and epistemological problems that surround the use of informants:

> Informants' insights into their own society are interesting, but generally the interest lies in the extent to which the informant grasps his own social environment. There are also other issues, such as the way in which an informant's account forms a conscious strategy for self-presentation and

the anthropologist's refutation of indigenous explanations, which have an obvious place in anthropological discourse.[26]

The traveller's ability to refute 'indigenous explanations' is further compromised by the transience of his/her passage. Travellers can marshall all the resources of enquiry including interpreter/informants but modern travellers are often (though not always) aware of the highly contingent and partial nature of their understanding of other cultures. When Hoffman is asked by a Bulgarian journalist whether she got her job at *The New York Times* because she was attractive, she has to explain that that is not how people get hired in American quality papers. This gives rise to the following observation: 'Explanations, mutual explanations; and sometimes, when I have glimpses of minute, telling differences, I wonder how fully we can explain ourselves to each other after all.'[27] The limits to knowledge for Dervla Murphy are marked out by tragedy. In *The Ukimwi Road*, few Ugandans she meets want to talk about their experiences during Idi Amin's reign of terror. This contrasts with Roumania where people talked endlessly about their experiences under Ceaucescu. She comments: 'Perhaps, the Ugandans' worst moments, involving much more physical violence, couldn't be shared with someone from another culture.'[28] Interpreters therefore can find themselves trying to communicate knowledge that people may not wish to offer or do this in such a way that the explanations for either party are sharply bounded by patterns of understanding and horizons of cultural expectation. The fact of bilingualism itself involving knowledge of a major European language sets interpreters apart from their compatriots who do not have access to this language. To what extent does this distancing from their own culture through the knowledge of the foreign language lead to an ambivalence about the culture that the interpreters come in some way to represent, as privileged purveyors of inside information? This question is rarely asked in contemporary travel writing but there are two possible perspectives on the cultural displacement of interpreters. The first is to argue that, as we saw in the last chapter in our discussion of the origins of theory, perception is concomitant with distance. Patterns, forms and practices can only be articulated when we see them at a remove, through the *regard éloigné* of another language and culture. The interpreter's exposure to another language in this view is a schooling in cultural self-awareness. The second perspective is haunted by a hermeneutics of suspicion that would see interpreters as dubious cultural transgressors, who give voice not to the authentic experiences of their compatriots but to the self-aggrandising views of pro-Western cosmopolitan elites. It is possible here to invoke the obvious categories of race and class in any analysis of the interpreter's positionality. Another category would be gender. This is the category that Dervla Murphy brings to bear on the interpreter's task when she describes being brought to the home of Moses, a Kenyan health-worker. Murphy is introduced to his wife, Jenny, and his mother-in-law: 'Neither she [Jenny] nor her mother spoke English but Moses proved a diligently non-sexist interpreter, keen for his womenfolk to have their say.'[29]

The travel writer's dilemma is the drama of human limits. The traveller can either use an interpreter and have an *heteronymous* or dependent relationship to translation, or s/he can learn the language of the country being visited and have an *autonomous* or independent relationship to translation. In the latter case, travellers do their own translation rather than having others do it for them, which presupposes, of course, that they know other languages. The traveller may decide that ethically the only appropriate form of travel is to travel in countries where they know the language, though even this, as we have seen in the previous two chapters, is often highly problematic. Even relatively short journeys can be linguistically formidable. To have used the autonomous mode in Eastern Europe, Eva Hoffman would have had to master Slovak, Czech, Hungarian, Roumanian and Bulgarian. As she was born in Poland, she speaks Polish but, if she came from elsewhere, this language too would have to be added to the list. The journey to the mountains of the Batu Tiban in Borneo turns out be something of a linguistic odyssey for Redmond O'Hanlon and James Fenton. The complexity of language negotiation is highlighted in a scene where O'Hanlon and Fenton leave a bottle of pills for a Kenyah woman who is seriously ill with gangrene. They are accompanied by two Iban speakers, Leon and Dana, but Dana has some understanding of Kayan, the language of the Kenyahs:

> James limped horribly, he acted a gangrenous leg, he indicated the popping of one pill in his open mouth per one traverse of the sun across the sky. Leon translated into Iban, Dana translated into pidgin Kayan; the chief's son appeared to understand.[30]

Genuine polyglots, who thoroughly master a large number of languages, are rare. They are usually figures of legend, people whose competence is exaggerated by monoglot vagueness. Even the most linguistically talented travellers will find their resources stretched by the multilingual complexity of many areas of the planet. The recourse to a heteronymous mode of translation appears inevitable in some cases, though the temptation is always there to affect an autonomous role by concealing the full role played by heteronymy in the form of interpreters.

Touch, taste, music, perfume

Sometimes, of course, interpreters are not to hand. The common alternative is the improvised language of gesture with all its attendant ambiguities. However, language and gesture do not exhaust the range of human possibilities for communication. All the five senses can be pressed into the service of understanding. Part of the experience of travel indeed is to discover the communicative potential of the senses. Dervla Murphy describes the importance of touch in *Muddling through in Madagascar*, where she recalls a Bekapitsa chief who helped her and her daughter Rachel in a potentially difficult situation. Murphy shakes hands with the chief and declares, 'When there are no words in common a handshake can be an important method of communication – something much more than a formality.'[31] Touching is a notoriously complicated and often highly encoded area of intercultural communication, as the French ethnologist Raymonde Carroll has shown in *Évidences invisibles*, her comparative study of Franco-American cultural differences.[32] However, even if we remain sceptical of a myth of unmediated universality, it is possible to see how touch – the embrace, the handshake, the kiss on the cheeks – allows certain kinds of meaning to be communicated between human beings that do not have a common language. This communication may not always be welcomed, however. In *The Politics and Poetics of Transgression*, Peter Stallybrass and Allon White describe the nineteenth-century male preoccupation with contamination and contagion. Public spaces were particularly dangerous, with their potential promiscuity of contact. Physically touching the other was to be avoided but, in that predictable paradox of transgression, touch became eminently desirable. Hence the increasing autonomisation of sight where desire is celebrated as gaze and touch is abhorred as contamination.[33] In her analysis of the white man's lament in modern travel writing, Mary Louise Pratt claims, 'In contemporary travel accounts, the monarch-of-all-I-survey scene gets repeated, only now from the balconies of hotels in big third-world cities.'[34] An advantage of the balcony, however, is not only the view (the 'survey') but the distance. Like VIP enclosures in sporting arenas or the class geography of cities, the others are kept at a remove, where they can be observed by, but cannot touch, the viewing subject. Touch is therefore, in many instances, deeply transgressive and, for that reason, all the more significant in the guest/host relationships of travel.

Taste has a twofold communicative significance in travel literature. Firstly, there is food itself and what food tells us about the cultures that produce or offer it. Hence the often detailed descriptions of meals eaten in travel accounts, no matter how spartan, as they reveal much about diet, agriculture, economy (distribution networks), standards of living, language (specific names for ingredients or dishes) and history (cultural influences on culinary tradition). Drink is part of this geography of the palate and when consumed in sufficiently large quantities has the added advantage of favouring wordless communion with others, as Murphy and O'Hanlon amply testify. The galloping gourmets of television food programmes make visible this nomadism of taste as food programmes move from the sedentary kitchen of the studio to the visual postcards of markets, vineyards, foreign restaurants and the cavernous kitchens of five-star hotels. The second dimension to taste in travel writing is how the food is eaten. In his essay, 'Two Suppers', George Steiner claims that 'To eat alone is to experience or suffer a peculiar solitude. The sharing of food and drink, on the other hand, reaches into the inmost of the social-cultural tradition. The range of its symbolic and material bearings is almost total.'[35] Julia Kristeva, for her part, is fully alive to the importance of the meal for the foreigner, for the stranger, even if the convivial promise is not always sustained once the dishes have been washed up:

> 'Miracle de la chair et de la pensée, le banquet de l'hospitalité est l'utopie des étrangers: cosmopolitisme d'un moment, fraternité de convives qui apaisent et oublient leurs différences, le banquet est hors temps. Il s'imagine éternel dans l'ivresse de ceux qui n'ignorent pourtant pas sa fragilité provisoire.'[36]

The hospitality that is offered to the traveller in the form of a meal allows not only access into public places (cafés, restaurants, hotels) but, perhaps more importantly, to private places that provide the traveller with information on how people live, where they eat, how they decorate their houses, what their standard of living is, what hangs on their walls, how different generations relate to each other and what the different roles played by men and women are. In strongly patriarchal societies, the domestic or family meal takes on a particular significance as it is a means for the traveller to meet women who are otherwise not present in public places of conviviality such as pubs and cafés. Language is often enhanced by the act of eating and drinking together, as Plato's garrulous revellers remind us in *The Symposium*. But the very fact of partaking of food and drink with others has a semiotic richness that does not always depend on the alibi of language.

The sounds of intelligible speech are not the only sounds reaching the human ear. Any country has its own specific aural landscape – the bells, sirens, means of locomotion, bird calls, to mention only a few of the sounds – that communicates its distinctness. Where the language is not understood, it becomes part of this aural landscape and approximates to the condition of music. When the content is opaque, there emerges a refreshing, poetic attentiveness to the signifiers, to the formal properties of language. Nicolas Bouvier is seduced by the beauty of the Persian language: 'La musique du Persan est superbe.'[37] The Friday market in Madagascar's capital city is for Dervla Murphy a total sensory immersion in the life of Tana, and she refers explicitly to the 'musical surging of the Malagasy language as buyers and sellers haggle, discuss, advise, tease, condemn, laugh, protest.'[38] Hoffman, a speaker of Polish and English, is charmed by the radical otherness of Hungarian: 'All around are the enchanting and utterly perplexing sounds of Hungarian language, with its Bartókian syncopations and sensuousness.'[39] Babel's symphony for these travellers is the phonetic poetry of foreign speech. Music is not the prerogative of language, however, and sound as expressed through musical instruments is another avenue of communication that opens up to the intersemiotic traveller. The journey of Nicolas Bouvier and Thierry Vernet from Yugoslavia to Afghanistan is an experiment *ante verbum* in multi-media. Along with painting and writing materials, they have a recording apparatus and end up playing French dance tunes on guitar and accordion in a bar run by a Welshman in Pakistan. In Macedonia, Bouvier notes:

> Ici, comme en Serbie, la musique est une passion. C'est aussi un 'Sésame' pour l'étranger: s'il aime il aura des amis. S'il enregistre, tout le monde, même la police, s'emploiera à lui racoler des musiciens.[40]

The apparent ability of music to transcend language difference is encapsulated in the holiday iconography of campfire sing-songs and groups of tourists crowded into Irish pubs listening to folk music sessions. Listening to music is not an experience that is predicated on knowledge of a language, though it may of course, as in the case of song, be enhanced by it.[41] The communion of interest that unites musician and listener is a way of establishing contact where language is scarce. In addition, music in its genesis, structure and development carries its own local histories, histories that the traveller may know about beforehand or explore later.

Bouvier compares music and laughter favourably to language in what he sees as the universality of the non-linguistic: 'Je crois que la musique et le rire, autres valeurs universelles, vont parfois plus loin dans la communication avec l"Autre.".'[42] Laughter is not only the best medicine but it is also the most effective form of travel insurance, 'Il n'y a pas de meilleure communication que le rire, pas de meilleur passeport.'[43] An intuitive appreciation of Bouvier's observation may indeed explain why when people do not understand a language or only understand it imperfectly they grin furiously or laugh out loud – on cue from the speaker or other listeners – at jokes they cannot comprehend.

If the sound of laughter reassures, smells can be more troubling but they too are essential elements of travel experiences. Patrick Süskind's *Perfume* begins famously with the stench of the European city in the eighteenth century; the smells of cow dung, urine, mould, rotten cabbage, animal fat, dust and perspiration filling the streets of the airless cities.[44] Commenting on the nineteenth-century city, John Urry and Chris Rojek argue that 'It was the sense of smell which enraged social reformers, since smell, while, like touch, encoding revulsion, had a pervasive and invisible presence difficult to regulate.'[45] The development of new middle-class housing in expanding industrial cities like London, Glasgow and Manchester was driven in part by a wish to get away from the rank smells of the masses. Zygmunt Bauman argues that 'Modernity claimed war on smells. Scents had no room in the shiny temple of perfect order modernity set out to erect.'[46] Travellers are highly ambivalent with respect to smell. Smells of food, the street, people's perfume, flowers, cigarette brands (*gauloises*), the sea and rivers are all highly evocative, and smell is conventionally seen as the mnemonic sense par excellence, a dramatic short-cut to memory of place. The fragrance of mimosa in a faraway garden brings the experience of North Africa more powerfully to mind than any number of snapshots.

Nevertheless, the dance of near synonyms in English – 'smells', 'odours', 'scents' – reflects the shifting status of the smell in culture. Privileged guardian of nomadic memory, it can also be the source of the traveller's lament, the unpleasant intrusion of the 'pre-modern' into the world of the Western traveller. Dervla Murphy avoids hotels aimed at the more affluent traveller on her journey from Kenya to Zimbabwe, but in many places that she stays there are comments on the frequently pitiful state of the latrines or the pungent odours from the piping in the showers and bathrooms of lodging-houses. Alexandra David-Neel is fully conversant with Tibetan culture and language but her tolerance is sorely tested by food that is brought to her and her companion, Yongden, by a Tibetan beggar. When he puts down his purchase, David-Neel exclaims, 'Oh! . . . une odeur épou-vantable emplit soudainement la pièce, un relent de charnier.'[47] The origin of the pestilential smell is explained by David-Neel as a Tibetan custom of letting the innards of a slaughtered animal macerate in its stomach for days, weeks or longer, the stomach then used in the preparation of a soup. David-Neel pleads ill-health and refuses to eat the soup. The incident is introduced by her observation that, 'ce qui était le plus fatigant et devenait même parfois pénible à l'excès, c'était le rôle qu'il me fallait constamment jouer pour ne pas trahir mon incognito.'[48] The smell of the macerating innards is much more intrusive and threatening to David-Neel's identity than many of the other more physical dangers to which she is exposed. Acceptance or tolerance of certain smells is an extremely potent parameter of identity, and the wretchedly poor, immigrants, and marginal groups – punks, 'crusties' – are placed beyond the pale of social acceptance by the invisible ring-fence of smell. The potent anamnesis of smell for the intersemiotic traveller is more generally part of the risk-taking that travel involves, notably travel that places itself outside the safety-net of organised tourism.

Describing the adolescent, Adam Phillips comments: 'One way the adolescent differentiates himself, discovers his capacity for solitude – for a self-reliance that is not merely a triumph over his need for the object – is by taking and making risks.'[49] Going to extremes is finding out, establishing one's limits, the limits that are constitutive of personal identity. Travel's almost mythical association with youth, from the young hero setting out in pursuit of divers grails to the EuroRail backpackers sprinting through the rail timetables of Europe, is partly grounded in this association of risk with self-discovery. Ageing will frequently involve the diminution of risk in travel; the shift from the hostel to the hotel, from the food stall to the restaurant, from the journey alone or *à deux* to the comforting and protective conviviality of the coach tour. Tolerance of dirty linen, malfunctioning toilets, rooms that have the lingering memories of previous inhabitants, diminishes as more stable identities are less likely to want to court the adolescent vertigo of risk. Writers of travel accounts are different in that their exposure to the perils of relatively unorganised travel maintains an element of risk, even if the risks do not take the highly coloured form of the rampaging rhinoceroses and festive cannibalism of *Boy's Own* narratives. A road accident or hepatitis is a more likely fate for the modern traveller. Dealing with other forms of communication in travel, whether this be touch, taste or smell, is thus an experiment with self, an exploration of the limits of personal and cultural tolerance of myriad otherness.

The world as picture

The Irish sociologist Eamonn Slater, in an essay entitled 'Becoming an Irish *Flâneur*', details the growing importance of images in late modernity:

> As the process of commodification penetrates deeper into the cultural realms of society, commodity production takes on a more visual character: this corresponds to a process of *visualisation*. Images and visual symbols become the universal language of commodity production across national boundaries. Television, movies and the advertising industry can replicate images endlessly and beam them virtually anywhere.[50]

Martin Heidegger claimed that 'the fundamental event of the modern age is the conquest of the world as picture'.[51] The implication of visual practices in travel is long established. From romantic landscape painting to the picture postcard and TV holiday programmes, travelling is often primarily projected as an activity of *seeing*. In *The Tourist Gaze*, John Urry describes changes in tourist practices as transformations of the ways in which people gaze upon or look at objects, peoples and places.[52] Discussing Mungo Park's *Travels in the Interior of Africa* in *Imperial Eyes: Travel Writing and Transculturation*, Mary Louise Pratt describes 'arrival scenes' as 'particularly potent sites for framing relations of contact and setting the terms of its representation'.[53] These 'scenes' are visual moments, where the colonial traveller sees the native other for the first time. The Baconian revolution in science had firmly established ocularcentrism in Western thinking. Observation was the touchstone of legitimacy in Western science and, where the eye could not see, visual metaphor stepped in.[54] Literacy and the advent of printing further strengthened visual and spatialised perceptions of experience.[55] If sight became the most privileged of the senses, Foucault demonstrated in a number of works that it also became the most sinister, with the sufferings of others on display as decontextualised spectacle.[56] The notion of gaze as culturally determined and politically coercive translates to colonial travel narratives. Here, natives in colonial contact zones are often presented as transfixed by the imperial gaze. As Sara Mills notes in *Discourses of Difference: An Analysis of Women's Travel Writing and Colonialism*, 'in travel writing the narrator gazes at the "natives" – and is irritated if they have the temerity to gaze back'.[57] The equivalent in contemporary travel settings is tourists gazing at local people as if they were objects in a visual landscape, as we saw earlier in Kenyan reactions to safari tourists. A curious effect of an understandable preoccupation with the visual in critical writing on travel literature and tourism is that it seems to have affected the writing itself. Neither Urry, Pratt, nor Mills links the predominance of the visual to the question of language or, more precisely, the absence of common language. Yet, the experience of travel in a country where the language is unknown to the traveller will be heavily informed by the visual. If you cannot speak, you can at least look. Sightseeing is the world with the sound switched off. Access is markedly different for an art gallery and a theatre as is testified by the multilingual crowds in the galleries and museums of the world. Similarly, the impetus to rely on a visual apprehension of the real must be in part stimulated by the temporary suspension of common language, whether the impetus takes the form of French Orientalist painting in North Africa or the photographic pilgrimages of modern tourists. Not speaking the language of the other can result in unease, and photography, as Susan Sontag pointed out, is often an effective way of dissipating the traveller's anxiety: 'The very activity of taking photographs is soothing, and assuages general feelings of disorientation that are likely to be exacerbated by travel.'[58] This not to suggest that people do not also visually interact with their own cultures where they do speak the language, but the incentive to do so is surely greatly enhanced where words fail. Nor is it to suggest that visual experience is somehow unmediated or does not have grammars or codes of its own. Nicolas Bouvier is accompanied on his journey by the visual artist Thierry Vernet. In a meeting with a group of Kurdish villagers, when sign language no longer proves effective, Vernet draws with a knife on the bottom of white tin bowls a sketch of their car, a section of their route and the bars of their temporary prison in Mahabad, Iran. However, visual communication has its limits. When a coffin maker in Macedonia asks Vernet the time in Macedonian, Vernet gestures that he cannot reply in Macedonian and shows him his watch-face. Clock-time as visual representation is of course highly coded and the coffin maker has not been taught to read the time. Bouvier's laconic comment is, 'Pour les impossibilités au moins, il y a toujours moyen de s'entendre.'[59]

In science fiction novels pictures are a standard prop in projects for communication with extra-terrestrial intelligence. The difficulty, as Brian

Mossop points out in 'The Image of Translation in Science Fiction and Astronomy', is that extra-terrestrials may have radically different conventions for relating forms to meanings.[60] The crucial role of the guide book or travel supplement or the voiceover in the holiday programme for earthbound travellers is to provide the tourist with the visual literacy necessary to distinguish 'important' or 'typical' sights from other less valued visual experiences. For Jonathan Culler, indeed, tourism is a branch of semiotics: 'All over the world the unsung armies of semioticians, the tourists, are fanning out in search of the signs of Frenchness, typical Italian behaviour, exemplary oriental scenes, typical American thruways, traditional English pubs.'[61] It is significant that Culler's semioticians are looking for visual not linguistic evidence of otherness. Engaging with the external signs of alterity may appear to involve less personal risk (signs seen from a distance) than the direct dialogical encounter of language. The panoramic window of the motor coach, the windscreen and the railway compartment window foreground the visual and filter out external smells, sounds, tastes and touch. Charles Musser sees travel as crucial to the emergence of fictional narrative in early cinema, especially as exemplified in the railway sub-genre in films like Edwin S. Porter's *What Happened in the Tunnel*, *Romance of the Rail* or *The Great Train Robbery*. Drawing on the work of Wolfgang Schivelbusch, Musser stresses the affinities between the rail and the screen:

> The traveller's world is mediated by the railroad, not only by the compartment window with its frame but by telegraph wires which intercede between the passenger and the landscape. The sensation of separation which the traveller feels on viewing the rapidly passing landscape has much in common with the theatrical experience of the spectator. The allusion of train window with the screen's rectangle was frequent within this travel sub-genre.[62]

Trains and films frame the world and, in a profoundly ambiguous sense (departure/distance), travel becomes an act of separation. The sensation of separation is elaborated on by Kate O'Brien in her Irish travel account, *My Ireland*, where she describes a childhood visit to the Bioscope theatre in Grafton Street, Dublin, in 1907. The seats in the theatre were arranged like those on a tram or a pullman train and O'Brien comments, 'in them we travelled by screen, far and high and dangerously, over mountain passes and by rocky shores, through gentle lanes and along busy streets. I remember only all the marvellous travelling. There can have been no story-telling, no human interest'.[63] The cinematographic streets are 'busy' but the spectacle is devoid of 'human interest'. Is this O'Brien's way of expressing the non-engagement of the traveller in the daily transactions of language that are a central element in our experience of the lifeworld? Does the era of silent cinema described here reflect more accurately than the 'talkies' our experience of travel in linguistically remote places (that may be close to hand, viz.

Bryson in Wales) where an important dimension to our usual comprehension of the world has effectively been silenced by the limits of our language abilities? The exponential increase in leisure travel in the developed world since the second world war means *inter alia* that travellers are opting more and more for foreign rather than domestic holidays.[64] The opportunities for contact with foreign cultures and languages are thus greatly increased. Tourists have become part of the accelerated movement of people, goods and services that is seen to be a characteristic feature of globalisation. Like Slater, Mike Featherstone argues that this movement is accompanied by a flow of signs and images that are present in all areas of everyday life. This aestheticisation of everyday life means that boundaries between art and everyday life are increasingly blurred, with reproduced imagery becoming omnipresent.[65] It could be argued that the aestheticisation of everyday life in late modernity and the primacy of the visual in many travel experiences is related, at least in part, to the minoritisation of language at the inception of the modern movement in scientific thinking. In a 1961 essay, 'The Retreat from the Word', George Steiner argued famously that in the seventeenth century significant areas of truth, reality and action receded from the sphere of verbal statement. He claimed:

> With the formulation of analytical geometry and the theory of algebraic functions, with the development by Newton and Leibniz of calculus, mathematics ceases to be a dependent notation, an instrument of the empirical. It becomes a fantastically rich, complex and dynamic language. *And the history of that language is one of progressive untranslatability.*[66] (his emphasis)

The history of the mathematicisation of scientific knowledge is also, however, one of radical and accelerated translatability. Gillian Beer argues that the use of mathematics has 'speeded up communication between scientists to a startling degree, as if the Tower of Babel had been built in a day once the workers found a common discourse'.[67] The Harvard mathematician Michael Guillen, in his *Five Equations that Changed the World*, uses the Babel myth to describe the 'inconvenient reality' of a multilingual world and the failure of efforts by the United Nations to have diplomats speak only one language, 'a restriction that would facilitate negotiations and symbolize global harmony'. Mathematics, on the other hand, has been the triumphant Esperanto of modernity:

> As measured by the millions of those who speak it fluently and by the historic consequences of their unified efforts, *mathematics* is arguably the most successful global language ever spoken. Though it has not enabled us to build a Tower of Babel, it has made possible achievements that once seemed no less impossible: electricity, airplanes, the nuclear bomb, landing a man on the moon, and understanding the nature of life and death.[68]

The construction of the nuclear bomb seems a rather dubious benefit of Guillen's cooperative utopia but the mathematicisation of enquiry has certainly resulted in that withdrawal from the word that Steiner sees at work as much in the human and social sciences as in the physical. It has also, in our view, determined the current hegemony of English as a source language in translation and as a target language in language teaching. The pre-Babelian promise of mathematics is mirrored in the *reineSprache* of English, as if, in a sense, the minoritisation of all language becomes the majorisation of one. The condition of mathematical transparency that allows topologists of different nationalities to gather together in a community of understanding around the blackboard or VDU is the globalising impulse behind English the world language. This communicative potential of mathematics as the 'global language' of science has arguably had another consequence that relates quite literally to the retreat from the word, the emergence of visualisation as a core feature of globalisation. As Crashaw and Urry note, 'Everyday expressions such as "seeing the sights", "capturing the view", "eye-catching scenery", "picturesque villages", "pretty as a postcard", illustrate the significance of the eye to both the traveller and the travel promoter.'[69] What Urry and Crashaw inadvertently highlight is the linguistic dilemma of the global traveller. The more countries the traveller goes to, the less languages s/he knows. The most common strategy is either to speak a global language, now almost invariably English, as French continues to lose ground, or rely on a largely visual encounter with other people and places – the 'sights' captured on cameras and camcorders. This must explain, in part, the desire of the 'anti-tourist' (see Chapter 2) to learn or give the appearance of having learnt the foreign language. Assiduously avoiding the famous 'sights' in favour of the linguistic interaction of the local bar or newspaper, the traveller as local linguist is distancing himself, herself from the traveller as global sightseer.

Guide books and complicated doubleness

The shift towards language autonomy is complicated, as we have seen elsewhere, by the cruel boundedness of human ability. Developments in tourism in the nineteenth century show a preoccupation with the problems posed by this language heteronymy. In a nineteenth-century French advertisement for the *Grand Hôtel Royal* in Cairo, one of the services offered by the hotel and clearly indicated in bold type is an 'Interprète parlant plusieurs langues.'[70] The *drogman* is a familiar figure in orientalist literature, but the presence of the guide/interpreter was not always welcome. Karl Baedecker, indeed, saw the advent of the guide book as a step on the road to freedom. In his preface to the eighth edition of the guide to Germany (1858)

Baedecker speaks of releasing the traveller from the

> unpleasant, and often wholly invisible, tutelage of hired servants and
> guides (and in part from the aid of coachmen and hotelkeepers), to assist
> him in standing on his *own* feet, to render him *independent*, and to place
> him in a position from which he may receive his own impressions with
> clear eyes and lively heart.[71] (his emphasis)

In *The Beaten Track: European Tourism, Literature, and the Ways to 'Culture'
1800–1918*, James Buzard devotes a whole section of his work to the genesis of
the guide book, in particular the pioneering works of Karl Baedecker and John
Murray.[72] The question of language, however, is not raised in the discussion.
The omission is all the more striking in that one of the main reasons for hiring
the guides that are the object of Baedecker's scorn was their knowledge not
only of local history but also of the local language. The guide book *translated*
the foreign culture into the mother tongue of the traveller. The traveller no
longer had to rely on the oral translation of the guide/interpreter as the guide
book provided the written translation. The Murray and Baedecker guides thus
facilitated the transition from heteronymous dependency on the oral interpreter to an autonomous mode of travelling grounded in literacy. The reliance
on the guide book has some predictable linguistic consequences. Dervla
Murphy stays at a guest house in Kalangala, Uganda, where she finds twenty-
five backpackers sharing the twenty rooms: 'All these backpackers seem to be
coming from or going to the same places and using the same guidebook – the
Lonely Planet, ironically.'[73] On a ferry from Brindisi to Piraeus, Lisa St Aubin de
Terán finds herself in the company of many young North Americans 'doing'
Europe: 'Because they had all been to, or were going to, the same places, they
had a common vocabulary that joined them in instant, if ephemeral, friend-
ships.'[74] With many others speaking your language the Planet is not such a
Lonely place. Not only do the guide books deliver the travellers to the same
places the world over but the language of the guide books creates a sensation
of linguistic homogeneity. The independent traveller armed with the divining
rod of the guide books finds by charmed coincidence that many of the other
travellers in the guest house/hostel/café speak his/her language. This is
hardly surprising if the same guide in the same language has brought the travellers there in the first instance. The autonomy of the printed guide (no local
interpreters) produces another form of heteronymy (global interpreters dictat-
ing itineraries). The independent traveller thus remains signally dependent on
the linguistic lifeline of the guide book and its attendant language hegemony.

In the middle of an informal evening with a group of Bulgarians in the city
of Burgas, Eva Hoffman is asked by a theatre producer if she is 'doing business' or enjoying herself:

> It's a question that has the power to confound me, because it has never
> been far from my mind in my travels. There is an element of a complicated

doubleness, or near-authenticity, of which every writer engaged in an enterprise such as mine is guilty. I like the people around this table; I am, in point of fact, enjoying myself very much. But there's no denying that out of the corner of my mind I'm observing what's going on from a slight distance.[75]

The 'complicated doubleness' of the travel writer is the shifting duplicity of the translator. At one level, there must be the full engagement with the text to be translated in order to capture all its nuances but, at another, there is always the observer in the corner of the mind who wonders how this text will be put into another language. The translation problems increase when the material to be conveyed in language arrives through avenues of information or communication that are not linguistic. We could argue that the play on the different senses that results from the sensuous geography of displacement means that we have not only a cerebral but a somatic memory of place. The difficulty for the travel writer is that sensual heterogeneity must somehow be translated into language. Language equivalents must be found for non-language experiences. Parallels with conventional descriptions of romantic love as ineffable, as being beyond the reach of language, are inescapable. All the more so in that holiday and romance are traditionally associated. The absence of a common language, and a consequent dependence on eye-contact, touch, smell and sight, implies an eroticisation of perception that fuels the desire of a thousand boulevard cafés. The difficulty, of course, is a reductive exoticism that empties the desired Other of autonomous identity so that they become one-dimensional objects of florid fantasy. In the absence of the symbolic mediation of language, can desire be anything more than ultimately unsatisfactory non-dialogical obsession? Similarly, for the intersemiotic traveller there is the bogey of misunderstanding, illusion or exoticism that threatens the whole enterprise of travel in foreign places. This self-doubt is externalised in Dervla Murphy's *On the Ukimwi Road*, where Westerners are assailed for their nomadic superficiality. In Jinja, Uganda, Dervla Murphy is asked her occupation by a retired teacher who frowns when he hears her reply:

> Travel writers ignorant of local languages, he opined politely but firmly, often give misleading impressions. 'Only about 20 per cent of Ugandans can hold a conversation in English. And no African can express *African* thoughts and feelings in any European language – not even people as fluent as I am. That's one reason why so many donors go astray, wasting billions of dollars – or turning our politicians into billionaires. Most expats plan on a false basis.'[76]

This message is reiterated in Uganda by an Irish doctor, Mike, who has spent thirty years working there and who says that it is only after spending half a lifetime in the country, 'speaking the languages', that anyone can hope to understand the cultural specificity of Ugandan society. A Ugandan friend, Jill, tells Murphy, 'To you a big area of the African soul is invisible – Whites can only see it after a lifetime here, speaking some of our languages.'[77] The time factor that we discussed in the context of time-space compression in Chapter 2 emerges as the dominant factor here. Mike and Jill talk about half a lifetime, a lifetime, and both use the word 'language' in the plural. In a sense, there is once again the tension between horizontal and vertical travelling, the change in fractal scale (see Chapter 1) that reveals the daunting complexity of any site at any particular moment on the planet. Robert Guillain, the Far East correspondent for *Le Monde*, once observed, 'Quand on passe huit jours en Chine on écrit un livre, quand on y reste trois semaines un article, et après un an, rien.'[78] The more time spent in a country, the greater the knowledge of the language or languages, the more apparent becomes one's ignorance. Hoffman is startled on reading a poem in Slovak to find an elaborate meditation on loneliness and female pain. Whereas Poland appears real to her, nearby Slovakia is remote. She comments, 'while we allow the inhabitants of imaginary remote corners the authenticity of savages or sufferers, we rarely suppose them to possess the authenticity of complex, sophisticated perceptions'. Her conclusion is bleak: 'Perhaps it is simply impossible to encompass the whole globe pulsating with authentic complexity; or perhaps the desire for simpler worlds is nearly ineradicable.'[79] The desire for simpler worlds is visibly articulated in national stereotype. At a conference in the Czech Republic attended by Hoffman, the Irishman is predictably drunk, the Englishman ironic and the Frenchman obscure. Busy human minds hunger for the economy of labels that make reflection on cultural difference a mindless subroutine. The challenge for the travel writer and, more generally, for any sensitive traveller is to resist the lazy shorthand of fixed equivalence and to engage with the cultural depth and linguistic intricacy of other peoples and places. The internal, human transcendence that we discussed in Chapter 2 has a role to play here. Faced with the complexity of human language and culture, two transcendent responses are possible out of a range of other responses, such as employing interpreters or speaking a global language. The first is *linguistic transcendence*, where the traveller, despite the manifold difficulties of the task, learns the language or languages of the country or countries s/he intends to visit. There are, of course, limits to our capacity to learn other languages but inner, human transcendence is precisely about human attempts to overcome these limits. Part of the goodwill that is often expressed to travellers for their knowledge of the indigenous language stems from that transcendent awareness, the knowledge that in crossing the external borders of countries the traveller has made efforts to cross internal borders of ability. Some linguistic performers are more skilled than others but language competence is asymptotic rather than absolute. There is always more to be learned in the foreign language (as intralingual complexity makes clear) so that limits are always there to test transcendence. The second response is what might be termed *semiotic transcendence*, where all the senses other than language are brought to bear on a travel experience. The limits in this case are the limits of not knowing the language and attempting to transcend these limits through the operations of the five different senses. Though knowledge acquired this way is of course *limited*, this limitedness should not always be judged, as we see in discourses on translation, as evidence of failure, but rather as the internal transcendent impulse of the language animal to go beyond his/her local condition. What semiotic transcendence assumes, of course, at some level, is that there is a common humanity that makes communication possible and that we are not irredeemably bound by the circumstances of our birth into a particular language. This tacit universalism underlies the practice of inter-semiotic travelling.

Critical universalism

The notion of the universal has become itself a universal object of suspicion in post-structuralist and post-modernist thinking. However, it is a notion that is inescapable in any discussion of translation or travel. In order to argue for an enabling rather than disabling concept of the universal in translation and travel, we may turn to the work of the French historian François Furet for a useful set of discriminations. In *Le passé d'une illusion* he analyses the particular appeal of totalitarian ideologies in the twentieth century and describes Nazism as a pathology of difference and communism as a pathology of the universal.[80] Translation, as we saw in the last chapter, can be seen as a form of triangulation or, to use Gillian Rose's terms, a 'broken middle' that prevents a violent and dogmatic synthesis of binary opposites.[81] Staying with translation as triangulation, it is possible to see translation as lying between the pathology of universalism and the pathology of difference.

The pathology of universalism is implicit in language triumphalism, the sense of manifest destiny that informs the comments by Dinesh D'Souza in his *The End of Racism* (to which we referred in Chapter 1), where he argues that there is the risk of an American Babel, a breakdown of communication, if everyone does not speak a common language. For 'reasons of practicality', the language must be English, 'which is rapidly becoming the global medium of intercultural communication'.[82] Here, pragmatism is the foot soldier of ideology and Babel a synonym for Armageddon. The nirvana of intercultural communication masks the violence of language loss. For the universalist, translation is an obstacle to, not an agent of, intercultural communication.

The pathology of difference, on the other hand, is parodied by the bilingual Irish novelist Flann O'Brien in *The Poor Mouth*, where the president of the Grand Feis (festival) in Corkadoragha addresses the crowd:

> Gaels! he said, it delights my Gaelic heart to be here today speaking Gaelic
> with you at this Gaelic feis in the centre of the Gaeltacht. May I state that I
> am a Gael. I'm Gaelic from the crown of my head to the soles of my feet –
> Gaelic front and back, above and below. Likewise, you are truly Gaelic. We
> are all Gaelic Gaels of Gaelic lineage. He who is Gaelic, will be Gaelic ever-
> more. I myself have spoken not a word except Gaelic since the day I was
> born – just like you – and every sentence I have ever uttered has been on
> the subject of Gaelic.[83]

Here, language is fetishised and all contact with the other is a form of contamination. The language is idealised and the speakers are ennobled. In *Mere
Irish and Fíor-Ghael* Joep Leerssen describes the response of Irish-language
poets to derogatory representations of their language and craft by Tudor
propagandists. For these poets, the speech of the English

> (both in its contents and its linguistic medium) stamps them as uncouth,
> blubbering, simpering, stupid blockheads and bullies – this is in complete
> contrast to the mellifluous and harmonious *Gaeilge ghlic* and the clever
> speakers of that well-wrought language.[84]

Here, Babel is betrayal, translation a form of capitulation. Languages that
are constantly under social, economic and cultural pressure must, of course,
often champion difference, if only to offer cogent reasons for their own
survival. However, the rhetoric of difference can ultimately breed a
conformism as stifling as the gospel of universalism. Post-structuralist
critics of translation have offered a cogent critique of the shortcomings of
fluent, naturalising strategies that obliterate difference in translation and
favour translations that are indistinguishable from other texts produced in
the target language.[85] The difficulty with making the otherness of the text
present in the translation is that this may not lead to greater understanding
but to a superficial exoticism that is akin to the shallower varieties of postmodern eclecticism. The German writer and translator Hans Erich Nossack
asked what attracts us to a book written in another country, in another
language:

> It is not the folklore or the exotic. That is all at best interesting, and like
> everything interesting, magazines and travel agencies will jump at the
> chance to make a profit from it . . . It is not the foreign living habits that
> differ from our own. It is not the foreign religions, foreign ideologies,
> foreign institutions. As I said before that is all very interesting and infor-
> mative material for comparative studies. But, like everything that is merely
> interesting, it is subject to fashionable trends and is quite transitory.
> However, we as readers immediately understand something over and
> above these superficialities: to use a hackneyed phrase, we recognize that
> things are no different anywhere else, which relieves us momentarily of
> our sense of isolation as human individuals.[86]

Difference does not have to result in the pathology of closure. Foreign reli-gions, institutions and ideologies are more important than Nossack allows in determining sensibility, and a translator must convey these cultural differ-ences in sensibility to the reader of a translated text. However, understanding the other may be enhanced less by a radical fetishisation of difference than by deepening a sense of shared humanity. The violence of ethnic hatred is predicated on the acknowledgement of difference; the result, however, is not sensitivity and respect but intolerance and destruction. The potential contri-bution of translation to society is to arrest the murderous process of *dehumanisation*. It is the imaginative empathy of the act of translation that restores humanity to the other, not the espousal of absolutist cultural sepa-ratism. In the context of travel and translation, it seems necessary to distinguish between *pathological universalism* and *critical universalism*. Patho-logical universalism is the translation movement that would end all translation. Everybody, everywhere, is translated into the dominant language and culture. The universal is the universal projection of the language and values of a hegemonic nation or class. Language and cultural differences are asperities levelled out by a global process of homogenisation that seeks an increasingly rapid circulation of signs and images.

Critical universalism is celebration of difference that leads to an embrace of other differences, the universalism lying not in the eradication of the other but in sharing a common condition of being a *human other*. Both terms are important and translation in the travel context can be seen as that negotia-tion between humanity and otherness. A travel and a translation practice that is informed by this critical universalism is one that posits the humanity of others and areas of commonality, while also taking full and proper cogni-sance of difference. This practice realises the immense potential for mistranslation, bogus equivalence and semantic discrepancy in human contact but sees the strength of translation in the acknowledgement, though not the acceptance, of limits. In other words, the incompleteness of transla-tion, the 'loss' in the passage across languages and cultures, is not a terminal admission of failure but a stimulus to further translation attempts, further efforts to transcend the limits of our culture, language and time.[87] Adam, a bar-owner in Bukoba, Tanzania, comments positively on this essen-tially human form of transcendence that is travel as translation, saying to Dervla Murphy: '"This is very interesting to write books about the countries you travel in. It is good for us to know about each other. Big problems happen when people make mistakes about other people, because they know not about them."'[88] Paul Ricoeur, drawing on the insights of philosophical hermeneutics, sees translation indeed as a model of imaginative exchange in the kind of universality required by citizenship in a new Europe. The polyglot nature of Europe brings with it translation demands, demands that are possi-ble or even conceivable because languages are not self-enclosed. Ricoeur, in the words of the Irish philosopher Joseph Dunne, argues:

> There may indeed be an ultimate incommensurability between any one
> language and the other; but short of this limit there is the perpetual chal-
> lenge of rendering in the one what is said in the other. In carrying through
> this process, there is no 'master' Language – supplying a kind of neutral
> template on which correspondences between the two languages might be
> registered – to which the translator can have recourse. Rather, as bilin-
> gual, the latter must live into the distinctiveness (at many levels –
> phonological, lexical, syntactical, stylistic, etc.) of the other language and
> try to bring this over, without semantic loss, into her own language.[89]

Translation is conceived of in a nomadic mode as a guest/host relationship.
The host opens up his/her house of language to the other but any attempt to
diminish the guest's otherness, to impose dominant norms of behaviour or
expression on the other, is to violate the laws of hospitality. Coercion is the
ultimate discourtesy. Post-structuralist suspicion of fluent translation strategies can be seen as complementary not inimical to the ethical project
envisaged by Ricoeur and Dunne. The willingness of a language to go out of
its way to accommodate another language takes on its full significance when

> the encounter extends beyond language to the other culture in all its
> density of meaning, custom and belief – when, in Ricoeur's words, it takes
> on an '*ethos* whose goal would be to repeat at the cultural and spiritual
> level the gesture of linguistic hospitality' implicit in the act of translation.[90]

Travel, in its most progressive form, carries the ethical project of translation
to the cultural and spiritual level as it seeks to engage fully with other
cultures. This engagement is all the more apparent in that the practice of
travel depends crucially on the exercise of hospitality. The fact that travel
writers are criticised for incomplete, inadequate, prejudiced accounts of
other peoples and places is further proof of a critical universalism, an inner
human transcendence, an ethics of translation that allows or drives us to
formulate the critique in the first place.

A prodigal art

We noted earlier the paradox of intersemiotic travelling, the complex encoding
of the experiences of the senses in language. The problem is more general in
that the primary difficulty in all travel writing is in accounting for the
heterogeneity of the real. In this sense, all travel involves translation, seen as a
search for equivalences. The question of language and translation foregrounds
a problem that is travel itself. It would be mistaken to believe that language and
translation problems end with the journey. In a sense, they just begin. Travel
writers in their study, as much as on the road, are required to tease out the full
implications of translation. Claudio Magris, in Slovakia, offers a markedly

masculinist representation of the writer's art: 'A writer is not the father of a family but the son, and he must leave home and find his own way.' Daughters too can leave home, despite the attempts in many cultures to control the movement of women. However, what is significant in Magris's conception of writing is that it is a *prodigal* art. It involves what Magris calls a 'stern distancing needed by every kind of art and every liberating experience'.[91] But distancing is not enough: writing, as we saw in Chapter 1, also involves a return to the language of home, the language of the mother, the language of the father. The language of the narration must somehow capture the foreignness of the experience in the familiar words of the tribe. Hans Erich Nossack offers unsurprising advice to younger writers. They should translate. As he admits, 'One does not necessarily learn more about the foreign language but rather learns to use one's native language more precisely.'[92] Looking for equivalents for a foreign metaphor or trying to capture a 'foreign linguistic gesture' with an adequate expression in the mother tongue exercises the mind and vocabulary of the writer. The experience of translation forces writers to transcend the limits of their normal expression. In his reflections on the art of travel writing, Bouvier acknowledges its imperfection: 'quoi qu'on puisse faire, on n'a finalement que ses carences et sa niaiserie à opposer à l'invention du monde qui est fabuleuse'.[93] It is this inventiveness of the world that tests the artist's resources. The writer explores the adequacy of language in conveying the fullness of the experience of an elsewhere; 'L'écrivain va chercher le mot juste pour une chose ou la chose juste pour un mot, et ces couples peuvent aussi bien être séparés par des années lumière que tout à fait voisins en s'ignorant complètement.'[94] *Le mot juste* haunts translators as they too search for words or expressions that will transmit a particular nuance in a text.

The difficulty but also the promise of translation and travel is unexpectedness. Hoffman quotes Stendhal at the beginning of her account: '"The *unexpected*, the divine unexpected is better found elsewhere."'[95] A text, because it has been authored in another culture and another language, is not what you would expect to find in your own language. If it is, it becomes less interesting to translate. An absence of obstacles produces a dearth of desire. The unexpectedness of the world, the multiple surprises of a day away from the familiar, means the challenge for the travel writer is to replicate this unexpectedness in writing. Travel writers need a world to journey through but the world alone is not enough. Magris in Austria claims that 'genuine literature is not of the kind which flatters the reader, by confirming him in his prejudices and certainties, but rather of the kind which presses close on his heels and forces him to make a fresh reckoning with the world and with his own assumptions'.[96] The writing of a travel experience must at some level be unexpected (even if travel writing as a genre has its own conventions) if Stendhal's divine unexpected is to appear on the page. Confirming readers in their prejudices does not make them *travel* in any real sense, in much the same way as translations that conceal the alterity of foreign texts and cultures do not make the reader move away from the aesthetic assumptions of their native language and culture. Finding the world means losing yourself, if only temporarily. The unexpected does not necessarily imply radical formal innovation in writing, though it may do. More usually, it is that 'fresh reckoning with the world' of which Magris speaks, the effort made by the writer to achieve a kind of provisional equivalence between the world and language that convinces the reader 'qu'il est beaucoup plus riche intérieurement et beaucoup plus intelligent qu'il ne le pensait'.[97] The reader discovers not only unknown elements of other cultures but also internal territories of the self that were lost, hidden from view, unexplored.

Resistance, power

Dean MacCannell sees contemporary travellers as typically in pursuit of authenticity and 'authentic' experiences. In particular, travellers from urban centres in developed countries seek escape from what they perceive as the inauthentic, alienating reality of their modernity. In pursuit of these experiences – the backstreet café, the forgotten village, the remote island – travellers intrude more and more into the lives of the people in the travel destinations.[98] One strategy for minimising the panoptic inquisitiveness of the tourist is the use of staged authenticity, providing the tourist with a carefully constructed and managed illusion of authentic experience.[99] Staged authenticity is a form of resistance, a distancing technique that keeps invasive others at bay. It is the illusion of hospitality when the commodification of travel makes hospitality increasingly difficult to sustain. Another form of resistance to tourist intrusiveness is *translation resistance*. This resistance can take two forms. Firstly, there is a strategy of opacity. The travelees (those being visited) can refuse to be translated into the language of the traveller. They keep their distance from travellers by refusing to speak a language other than their own, even if this language is not understood by the traveller. In this way, areas of experience are shielded from the meddlesome curiosity of others. The second form of resistance is a version of staged authenticity. This is the strategy of limited entry. Here, the travelees speak the language of the traveller and offer apparent access to areas of their native culture but these areas are sharply circumscribed. Murphy encounters many examples of the first form of resistance in Tanzania and the second form is evident in a number of the interpreting situations we described earlier. The opaque strategy of translation resistance is an unwillingness to translate or be translated as a means of protecting an identity that is perceived to be under threat from another language group. Translation theoreticians aware of the politicised nature of the translation transaction have seen resistance to hegemony as taking the form of refractive or non-fluent or exoticising strategies. This saves translation while correcting the politics. However, a language group can view any concession to translation as a form of negotiated surrender and see its political survival in simple opacity. Translation resistance would appear to signal the demise of translation as a meaningful activity – zero equivalence as *Stunde Null*. In 'Pas de deux: le mésocosme de la traduction comme matrice d'une sémantique frontalière', Laurent Lamy claims that *'l'impossibilité de la traduction est sa condition de possibilité'* (his emphasis).[100] This type of affirmation is usually based on a Derridean act of faith in the necessary translatability of prestigious literary texts. However, it is possible to advance a very different analysis of the translation situation that would arrive at broadly similar conclusions. It is resistance to translation, not acceptance, that generates translation. If a group of individuals or a people agree to translate themselves into another language, that is if they accept translation unreservedly, then the need for translation soon disappears. For the *translated* there is no more *translation*. On the other hand, if they refuse to translate themselves and insist on speaking and writing in their own language, then the need for translation becomes imperative if communication of any kind is to be established. Hence, there may be a fundamental misconception of the universalising role of translation both among its supporters and its detractors. Speakers of minority languages, for example, who are hostile to the continual pressure to translate what they say, can be caricatured as regressive, ethnocentric or essentialist for refusing to embrace the enlightenment mission of translation. Identity is, however, predicated on difference. Translation would not have an identity if non-translation did not exist. Translation services are supplied because groups or peoples refuse translation. Translation as a universal phenomenon does not exist *despite* particulars but rather *because of* particulars. This must explain the apparent paradox of translators as the agents of a universalising process also being the spokespersons for an ardent defence of the local and the particular.

The primary difficulty in traveller/travellee language relationships is the question of power. Speakers of major languages are more likely to expect others to speak their language than speakers of minority languages. In other words, for powerful languages, the Other is always already translated. Úna Ní Mhaoileoin as an Irish speaker does not even consider that she might meet foreigners on her travels who speak Irish and is surprised when she does in Tunis, though the suprise is short-lived, as the few words her Tunisian friend has have disappeared. Travellers who are speakers of a non-global language or a minority language travel continuously in translation. They must continually translate themselves into another language to establish communication and, unless they meet compatriots or foreigners who have opted to learn a less powerful language, they rarely have the luxury of mother-tongue usage in communicative situations. Hence, complete or partial resistance to translation in travel encounters is arguably a plea for translation, but translation that is based on reciprocity not domination. The host welcomes the guest but – crucially in Ricoeur's model – the host welcomes the guest into the language of the host. The guest, therefore, has obligations. One obligation is respect for the language of the other by not systematically imposing the language of the guest.

Systematic imposition can have unforeseen consequences. Eva Hoffman interviews a Roumanian general about the situation in his country and he makes oblique references to alleged Hungarian machinations:

> 'A Hungarian', 'a Romanian', 'a Pole,' 'a Czech': after they've been invoked again and again, as if they were concrete entities, they begin, on the contrary, to seem like figures of allegory, hobbling across an abstract worn landscape of the mind. What can such designations mean in a world in which it takes less time to go from Poland to Hungary than to sit through a Woody Allen movie, and in which most computers in Slovakia are IBM compatible.[101]

The figure of speed is a familiar metaphor of dismay. The quicker you get there, the less differences you should find, so you are shocked when the differences persist. Rapid displacement should relativise difference and show the profoundly contingent nature of ethnic essentialisms. However, there is not only the question of history, as Hoffman herself readily admits, there is also the question of language. Polish, Roumanian, Czech and Hungarian are four separate languages. In the 'Afterword' of *Exit into History*, we are told that Polish is now one of the seven languages to be routinely heard on the streets of New York, 'evidence that the world is becoming utterly nomadic and interpenetrated, even while it becomes more separatist'.[102] Contact with others is always an ambiguous process. On the one hand, the contact produces the mixed realities of urban melting pots and the relativism of Enlightenment Travel, and on the other, contact sharpens a sense of difference, acts as a foil for the emergence of separate identity. Claudio Magris and Angelo Ara detail this tense ambiguity in their study of Trieste, where they contrast sections of a polyglot, multicultural elite with the self-enclosed communities of German, Italian and Slovenian speakers in the city.[103] The centripetal dominance of one language can generate the centrifugal affirmation of other, excluded languages or, within a language, heteroglossia can become more pronounced as dominant varieties of the language are contested.[104] Translation is a valuable ally in the construction of separateness and the primary architects of national literatures have often been translators.[105] This 'separatist' vocation of translation would seem to run counter to the ethical openness and universalist ambitions that were attributed to the practice earlier. However, the dual functions of translation are not incompatible and are best articulated in terms of a common trope of travel. The traveller goes elsewhere to encounter other people, places, cultures, languages. This is the ethical imperative, the exercise of critical universality. However, the journey often leads not only to greater self-awareness but also to greater cultural self-definition. You become aware of regional, national, continental distinctness (depending on the geographical area of engagement). Translation as travel is the link here between the local and the universal. The movement outwards is the translation effort of broadening the space of experience and the horizon of expectation through communication with others outside one's own culture. The movement inwards is the translation of extraneous material into one's native language and culture and not only extending the courtesy of translation to others but expecting that your language, in particular situations, be extended a similar courtesy. Translation like the practice of travel does not posit the local and the universal as mutually exclusive terms but sees the pair as genuinely liberatory in their mutual interdependence. Paul Fussell might be describing translation when he declares in *Abroad*, 'A travel book is like a poem in giving universal significance to a local texture.'[106]

Chapter Four

Babel Express

James Joyce never missed his rendez-vous at half-seven each evening in the railway station in Zurich. His appointment was with the Orient Express. When the train came to a halt, Joyce rushed to inspect signs in French, German and Serbo-Croat on the side of the train. His sight an uncertain ally, he often traced the outlines of the letters with his long, sensitive fingers. Joyce asked Eugène Jolas questions about people getting on and off the train and scanned the languages he overheard for dialectical differences.[1] For Joyce, travel was language in motion. The train brought its freight of languages and cultures to the Zurich station and, for ten minutes, he remained absorbed in the manifold possibilities of 'transluding from the Otherman'.[2] Joyce's homage to plurality in the shadow of a train continues a long tradition of associating mobility with mediation in the figure of the translator-nomad.

Burgundio of Pisa, the great twelfth-century translator, in the preface to his Latin translation of St John Chrysostom's *Homilies on the Gospel of John*, declared:

> I, Burgundio, in fear that, if I wrote in my own idiom when translating this holy father's commentary, I would be changing the meaning of one or more propositions of these two very wise men, and would be incurring the risk of altering so great an original (for these are words of faith) through my own error, I resolved to take a more difficult journey and preserve in my translation not only words with the same meaning as in the original Greek but also the same style and order of words.[3]

The notion of translation as a difficult journey had been anticipated by St Jerome in AD 395 in his famous letter to Pammachius, where the translator of the Vulgate quotes from the preface to his translation of Eusebius of Caeserae's *Chronicle*: 'Possibly, I have no equivalent by which to express some word, and if I then must go out of my way to reach the goal, miles are spent to cover what is in reality a short distance.'[4] If translation is construed as a nomadic practice, how is the translator to be configured as nomad?

The third world, origins, infidelities

For Rajendra Singh, translation is an activity undertaken by bi/multilinguals who 'live in a third world, which requires owning two or more languages without being owned by either of them'.[5] The temptation for the translator is to remain in this world and develop an idiolect that is incomprehensible to others outside the charmed circle of bi/multilingualism. Translatorese and the emergence of Eurospeak are the potential idioms of this third world. However, it is worth considering further the nature of this twilight zone where translation takes place, if only because the profession of translator and the discipline of translation studies can often underestimate the affective and cognitive complexity of its own practices. Andreï Makine in *Le testament français* describes the return of the Russian protagonist to the town in the steppes where his French-born grandmother lives. The young man is full of resentment at the French elements in his identity which, he feels, isolate him from his Russian peers:

> Je voulais qu'elle s'explique, qu'elle se justifie. Car c'est elle qui m'avait transmis cette sensibilité française – la sienne –, me condamnant à vivre dans un pénible entre-deux-mondes.[6]

The notion of difficulty or risk emerges in a different though related context in an article by Daniel Simeoni, 'Translating and Studying Translation: the View from the Agent', where he argues that:

> the translating agent straddles the borderline between cultures. Although various pressures associated with practice force him/her to 'stay home' – on the target side – s/he cannot afford to ignore the source field a long time without being at risk.[7]

Translation is a profoundly paradoxical operation. In order to respect the integrity of the source text, the translator is duty-bound to have as full an understanding as possible of it, an understanding that is at least comparable to that of a competent (in the domain) native speaker of the language. 'At least' is used advisedly here, because in many instances, owing to poor formulation, the translator has to be even more sensitive or ingenious than the native speaker to arrive at a suitable basis for transferable meaning. This applies as much to promotional material for trade fairs as it does to poetry. Thus, effective understanding requires extensive travelling into the other culture, regular contact, often long periods of residence. Travel must not, however, become exile. Translation only makes sense if Ithaca is in sight, if there is homecoming in the target language. Translators must then be alive to the full emotional, cognitive and referential range of their mother tongue. The danger for the translator, as Descartes warns in the *Discours de la méthode*, is that 'lorsqu'on emploie trop de temps à voyager on devient enfin étranger en son pays'.[8] The translator must become the Other while remaining the One (albeit, as we shall see, a fragmented One). There must be proximity without fusion, distance without remoteness.

The intrinsic paradox of translation, being simultaneously *a* and not-*a*, can be intolerable. In Gregory Bateson's terms, translation can be a double bind where the contradictory demands generated by the two languages lead to considerable stress as the translators find that they are unable to satisfy either demand. They can find themselves in a no (wo)man's land with no homes to go to.[9] This No (Wo)Man's Land is also a NoMad's Land. In *Entre-Deux: L'origine en partage*, Daniel Sibony points up the nomadic potential of 'l'entre-deux-langues':

> Comme franchissement, il consiste à inhiber dans une langue son collage à l'origine, sa prétention à être La langue-origine. Il s'agit de se dégager de ce qui, dans la langue où l'on baigne, fait qu'elle se pose comme l'Origine du langage; et de pouvoir donc la traduire, la trahir dans d'autres 'langues' qui la 'déforment.' Alors on peut passer à d'autres langues; d'autres langues [. . .] deviennent vivables et sont appelées à 'vivre.' L'origine comme parlante éclate alors dans l'entre-deux-langues qu'elle nourrit sans l'envahir. Faute de cela, le sujet ne peut parler et inventer dans d'autres langues; la première lui tient lieu de toute l'origine.[10]

Sibony claims that his work 'commence par l'entre-deux-langues et finit par le voyage', but one could equally argue that travel is there from the beginning, already inscribed in the movement between languages.[11] Travel here is conceived of ontologically as a reinvention of the self, a possibility of generating something other than the familiar from which the self emerges strengthened, 'à travers quoi on puisse fuir l'horreur de soi, apaiser sa soif d'autre, d'autre chose, et pourtant donner au soi une certaine consistance'.[12] Travel, in this perspective, is not the temporary *frisson* of displacement but a profound engagement with the basis of identity:

> l'impuissance à voyager, c'est-à-dire à intégrer de nouveaux 'lieux' non reconnus, à intégrer l'inconnu, voire l'inconnaissable, est la même que l'impuissance à faire alliance et partage, ou à supporter l'origine multiple. Il ne s'agit pas d'aller vers l'origine mais de voyager avec l'idée de l'origine, de *faire voyager l'origine*.[13] (his emphasis)

The implicit purpose of translation is to make the 'original' text travel. The text travels into other languages and, in this movement, the multiplicity of origin is revealed. It is precisely because texts are translated into many languages that origins are shown to be intrinsically plural. Indeed, the more 'originary' or foundational a text, the more translations are generated (Shakespeare, Homer, the Bible), the translations paradoxically affirming the primary, founding importance of particular texts. The translator goes to the text in the original (foreign) language and in the act of translation *explores* his/her original language. Translation makes visible a dual set of origins (source/target – foreign/domestic) in the movement between languages. The process of moving away from one's origins can of course be extremely fraught – witness the *bildungsroman* and the drama of maturity as heroes and heroines leave kith and kin. This trauma of departure often excites suspicion. As John Edwards, the British linguist, says, 'The translator, the one whose multilingual facility permits the straddling of boundaries, is . . . a type of quisling, but a quisling who must be allowed to do his spying, for obvious and practical reasons.'[14] Translators who leave the mother tongue to travel into other languages are engaged, at some level, in an act of betrayal vis-à-vis their linguistic origins. It is hardly surprising, therefore, that the accusation of unfaithfulness is routinely levelled against translators and that the Italian expression, *traduttore-tradittore*, is repeated *ad nauseam* in popular discussions of translation. Fidelity has been a conventional benchmark throughout translation history for evaluating the quality or legitimacy of translation. However, it is possible to argue that it is not fidelity but *infidelity* that is the fundamental condition of translation. Or rather, that any notion of fidelity (to a text, language, culture) must be preceded by initial infidelity (moving out of the language-house of the parents). For the fanatic and the purist, fidelity is the supreme value and memory is the guarantor of faithfulness, history giving way to rites of commemorative repetition. Identity is fixation, an obsessive recapitulation of the past. By moving across boundaries of language and culture the translator is 'unfaithful' to his/her language and culture, but this is in order to revitalise the original culture and language, open up texts and history to the new and unknown. The primary infidelity is the *sine qua non* of a fidelity to the creative energies of the host language. Hence, the figure of betrayal that colours conventional presentation of translation is not as disparaging as it initially appears.

Drive, analog modes and forgery

In *Freud en Italie: Psychanalyse du voyage*, Antonietta and Gérard Haddad argue that the notion of 'drive' in psychoanalysis implies activity, movement, displacement:

> Cela nous conduit donc à poser l'existence d'une cinquième pulsion, plus fondamentale que les autres puisqu'elle en est la condition, la pulsion *viatorique*, pulsion de la marche et du voyage. Quels en seraient les paramètres? La poussée provient de l'énigmatique appel de l'Ailleurs, de l'Inconnu, de l'Autre, que l'homme perçoit du fait même d'être sans cesse aiguillonné par le signifiant et la parole.[15] (their emphasis)

The *viatorial drive* in translation is fundamental. The task of the translator is to seek out what goes on elsewhere, what is unkown, what the other has written or produced. In common with travel, this work is as much self-exploration as it is the charting of new textual territories. Describing the translation work of Antonin Artaud, Jean-Michel Rey claimed that all translation is 'une façon de revenir à soi par le biais de l'autre, par l'épreuve de l'étranger'.[16] The initial movement in translation is one of openness, leaving one's own culture and language if only to return later. Marc-Alain Ouaknin, in *Bibliothérapie: Lire, c'est guérir*, sees translation in therapeutic terms as curative. Illness is enclosure, blockage, the inability to escape from the prison of the self. Translation brings with it an opening up towards another language, culture, world. If '*Guérir, c'est traduire*' [his emphasis], this is because, 'la guérison est passage, voyage et métaphore, sortie de soi, modalité d'être dynamique, qui nous fait homme, différent de la passivité ontologique de l'animal et de l'objet.'[17] Further on, he argues that 'La trans-duction de l'entre-deux-langues ouvre l'être à son "pouvoir être autrement", à son projet d'être.'[18] In the space between languages, there exists the opportunity for change, for the transformation of identity. Identity is not so much a fixed site as a locus of multiple origins.

The centrality of translation to the practice of travel and the figure of the translator-nomad is often strangely absent from the critical literature on travel. Major works on the subject over the last two decades by Sara Mills, John Urry, Mary Louise Pratt, James Buzard, Jean-Didier Urbain and Paul Fussell, to name but a few, pay scant attention to the phenomenon of language and translation in the travel experience. Even when the word 'translation' is included in the subtitle of a work, there is no guarantee that the subject will be discussed in any detail. James Clifford's *Routes* has as its subtitle, *Travel and Translation in the Late Twentieth Century*. The American scholar is eloquent on travel but is oddly silent on translation. He defines a 'translation term' as a 'word of apparently general application used for comparison in a strategic and contingent way'.[19] Travel is one of these trans-lation terms. The Italian tag *tradittore, traduttore* makes its inevitable appearance but there is no further attempt to offer a more discriminating concept of translation. Reading the literature of translation studies would have produced a more sophisticated understanding of the phenomenon but surprisingly, of the 437 items in the bibliography, not one single item is drawn from the discipline of translation studies. There are 1,971 items listed in the bibliography of the *Routledge Encyclopedia of Translation Studies*.[20] In the anthology of writings on Western translation theory from Herodotus to Nietzsche edited by Douglas Robinson, there are 124 texts by 90 different authors. Thus there is no shortage of material upon which Clifford can draw. He does, however, make a number of references to language learning by the anthropologist as a key gesture in the establishment of the persona of the fieldworker. In the first essay, 'Traveling Cultures', he asks useful questions about language in fieldwork situations: 'Can one speak of the language, singular, as if there were only one? What does it mean to learn or use a language? How well can one learn a language in a few years?' He challenges the 'nationalist' notion that (singular) language equals (singular) culture and posits a Bakhtinian plurality of discourses. Clifford claims that the 'subject [of language] deserves a full study, which I am not yet able to offer'.[21] The American anthropologist's honesty is welcome, but how can translation appear in the title of a work and the question of language be largely ignored?[22] It seems inconceivable, for example, that a translation scholar would produce a work subtitled, *Translation and Fieldwork in the Twentieth Century* and not refer to anthropology or ethnography. This reaction could be seen as the anxious touchiness of a new discipline but, at a more profound level, it points to a persistent failure to take translation as a language phenomenon seriously, quite apart from the inexplicable oversight of an entire body of writing on one of the central concepts in Clifford's arguments.

The failure to engage with the problematic of translation is not simply a matter of referential inclusiveness. Sensitivity to translation implies a self-reflexivity that is absent in Clifford's arguments. It is apparent from Clifford's texts that he has some familiarity with French and Spanish, yet the reader is given no sense that s/he is operating in a world of translation, a world of languages other than English. At one point in the collection, there is a quotation from Maruch Komes Peres and Diane L. Rus's *Ta Jlok'ta Chobtik Ta K'u'il (Récit d'une tisserande de Chamula)*. The English extract would appear to be a translation, given the title of the original work, but there is no indication of either the text as translation or the identity of the translator. Further on, there is a verse from an Alaskan song with the source text and English language translation. The source of the song is indicated but we are not told in Clifford's text who did the translation. The invisibility of the translator (even when it is possible to surmise that the translator is Clifford himself) and the failure to foreground the material presence of translation through identification and attribution generates an illusion of understanding and immediacy, as if the world is always already translated into English. The translation strategies of the texts replicate the classic trope of colonial subordination where the mediating presence of a translating other (native and foreign) is erased and the texts are presented as 'natural' and self-evident in their attributive anonymity.[23] The self-reflexive shortcomings are mirrored at the level of disciplinary engagement. When Clifford lists the disciplines anthropology has engaged with over the years, he mentions sixteen.[24] Linguistics is in the list but there is no reference to translation studies, again despite the repeated references to 'translation' (as metaphor rather than practice) throughout the texts. The sociocultural anthropology that Clifford practises may in fact be even more selective than he himself realises.

Clifford's blindness, however, generates its own insights. He quotes the claim by Eric Wolf in 1964 that anthropology was a 'discipline between

disciplines'.[25] Clifford points up the consequences of this liberality of definition: 'this openness poses recurring problems of self-definition. And partly
because its theoretical purview has remained so broad and interdisciplinary,
despite recurring attempts to cut it down to size, the discipline has focused
on research practices as defining core elements.'[26] Clifford's observations
could apply equally well to translation studies. Here too, problems of self-
definition abound. To take one example, a recent volume of essays on
research in translation studies included essays from the fields of machine
translation, interpreting, feminist theory, computer-assisted translation,
advertising, literature, linguistics, screen translation and pedagogy, and this
is by no means an exhaustive inventory of the possibilities for different
disciplinary interventions in translation studies.[27] As commentators like
Edward Said and Clifford himself have already remarked, all theories travel;
they all involve an act of critical displacement.[28] However, one could argue
that certain disciplines such as anthropology and translation studies are
particularly prone to nomadic restlessness. In other words, it is not just the
translating subjects of the discipline that are engaged in a nomadic practice
as they translate; rather the discipline itself is nomadic in its disciplinary
journeying from subject area to subject area. The journeying is not without
its risks. If history is often more comfortable with the fixed chronicle of
settlement than the unstable traces of nomadic passage, then nomads
become less visible in the record of time.[29] Similarly, a discipline that is
markedly nomadic in its operations may experience the difficulty of 'self-
definition', the crisis of identity, to which Clifford refers, and a consequent
lack of visibility. The fact that a major thinker in cultural studies can
produce a work that has translation in the title and not have one reference
to works in translation studies does point to a problem of disciplinary presence in the wider sphere of intellectual activity. Conversely, another
response to the theoretical nomadism endemic in translation theory is to
eschew theory altogether and concentrate on 'research practices' or translation practice. The aggressive dismissal of theory that has been a standard
feature of much public debate in translation studies since its inception is
arguably rooted at some level in an uneasiness with the labile nature of
translation theories and a desire for pragmatic certainties that will 'settle'
the discipline once and for all.

In *Nomadic Subjects: Embodiment and Sexual Difference in Contemporary
Feminist Theory*, Rosa Braidotti has the following to say about the polyglot,
whom she defines as a 'nomad in between languages':

> The nomadic polyglot practices an aesthetic style based on compassion
> for the incongruities, the repetitions, the arbitrariness of the languages
> s/he deals with. Writing is, for the polyglot, a process of undoing the illu-
> sory stability of fixed identities, bursting open the bubble of ontological

security that comes from familiarity with one linguistic site. The polyglot exposes this false security.[30]

Exposure of false security does not imply relativist free fall. Bruce Chatwin notes in an essay on nomad invasions that nomadism is not synonymous with aimless wandering. For him, 'a nomadic migration is a guided tour of animals around a predictable sequence of pastures. It has the same inflexible character as the migrations of wild game, since the same ecological factors determine it.'[31] For Braidotti, 'nomadic consciousness combines coherence with mobility'.[32] A translator does not wander aimlessly from source text to target text. A given text exists in the source language (in most, though not all, instances written by someone other than the translator) and it is that text, not any other, which the translator is asked to translate. In the target language, as the polysystems theorists have shown, there is a plethora of norms and procedures that govern the translation of the text into the target language.[33] Thus, translation is mobile but it does not lack coherence. The fact of translation is testament to multiplicity but it does not follow on from this that in a spirit of postmodernist relativism any old translation will do. What a nomadic concept of the translator does account for is the apparent paradox of dual empowerment in the act of translation. Thus Braidotti claims:

> The nomad's identity is a map of where s/he has already been; s/he can always reconstruct it a posteriori, as a set of steps in an itinerary. But there is no triumphant *cogito* supervising the contingency of the self; the nomad stands for movable diversity, the nomad's identity is an inventory of traces.[34]

Translators can be drawn to particular writers or to particular types of translation (legal, administrative, technical) but the experience of many translators is that a variety of different authors and text-types passes through their hands. For a translator to translate, for example, three different authors or three different texts by the same author, in much the same fashion, would be seen to be remiss. S/he would affirm the presence of a triumphant *cogito* in the target language but at the expense of the diversity of the texts, languages and cultures from and into which s/he is translating. If each translation is a journey, then no one translator ever gets to the target language by the same route, as even the most basic perusal of translation examination scripts shows. It is the cumulative 'traces' of the target-language choices that generate the identity of the translation that make it read as a different text. So each translation is a map of where the translator has been but the map shows us not only the translator but the author. The translator needs the fluid openness of the nomad not as a licence for unbridled narcissism, but, on the contrary, as the precondition for an act of disciplined attention that provides the reader with a reliable guide to the specificity of a text or style(s).

The movable diversity of translation does not in our conception of the translator-nomad empty out the subject as appears implicit in the post-Derridean expression of an 'inventory of traces'. The translator is a situated subject, positioned by contexts of race, gender, class and history, but not reducible to these contexts, just as no text is merely the sum of its contexts. This is not to argue that the contexts are not important or marginal. On the contrary, as we have seen in the first three chapters, contextual understanding can often provide invaluable clues to understanding many different kinds of travel experience and translation practice. However, a purely historicist analysis of the phenomenon of translation is never fully adequate. Michel Le Bris, philosopher, critic and travel writer, describes the foundational experience of looking at and being looked at by another:

> Ce visage là, devant toi cesse d'être une simple masse de chair, devient véritablement humain lorsque tu réalises qu'il y a derrière ses yeux des mondes, dans lesquels tu pénétreras jamais. Et c'est cette transcendance de l'Autre qui te révèle en retour la tienne, c'est le 'Tu', en somme, qui me fait 'Je'. C'est par cet arrachement à la bulle du Même que nous entrons en humanité. C'est cet écart, que nous n'avons cesse de combler, qui nous permet de vivre avec autrui – et d'habiter un lieu sans qu'il se referme en prison. Parce que c'est dans cet écart que peut se déployer l'imaginaire, et ses puissances.[35]

Travel in a foreign language is a heightened experience of this fundamental unknowability of the other. The lack of or poor grasp of a foreign language makes palpable the distance from the other, the feeling that there are worlds you may never enter. The other will always transcend your understanding of his/her contexts. It is precisely this transcendent incommensurability that drives translation and travel. Both are situated in the gap, the 'écart', that motivates the perpetual effort to know a country better, to render a text more fully, but the effort only succeeds because it fails. In other words, total knowledge of a country and its people (a manifest absurdity) and a perfect translation signal not the triumph but the undoing of translation and travel. The gap of the 'entre-deux' here should be conceived of less as a space, a reified entity tending towards stasis than as a constant movement backwards and forwards in which there is no fixated identification with either of the poles. The continuous oscillation between source text and target text, between home culture and foreign culture, native language and foreign language, define both translator and traveller as figures in motion. The translator/traveller embraces the analog mode of both/and rather than the digital mode of either/or.[36] In *Questions of Travel: Postmodern Discourses of Displacement*, Caren Kaplan describes the pitfalls of binary oppositions that restrict arguments and overdetermine narratives. In Jean Baudrillard's American travel account, *Cool Memories*, binary oppositions such as city/desert, natural/artificial, woman/man, Europe/America generate reassuring stereotype rather than radical insight. Kaplan draws on an observation by Douglas Kellner that Baudrillard's predilection for binary oppositions and extreme differences 'produce[s] racist thinking by exaggerating differences to the point of stereotype "while covering over or erasing similarities"'.[37] Travellers or translators beholden to exoticism will exploit binary contrasts, a temptation difficult to avoid, given the importance of difference as a trope in the formulation of both translation and travel. On the other hand, it is the positing of some degree of 'similarity' that makes travel conceivable or translation practicable. In the absence of the common ground of similarity the traveller would be condemned to solipsistic isolation and the translator to a prison-house of (native) *langue*. The Other may in a fundamental sense be unknowable but that does not mean that we have nothing in common. The analog operation of the translator/traveller is that pulsation, the oscillation between what we know and do not know, positing neither total familiarity (imperialism) nor total difference (racism).

An instance of the baleful influence of binary thinking in translation studies itself is the centuries-old debate between scholars who favour fidelity to the source text and those who favour the target audience. One of the difficulties with this eternal *sourcier/cibliste* controversy is that, rather than eliminating the translator's invisibility, the polemic in fact maximises it. The danger is ideological overdeterminedness, where the translator is seen as either the pawn of the values of the target-language culture, an idea expressed in the concept of fluent strategy, or as the successful conveyor of the linguistic and cultural values of the source culture (Meschonnic/Berman). In both instances, it is the source or target language and culture that become the objects of debate and the translator an entity that becomes subsumed under source-oriented or target-oriented translation. The translator's signature becomes that of the hostage held at metaphorical gunpoint by the *sourciers* or *ciblistes*. However, what is striking in the teaching of translation or the history of successive translations of similar texts is the importance of what we might term *proactive translation*. This refers to the *imaginary* dimension of translation. The translator differs from the conference interpreter in that s/he does not usually have direct or immediate contact with the audience. The translator can of course and does make assumptions about what the audience knows and wants. Ultimately, however, they remain assumptions, and feedback mechanisms are rarely so sophisticated that the translator can effect a perfect translation homeostasis. Therefore, there is a sense in which translators are not mere ciphers of the source and target cultures. They are proactive in that they possess an imaginative autonomy which means they do not so much find audiences as create them. In that gap between source and target text, 'peut se déployer l'imaginaire, et ses puissances'. It is the exercise of proactive translation, the existence of the imaginary dimension, that points to the importance of the analog agency of the *translating subject*.

Imagination has not only excited admiration, however, in aesthetic and religious life, it has also invited reproof, censorship, condemnation. Travel writing was long derided for its associations with 'imaginary' tales of travel to far-flung places and improbable accounts of the improbable. Translation has been viewed with profound suspicion by monotheism from Judaism to Islam to Christianity (cf. the Roman Catholic attachment to the Vulgate, itself paradoxically a translation).[38] The fear is of the imaginative interposition of the translator who will alter, deform or mutilate the sacred wholeness of the original. The treachery of fancy is the seedbed of heresy. Is there, we may ask, something about the activity of translation that is vaguely fraudulent? Translation history, indeed, has many examples of fictitious translation, from Macpherson's eighteenth-century Ossianic forgeries to a number of nineteenth-century 'translations' from the German by the Irish poet James Clarence Mangan. Mangan attributed the original poems to the German poets 'Selber' and 'Drechsler', who did not, of course, exist.[39] If we take Jean-René Ladmiral's definition of the function of translation – 'Ça sert à nous dispenser de la lecture du texte original' – we could argue that the end-user of a computer manual who has no idea that it was written in another language (and is this not one of the criteria for good pragmatic translation?) has a copy that is as good as the original – in other words a successful forgery.[40] Translators may feel that the analogy belittles their expertise but good forgers are enormously skilful and bad translation bears all the hall-marks of shoddy imitation. Indeed, might it not be asked to what extent do target audiences want the self-reflexive traces of transformation in transla-tion or do they prefer, to quote the English-language title of an Umberto Eco collection of essays, Faith in Fakes?

Translation, at one level, is self-evidently a lie. It is not what it purports to be. It is not the original. The reader who reads a translation is engaged in a willing suspension of disbelief. S/he reads the text *as if* it were the original text. The proximity of translation to fiction lays it open to the same charge of misrepresentation and mendacity as fiction itself. George Steiner has referred to the unsilenced query as to whether fiction is really a serious pursuit: 'An undermining puritanism nags at the history of fiction: the idea, advanced first by Calvinist rebuke to all licence of feeling, then by the *bourgeois* stress on utility and parsimony of emotional commitment, that fiction was not an adult or serious thing.'[41] If fiction is not adult or serious, it is frivolous, wasteful and corrupting. It is precisely these fears that Oscar Wilde plays on in his dialogue 'The Decay of Lying', where he berates nineteenth-century fiction for seeking the alibi of fact and failing to remain true to the truthful untruths of art. Vivien claims, 'if something cannot be done to check, or at least to modify, our monstrous worship of facts, Art will become sterile, and beauty will pass away from the land.'[42] The translator is akin to the travel writer in that they both have a prior text of experience or of reading; there is therefore a certain level of verifiability and answerability. Translation is, however, a supreme fiction in that it is an untruth – pretending to be the original – that is articulating a truth: 'Far from traducing the original, the translation injects new blood into a text by bringing it to the attention of a new world of readers in a different language.'[43] The radical literalism of Vladimir Nabokov that eschews the 'prettiest paraphrase' is haunted by this fictional dimension to translation. For him: 'The person who desires to turn a literary masterpiece into another language, has only one duty to perform, and this to reproduce with absolute exactitude the whole text, and nothing but the text.'[44] The most exact reproduction is nonetheless radical transformation. The reader is reading *Onegin* not in Russian but in English. Therefore, s/he is in the simulative, as-if mode of translation that generates a fiction of proximity. The essential falsehood of translation is inescapable.

Trade, speed limits and machine translation

A well-documented feature of late modernity or postmodernity has been the reorganisation of capitalism and the accelerated flow of goods, signs and people around the planet.[45] Inderpal Grewal and Caren Kaplan have argued that the increasingly transnational and mobile nature of capital accumulation demands new shifts in critical thinking.[46] Another way of approaching the changes that characterise the post-Fordist era is the concept of globalisation. Global movements and exchanges of people, commodities and ideas did not begin, however, in the late twentieth century. The Ottoman, Muscovite, Aztec, Inca, Mali, Ethiopian and Mwene Mutapa empires, the history of the Venetian and Dutch Republics, the metamorphoses of colonialism, all attest to globalisation as a phenomenon that is geographically broad and historically ancient. Stuart Hall situates England in a long history of globalisation that has been the experience of empire and he notes that 'we suffer increasingly from a process of historical amnesia in which we think that just because we are thinking about an idea it has only just started'.[47] One ancient if enduring figure of globalisation has been the figure of the trader. For Georg Simmel, the trader is a special case of the more general type of the stranger. The stranger for Simmel is not the wanderer who comes today and is gone tomorrow, but rather the person who comes today and stays tomorrow, 'the potential wanderer so to speak, who, although he has gone no further, has not quite got over the freedom of coming and going'.[48] Simmel points out that in economic activity the stranger is omnipresent as trader. As long as people produce goods for their own needs or goods are circulated within a small group, there is no need for a middleman:

> A trader is required only for goods produced outside the group. Unless there are people who wander out into foreign lands to buy these necessities, in

which case they are themselves 'strange' merchants in this other region, the trader *must* be a stranger; there is no opportunity for anyone else to make a living at it.[49]

In an 1828 article on Thomas Carlyle's *German Romances*, Johann Wolfgang von Goethe draws an explicit parallel between the trader and translator. He claims that anyone who studies German finds himself/herself in the market-place where all nations offer their wares and he goes on:

> And that is how we should see the translator, as one who strives to be a mediator in this universal, intellectual trade, and makes it his business to promote exchange. For whatever one may say about the shortcomings of translations, they are and will remain most important and worthy undertakings in world communication.[50]

Central to Simmel's notion of the trader is mobility. The trader is a stranger on the move. If we examine much translation theory and history, we tend to find the following division. Translation theory and history deal with literature and religion, whereas translation pedagogy and practice deal with economic and scientific translation. Commercial translation is seen as an application of translation principles, but is it not possible to view *commerce as translation* – not simply in the sense of translation as an ancillary activity, or in a loose metaphorical sense, but envisioning translation and commerce as two forms of nomadism whose fortunes are inextricably bound up with each other?

Goethe is eager to point out that the translator/trader can play the role of interpreter while enriching himself. The connection between money and translation is not a fortuitous one, and the link has been established by many commentators over the centuries. In his essay on Dante's *Divine Comedy*, August Wilhelm von Schlegel describes the importance for numismatists of *aeruga nobilis* (noble rust) in establishing the authenticity of an old coin. Cultures and peoples have a similar noble rust. The translator must conserve this rust and not sacrifice antiquity to fashion: 'Only an erstwhile Frenchman would coldly polish off that rust while describing or translating the work, just so he could smugly show off his new penny.'[51] It is, however, an eighteenth-century Frenchman, Charles Batteux, who brings together money, trade and translation in his *Principes de littérature*. In this work, he recommends the use of what we would now call transposition in translation practice and declares:

> Let him [the translator] take the scales, weigh the expressions on either side, poise them every way, he will be allowed alterations, provided he preserve to the thought the same substance and the same life. He will act only like a traveller, who, for his conveniency, exchanges sometimes one piece of gold for several of silver, sometimes several pieces of silver for one of gold.[52]

A salient feature of globalisation is time–space compression, the ability of goods, people, currencies and bits of information to circulate at ever greater speeds. The dematerialisation of money has been a hugely important factor in the advent of the post-Fordist economy and the consequent acceleration of exchange.[53] In his essay 'On the Psychology of Money', Georg Simmel argued that any uniform and generalised means of exchange was a means of lengthening the teleological chain and that money was one such form of exchange. The teleological chain represented the difference between what he called a 'primitive' and 'cultivated' human condition and the chain could be measured by the number of links that lie between an immediate action and its ultimate end.[54] A characteristic of modernity that is frequently cited is its growing abstraction, the increasing number of links between actions and ends.[55] However, something must link the links and Simmel sees money as a prime example of the intermediate link. Money, as a means of exchange, is a way of converting personal volition into goods and services, whereas in a direct barter system you are dependent on person B wanting your good a at the same time as you are attracted to their good b.

> Therefore it is of the greatest value for the attainment of our goals that an intermediate link be inserted into the teleological chain, one into which I can convert b at any time and which can, in turn, be converted into a – roughly in the same way that any particular force, for instance, falling water, heated gas, or windmill sails, can be converted into any particular type of energy once it is introduced into the dynamo.[56]

Once equivalence is established and one has the equality of all things through an accepted means of exchange, there results a certain smoothness, a grinding down of sharp corners, that eases and accelerates the circulation of things. Batteux's analogy between translation, trade and money takes on a new significance then in the context of the speed revolution of modernity. The new information economy of signs and spaces, with the rapid movement of symbols and bytes, is generating pressures on translation to become a uniform and generalised means of exchange, a transparent medium of fluid interchange. The translator becomes, like the demon in James Clerk Maxwell's *Theory of Heat* (1872), a perfectly neutral space of transmission. Eurospeak becomes in more ways than one the speech of the Euro. The drive towards zero resistance, full equivalence and transparent immediacy that is implied in this reading of translation as intermediate link generates real translation pressures.

The first point to note is that English is adopted increasingly as the kind of universal means of exchange envisioned in Simmel's theory of money. The advertisement for *Visa* credit card in Guarulhos airport in São Paolo proclaiming 'It's fluent in every language' is articulating a deep truth. Credit cards are emblematic of the new paper economy in which money circulates at greater velocity, and the language of the advertisement is not Portuguese but English. If the credit card is the universal means of financial exchange, then English is the universal means of linguistic exchange. The *Visa* vision of polyglossia is frictionless monoglossia.

A second feature of a globalised translation environment is the tyranny of real-time, where translators have increasingly short response-periods for translation assignments. There is less and less time; partly because there is more and more translation. Figures for the size of the world translation market are notoriously difficult to come by, but it is estimated that around 250 million pages of technical and commercial text are translated each year and the amount increases all the time.[57] Time pressure has always existed but modems and Computer-Aided Translation (CAT) tools such as translation memories and glossary managers have greatly increased temporal expectations in a world of short-batch production and time-to-market constraints. Sharon O'Brien highlights the time factor in an analysis of the benefits of CAT tools for software localisation (the translation of complete software packages, including manuals, codes and help systems). CAT tools principally allow translators to use what they have translated before in a new translation where there is overlap or repetition from previous documentation, as is frequently the case in localisation. O'Brien claims:

> Traditionally, machine translation and even computer-aided translation were seen as a threat to the translator. However, the re-use of previous translation in the localisation industry simply frees up more of the translator's time to allow him/her to translate a greater number of words per annum in total.[58]

Software localisation provides many examples of growing time constraints. Localising *Windows '95* and *Office '95* meant the release of the products in twenty languages within 165 days of the US original version. The office documentation entailed the translation of 134,00 words and the Help functions involved the translation of over 1,200,000 words.[59] The localisation ideal of 'sim-ship', where all language versions are released at the same time and if possible at the same time as the original language version, means there is less and less time to do a translation. Any resistance offered by the text or translator slows down the process. If accelerated velocity is the chief characteristic of the post-industrial economy, then the pressure is on the translator to approximate more and more to the ideal of *instantaneous transparency*. Here, time (speed of execution) annihilates space (the place of the translator).

Between Caesar and Napoleon, armies did not move appreciably faster. Men and horses became tired, were injured, needed a rest. The Machine Age, as Wolfgang Sachs points out, changed everything: 'neither the body nor the topography any longer define a natural limit for speed'.[60] The

German philosopher Peter Sloterdijk has coined the term 'tachocracy' to define the continuous acceleration of modernity. He contends that, 'the great self-movement towards surplus-movement leads to a tendency towards motorisation, towards the installation of automatic process units and their continual acceleration.'[61] If we can speak of translation as an element of tachocracy, then there are obviously variable translation velocities, from the lifelong labour on Dante to the 'automatic process units' of machine translation. We argued above that English has become a privileged intermediate link in the teleological chain of globalisation. Machine translation is another potential agent of universal linguistic exchange. Indeed, David Crystal, the British linguist, sees machine translation as the only serious long-term threat to the global dominance of English. In his *English as a Global Language*, he envisages the future a century hence:

> It will be very interesting to see what happens then – whether the presence of a global language will eliminate the demand for world translation services, or whether the economics of automatic translation will so under-cut the cost of global language learning that the latter will become otiose.[62]

Crystal sees the need for a global lingua franca as the facilitation of communication within multinational regional or political groupings that have become increasingly numerous since 1945. The alternative to a common language, he claims, is 'expensive and impracticable multi-way translation facilities'.[63] The presence of a global language removes the translator but leaves translation. In the case of English, for example, outside of the 337 million people who speak it as their first language, other speakers of the language will be translating at some level from another language when they use English. The translator as intermediary will, however, be absent from the exchange in a lingua franca even if translation problems *per se* do not disappear. The translator is a similarly endangered species in the area of machine translation. At one level, the statement appears self-evident. The whole point of Fully Automatic High-Quality Translation would appear to be to dispense with the human translator and to automate the translation process. However, it has been commonly supposed that translators will still be involved at the pre-editing and post-editing stages of MT because of the generally unsatisfactory nature of MT output outside sharply circumscribed sublanguages. In an essay entitled 'The Problem with Machine Translation', Reinhard Schäler, the director of the Localisation Resources Centre in Ireland, has challenged this assumption. Schäler describes the rapid growth in the use of MT systems and argues that increasingly MT users are not concerned with the quality issues that exercise the minds of professionally trained translators:

> This is especially true when companies have to deal with short turn-around cycles and frequent updates of technical texts, and when accuracy

and consistency of the translation (features associated with MT output) take precedence over style, readability and naturalness, all associated with the traditional values and reference system of the human translators.[64]

A consequence of this development is that increasingly translation is being done by machine and being used by non-translators. For example, a study showed that 80 per cent of the users of the European Commission's Systran system were from outside the Translation Service.[65] The US National Air Intelligence Center (NAIC) which has been using MT for over thirty years does not employ translators but computer scientists, post-editors and language specialists. The NAIC hires subject specialists with some knowledge of the source language as pre- and post-editors in preference to more linguistically skilled translators. It is significant that it is the dimension of accelerated time, 'short turn-around cycles and frequent updates', that is a powerful argument for MT use. In the contemporary tachocracy of the Western world, human translation is an impediment: it slows down the circulation of goods, sevices, peoples. Translation has had to adapt to what Paul Virilio calls the 'dromocratic' or speed revolution.[66] The intensive time of telecommunications as opposed to the extensive time of the postal system has allowed translators to greatly speed up delivery of translated work, and Internet access has cut down the preparation time involved in consulting background material. The increased velocity of translation lessens the resistance of duration. The end-point of acceleration, instantaneous transparency, is simultaneous real-time translation. However, the dromocratic nirvana of instaneity is the translator's exit from history. Machine translation or a global language provide us with instantaneous translation without the translator. This is the dream of science fiction and the tachocratic ideal of modernity. The translator nomad travels so fast that s/he becomes increasingly invisible (transparent) and is eventually annihilated.

Fast castes, kinetic resistance and the Grand Tour

Speed may be destructive but it is also a powerful source of prestige for what the development theorist Susan George has called the 'fast castes'.[67] To be on the move, to be going places, is to be on the way up. The rapid check-in facility for the business-class air passenger, the expensive car with the powerful engine and acceleration, the instant gratification of desire ('I want room service, now!'), are the more visible attributes of a power over time and space (and over the time and space of others) that equates to social status. In the world of translation, conference interpreters are the most conspicuous members of a 'fast caste'. Unlike translators, they are often on the road, travelling from conference to conference, flying from one meeting/conference to the next. These are also the nomads who approximate most closely to the tachocratic ideal of simultaneous real-time translation. Thus, conference interpreters are doubly invested with the prestige of speed, at the level of lifestyle and at the level of professional practice. In addition, at meetings and conferences they encounter and work with other members of the global fast caste. It is hardly surprising, therefore, that interpreting is traditionally thought of as more 'glamorous' than translation and has, on the whole, been more successful in achieving professional status. The myth of speed needs, of course, to be distinguished from the reality of speed. Few interpreters would claim that simultaneous interpreting is always, everywhere possible and unfailingly accurate. Too many intrinsic and extrinsic factors are there to affect an interpreter's performance.[68] Commenting on the photographic work of Martha Rosler, Edward Dimendberg, a film scholar, describes how she details the profoundly dysfunctional character of the centrifugal space of the American motorway. Using photographs of the New Jersey turnpike and the approach routes to New York City, Rosler shows how 'images of traffic jams, construction blockages, road obstructions, and automobile accidents effectively refute the myth of frictionless circulation'.[69] Acceleration ends inevitably in congestion. Wolfgang Sachs notes that, 'despite the ever-expanding number of time-saving machines we feel more pressured and driven by lack of time than ever before'.[70] The new car owner does not rejoice in extra hours of leisure. S/he drives further. The more people move about, the more difficult it becomes to meet them: 'Great efforts at scheduling and synchronisation come in the wake of increased circulation.'[71] Hence, the more rapid the circulation, the more counter-productive the effects and the greater the friction/resistance in different systems. As we have seen in the first three chapters, travellers moving in a world of language(s) do not move in an ideal, unmediated space of pure mobility. The multiple negotiations of language and translation attend their passage through different lands. They slow down, and make complicated the journey through the lives and cultures of others. It is in this aspect of language, translation and travel that it is possible to outline a liberatory politics of polyglossia and translation that is based neither on nervous particularism nor overweening universalism.

'Where acceleration is the everyday norm, slowness becomes a non-conformist adventure':[72] this is the basic contention of Sachs. Therefore, forces of deceleration open up spaces of critical possibility that are denied by the blind compulsion of speed. To some extent, the focus of capitalist modernity has been resolutely on removing the obstacles of space and time. As Karl Marx noted in the *Grundrisse*:

> While capital on one side must strive to tear down every spatial barrier to intercourse, i.e. to exchange, and conquer the whole earth for its market, it strives on the other side to annihilate this space with time, i.e. to reduce to a minimum the time spent in motion from one place to another.[73]

To express this project somewhat differently, market expansionism, like imperialism, seeks the eradication of the '*entre-deux*'. Far is always too far and long is always too long. Anything that takes time is a waste of time. The aim is to remove anything that lies in the way, to reduce to nought the obstacles of space, time, culture and language. Daniel Sibony describes the originary fantasy of the '*entre-deux aboli*'. Examples of the fantasy are

> voir la mère vous concevoir; génération surmontée; arriver le *premier* au Nouveau Monde, premier nouveau-né du monde, arriver en Amérique, but du voyage, pour constater que c'était vierge, au besoin tuer tout le monde pour faire en sorte que ce fût vierge.[74]

The fantasy of return to pure origin is played out in countless holiday brochures with empty beaches washed by primordial seas. The violence that is implicit in the mythical fabrication of a *tabula rasa* on earth indicates that eradication of the *entre-deux* comes at a cost. Speed kills. However, it is not only that the proximity promised by the dromocratic revolution may be lethal, it may also be fundamentally deceptive. Martin Heidegger saw television as the quintessential medium for the abolition of remoteness, a medium that would come to dominate the whole machinery of communication. He expressed scepticism, however, as to the possibilities of understanding brought by televisual proximity:

> this frantic abolition of all distances brings no nearness; for nearness does not consist of shortness of distance . . . despite all conquest of distances the nearness of things remains absent.[75]

Learning a language takes time. Translation often involves the investment of many hours, days, weeks, months and, in some cases, even years. In both instances, we have what we might term *kinetic resistance*. The profound engagement with language and culture that is implied by in-depth language learning and attentive translation represents a substantial commitment of time. It is the acknowledgement of the extent of the *entre-deux*, of the time necessary to chart differences and find points of contact. Kinetic resistance involves the recognition not only of the infinite complexity of a multilingual world but of the fractal dimension to language that makes for the apparently infinite complication across contact zones within any one language (see Chapter 1). As a learner or translator becomes more and more familiar with the foreign language, interlingual complexness gives way to intralingual intricacy. Language learning and translation bring nearness, a deepening knowledge of another culture and people, but they also reveal distance, how much there is still to learn, how all translations are approximate. Caren Kaplan is deeply critical of the romanticisation of speed and distance in the American travel writing of Jean Baudrillard. She argues that it is necessary to conceive of distance in less binary and more complicated ways:

> In the age of telecommunications and transnational cultural production this might mean that distance does not inevitably lead to exile or war but to new subjectivities that produce new relationships to space as well as time so that distance is not only a safety zone or a field of tension but a terrain that houses new subjects of criticism.[76]

The kinetic resistance of language in translation and foreign-language acquisition institutes a notion of the in-between, the *entre-deux*, that allows for a more complex representation of distance. Distance here is not so much a terrain as a figure of movement. In other words, the pulsation, the oscillation of the *entre-deux* brings a subject near to and away from the Other. There is no absolute proximity but neither is there absolute distance. A dynamic conception of the in-between thus avoids a spatialisation of contact that haunts reified notions of distance. Marc-Alain Ouaknin, drawing on the cabbalistic concept of *Tsimtsoum* or contraction, relates the empty space of creation to the notion of a necessary distance that allows the Other to emerge:

> La création à partir de l'espace vide rend possible l'altérité à partir de la séparation. Séparation, distanciation, différenciation, à partir desquelles aucune fusion ne sera possible. Seuls des ponts pourront être jetés pour essayer de franchir l'abîme sans d'ailleurs jamais y parvenir.[77]

In personal relationships, a fusional totality prevents the emergence of the individual self and the notion of a relationship itself is predicated on the idea of separation, distance. This is what Ouaknin calls after Lévinas the paradox of a 'relation sans relation'.[78] The distance involved in translation is situated at an extrinsic and intrinsic level. The extrinsic level is the most obvious; texts in different languages are separated from each other in terms of history, culture, syntactic, lexical and textual conventions. The intrinsic level is the separation or distance that the translators feel with respect to their own language in translation. As the Canadian writer and translator, Joyce Marshall, claimed: 'I'm told my translations don't sound like me'; and Sherry Simon and David Homel, summing up Marshall's attitude to the translation process, see her approach to translation 'as a means of estrangement from the self, of taking leave of a too-familiar language'.[79] In the age of telecommunications and transnational cultural production to which Kaplan refers, the necessary distancing of the *entre-deux* frustrates expansionist fictions of total knowledge, often expressed in the mandarin dismissiveness of, 'I am assuming that travel is now impossible and that tourism is all that we have left.'[80] Michel Serres believes not only that travel is still possible but that it is vital: 'Qui ne bouge n'apprend rien.' Further on, he declares: 'Aucun apprentissage n'évite le voyage. Sous la conduite d'un guide, l'éducation pousse à l'extérieur.'[81] It was of course this belief that acted as an initial incentive for the sixteenth- and seventeenth-century Grand Tour. The evolution of the Tour, however, points to an element of travel that still remains decisive. Originally conceived as a preparation for a diplomatic career, the Grand Tour evolved into a more generalised form of instruction for young aristocrats. Jennifer Craik refers to two stages in the development of the Tour: 'first, the age of reading and speaking, when tourists actively engaged with guides, locals, and each other; followed by an age of observation, in which people learned by looking or visually taking in the vistas and splendour of continental culture.'[82] If travel in the first stage was to facilitate national and international relations by making contacts and learning foreign languages, the second stage saw a marked preference for the eye over the ear and the increasing predominance of sightseeing. Changes in modes of transport further encouraged a visual appropriation of the world through the panoramic vision of the train carriage, motor coach and private car. The windscreen makes the world transparent to vision but opaque to sound. In the case of train journeys, as we saw in Chapter 2, there is frequently a displacement from language interaction without to language interaction within, where the means of transport itself becomes as much a privileged point of language contact as the destination. However, in general historical terms, the visualisation of the world has been at the expense of foreign-language interaction.

Where there is language interaction, the interaction is often in a global lingua franca, increasingly English. In other words, as more and more of them for economic and political reasons learn English, non-Anglophones experience foreign-language interaction, but for English speakers foreign-language interaction correspondingly diminishes. There are arguably two baleful effects of this development, one of a more general and the other of a more private nature. The first consequence is the growing impoverishment of the world's linguistic ecosystem. According to the UNESCO *Atlas of the World's Languages in Danger of Disappearing*, up to a half of the 6,500 languages spoken on the planet are endangered or on the brink of extinction. Some linguists claim that a language dies somewhere in the world every two weeks. In 1788, there were around 250 aboriginal languages in Australia, now there are 20. The arrival of Portuguese in Brazil led to the disappearance of 75 per cent of the languages spoken in the country, and, of the 180 indigenous languages still remaining, few are spoken by more than 10,000 speakers.[83] Language change is a constant feature of human history but the rate of language loss in more recent centuries is distinctly alarming. Although linguists like David Crystal and John Edwards have quite understandably argued for the virtues of bilingualism (one local language plus one global language), languages do not exist in ideal symmetrical relationships and the coefficient of power is higher for some languages than others. In contemporary circumstances, this power is generally related to economic pre-eminence. Money talks. Edwards's contention is that, in matters of linguistic survival and language maintenance, 'economic considerations are of central importance'.[84] The domains of use that are least susceptible to intervention by language activists are domains of necessity, those domains where people feel compelled to speak a particular language for reasons of economic and social survival or betterment. Edwards concludes bleakly, 'One is tempted to frame an iron law in these matters: people will not indefinitely maintain two languages when one will serve across all domains.'[85]

A second and further consequence of global monolingualism relates more specifically to speakers of a global language. Travel presupposes, at some level, a quest. The quest can be for the simple abandonment of routine or a more strenuous exploration of personal meaning. The fundamental figures are those of departure and return, but the motion of exploration can only be initiated if there is a primary move away from origin, a move that in turn heightens sensitivity to the question of origins. As Sibony notes: 'pour avoir une origine il faut pouvoir s'en écarter, y revenir, et instaurer avec elle un entre-deux qu'on puisse *franchir*.'[86] In the biblical account of genesis, man and woman enter humanity at the moment that they are expelled from the Garden of Origin. They seek to recover that Paradise in the *entre-deux* of their human existence but the moment they re-enter Paradise is the moment that their humanity is annulled. At this moment the quest ends, there is no more newness or change or unexpectedness. Paradise renders these notions meaningless. Hence, the human necessity of a myth of expulsion, a wandering away from origin so that knowledge as quest, curiosity, can be instituted. For speakers of a global language, pragmatic or instrumental arguments for speaking other languages are less pressing than for those who do not speak a global language. Motivation and interest must come from elsewhere. If we conceive of knowledge as nomadic, as predicated on a primary exile from origin, then learning another language is more than simply instrumentalist in its consequences, it sets up an initial distance with respect to language origin that both strengthens our awareness of the origin and complicates our sense of it. The engagement with another language, the transactions of translation, increase the self-reflexive awareness of the extent of translation within the language of origin itself.

There is a danger in emphasising intralingual complexity at the expense of interlingual possibilities. If the former defence of the hegemony of English was unapologetically imperial, as in American language policy in the Phillipines or British language policy in Ireland, the latter-day defence of English-language hegemony has all the semblance of radical critique. For example, Stuart Hall claims English is the language of global mass culture but that this language is international English, an English that has been broken and invaded by the languages that it has tried to hegemonise. The new international language is not the same as the 'old, class-stratified, class-dominated, canonically secured form of standard or traditional high-brow English.'[87] In his *Language in History* Tony Crowley looks at the fiction of a standard language within Britain itself and how a particular vision of class, nation and empire was articulated through hegemonic varieties of the language.[88] Crowley also examines the language revival movement in Ireland that began in earnest in the 1890s and is extremely critical of what he views as the essentialist and racist views of Irish-language activists of the period. He concludes with an analysis of an essay by Seamus Heaney on John Alphonsus Mulrennan which considers the cultural effects of the impo-sition of the English language on Ireland.[89] Crowley takes Heaney to task for his monoglossic view of the English language but notes approvingly Heaney's celebration of Joyce's decision to make the demotic English of Dublin the language of a new European art:

> What Heaney describes here of course is the forging of heteroglossia, the process by which this Irish writer does not fall prey either to the blandish-ments of monoglossic Gaelic culture with its accompanying nostalgia and reverence for the epic past or to the terrors imposed by cultural domina-tion by the monoglossic English language, the instrument of everyday humiliation. What occurs instead is a revelation of the heteroglot nature . . . of all languages and consequently all forms of identity. Rather than a secure form of purity, what Heaney ends with is the hailing of the creativ-ity and novelty of a new form of language, inherited from the past and made new in the present. It is a language which scorns the policing of linguistic and cultural borders and even questions their very necessity.[90]

Crowley's incorporation of the Bakhtinian notion of heteroglossia – Bakhtin is the subject of a chapter in the book – is a prelude to a lyrical evocation of the progressive and emancipatory possibilities of a 'new form of language'. Like Hall, Crowley is attracted to the radical promise of English heteroglos-sia. However, it is not only revolutionaries that scorn 'linguistic and cultural borders'. Despots from Napoleon to Hitler have shown an equally scant regard for borders, linguistic or otherwise. The question is whether in the global system a heteroglossic discourse of translation is not being used to evacuate a polyglossic reality of translation so that eventually heteroglossia and hegemony become synonymous – sameness through difference. Poly-glossia invites that radical departure from origin that endlessly complicates the world. In signalling the demise of a common language the classic Babel account is also a tale of expulsion from an originary state, the Adamic speech of Eden, the *Ursprache* of a pre-Babelian world. Our purposive consciousness, concentrating on its immediate environment, can make our mother-tongue into another language of origin and ignore polyglossia (particularly if the mother-tongue is a dominant language). Translation, learning another language, is a constant reminder of the fragmented origin of human language, of the language-animal as a creature of multiple origins.

The encounter with other languages reveals the prodigality of Babel by opening up the *entre-deux* between languages as an area of exploration, discovery and surprise. George Steiner, for his part, claims that Babel was not a curse but a gift:

> The gift of tongues is precisely that; a gift and benediction beyond reckoning. The riches of experience, the creativities of thought and of feeling, the penetrative and delicate singularities of conception made possible by the polyglot condition are the pre-eminent adaptive agency and advantage of the human spirit.[91]

Risk and the nomadic dynamic

A recurrent concern of modernity has been the category of risk. One of the key features of the modern age has been the disembedding of social relations from local contexts of action.[92] To disembed is to remove social relations from local involvements and to recombine them across larger stretches of time and space. As Urry and Lash point out, such disembedding implies trust:

> People need to have faith in institutions or processes of which they possess only a limited knowledge. Trust arises from the development of expert or professional knowledge, which gives people faith, including forms of transport which convey them through time-space.[93]

Systems of mass travel and transport that developed in the nineteenth century saw the emergence of a whole new category of travel professionals, beginning with Thomas and John Cook, whose primary function was to minimise the risk, inconvenience and unpredictability involved in travel from one place to another. The increasing abstraction and complexity of modernity, with the extension in space and contraction in time implicit in globalisation, leads to an increasing devolution of trust on to expert systems – trains, planes, itinerary planners, hotels – that will 'simplify' our journeys and eliminate attendant risks. For George Ritzer and Allan Liska the result is the increasing 'McDisneyization' of the travel industry. Drawing on Ritzer's previous work in *The McDonaldization of Society*, Ritzer and Liska apply a neo-Weberian theory of rationalisation to Disney World.[94] In this view, society is seen as growing increasingly calculable, efficient, predictable and more and more controlled by non-human technologies. The putative rationality of modernity, however, generates its own irrationality. Not surprisingly, they find all these features present in the rationalised theme park of Disney World. Ritzer and Liska claim that, because of the McDonaldised lifeworld that is increasingly becoming the norm in the West, tourists want highly predictable (no smelly bathrooms), highly efficient (lots to do), highly calculable (no hidden expenses) and highly controlled (aerobics classes at two) holidays.[95]

Language is a key element in the predictability of McDisneyised tourism, as is apparent in a quote from an Hawaiian hotel official: '"The kids are safe here; there's low crime, you can drink the water and you can speak the language."'[96] The official means English, of course, which is hardly surprising given the relationship of Hawaii to the United States. However, as David Crystal points out, English is increasingly the language of international tourism and travel, if only because the world's leading tourism spender and earner is the United States.[97] Language is important in tourism if only because of the highly personalised nature of the employee/tourist encounter, whether this be in hotels, bars, restaurants or shops. The personality of the tourist worker is an integral part of the tourism 'product'.[98] Therefore, inability to communicate with the 'local' staff would be seen to diminish the quality of the holiday experience. An element of predictability is the ready assumption that the locals will speak the global language of the visitor. In addition, motorists' organisations, travel health insurance companies and credit card providers increasingly advertise services where the distraught traveller can telephone their way out of catastrophe to 'someone who speaks your language'. If polyglossia emerges as a risk in late modernity, it is also apparent that language knowledge and use can function as a form of resistance to the hegemonic spread of global language entailed by a theory of McDisneyisation. The resistance can occur at two levels, at the level of the tourist workers and at the level of the tourists themselves. In the case of those working in the tourist industry, the distinction between 'backstage' and 'frontstage', most notably suggested by Dean MacCannell, can help to clarify the role of language in worker–tourist interaction.[99] Workers in the frontline such as waiters, hotel receptionists and tour guides will speak a common international language as they interact with tourists in the foreign setting. Frontstage the language of work is the language of the tourist. However, backstage, cooks, kitchen helps and maintenance staff are not normally expected to have competence in a language other than their own. The language of interaction between frontstage and backstage will be the language of the country. As we already mentioned in Chapter 3, tourists in pursuit of the authentic often wish to go backstage and the response of workers in tourist destinations may then be to stage authenticity and produce a fake backstage (the weaving demonstrations in craft shops) in order to escape the intrusive gaze of the tourist. One of the signal advantages of 'local' languages is to render the gaze ineffective. The cooks swear, the waiters banter between themselves, the receptionist ironically comments on a guest's rudeness to his/her colleague; language has the potential in the theatre of tourist encounter to act as a protective mask, a barrier to unwelcome invasiveness. For immigrant workers their native language performs partly the same function (though language also functions in these situations as a code of belonging and a source of identity). In his essay, 'Performing the

Tourist Product', Philip Crang correctly identifies 'talking' as one of the neglected aspects of tourism production and consumption.[100] However, he does not (typically for much of the literature on tourism) mention the issue of 'foreign talking' or talking between languages. The resistance of language difference in the performance of the tourist product highlights a fundamental feature of language, a talent for concealment. Ludwig Wittgenstein claimed in the *Tractatus* that, 'die Sprache verkleidet den Gedanken', and John Edwards has latterly argued that 'concealment is as much a feature of language as is communication'.[101]

Translation in these circumstances may often be unwelcome. The tourist who speaks the host language breaches the buffer zone of distance and there may be discomfort at what is felt to be the prying proximity of the translator/linguist. However, there can also be welcome surprise as the McDisneyisation of tourism increasingly marginalises non-global language. The tourist who speaks the language of the other resists the facility of global-speak for the perils of nuance. Crystal points out that, while one-third of the world's population are regularly exposed to English, two-thirds are not: 'Move away from the regular tourist routes . . . and English soon becomes conspicuous by its absence.'[102] A factor that is complicit in the resistance of the tourist as linguist is the relatively sedentary lifestyle of large sections of the world's population. Geraldine Pratt and Susan Hanson have argued that excessive emphasis on the phenomena of mass media, tourism and global financial capital has stressed transnational mobility and time-space compression at the expense of the intense localness of the lives led by many people:

> Although the world is increasingly well connected, we must hold this in balance with the observation that most people live intensely local lives; their homes, work places, recreation, shopping, friends, and often family are all located within a relatively small orbit. The simple and obvious fact that overcoming distance requires time and money means that the everyday events of daily life are well grounded within a circumscribed arena.[103]

These intensely local lives will be largely conducted in the local language. Only 8 per cent of the world's population have access to cars, 3 per cent to a personal computer.[104] The media of real or virtual mobility are still the possessions of the privileged. In other words, local languages are still powerfully present in the lives of many human beings. For this reason, contact with millions of others on the planet is still primarily (though not exclusively, as we have seen in Chapter 3) a labour of linguistic love. If romantic fiction is conventionally the chronicle of impedimenta that must be overcome by the lovers before the bliss of (re)union, then the courtship of language is a risky and uncertain enterprise. The most obvious risk is failure. The risk is a real one given the complexity of all languages. Linguists have estimated that, given the four basic skills (understanding, speaking, reading, writing the foreign language) and their subdivisions, there are at least twenty dimensions of language that would have to be tested to determine an individual's bilingual proficiency.[105] Competence will vary, of course, in relation to the demands of the situation. Travellers will not usually find themselves producing texts in the foreign language. However, the range of skills does point up the potentially infinite difficulty of the task, with the attendant risks of humiliation, misunderstanding, fatigue and frustration (see Chapter 2).

A further risk is felt to occur at a more advanced stage in the learning process, the fear of assimilation. This is typically the experience of immigrant groups, a recurrent tension between integrative motivation and the anxiety of absorption. In the general context of travel, Eva Hoffman sees Thomas Mann's *Death in Venice* as a parable of disorientation. She re-reads the novella on a train back to Warsaw and comments: 'in Mann's fiction, and undoubtedly in reality as well, to travel towards Otherness, even if it is most ardently desired, is to risk disintegration; it is to lose the firm certainties of yourself.' Hoffman sees Mann's short fiction as 'a cautionary tale about the dangers of travel'.[106] The sensation of dissolution of the self is not confined to travel writing or literature but also surfaces in anthropological writing. Dorinne Kondo describes the experience of seeing her reflection as she was out shopping for her Japanese host family and how she resembled in every way – clothes, gesture, body – a typical Japanese housewife. She was doing fieldwork in Japan on Japanese workplace relations but the process of assimilation secreted its own terrors: 'Suddenly I clutched the handle of the stroller to steady myself as a wave of dizziness washed over me ... Fear that perhaps I would never emerge from this world into which I was immersed inserted itself into my mind and stubbornly refused to leave, until I resolved to move into a new apartment, to distance myself from my Japanese home and my Japanese existence.'[107] The dissolution that Hoffman and Kondo describe could be seen, in terms of our conception of the in-between, as an exclusive identification with one pole of the language interaction. In other words, the pulsation, the oscillation of the *entre-deux,* has given way to a fusion with one end of the exchange. This is the risk of language learning, but learning without risks seems properly inconceivable as knowledge must involve the unknown, the unforeseeable. Only movement towards the Other can allow self-knowledge to emerge, as the 'natural' reveals itself to be 'cultural' and change becomes possible through distance from the *délire identitaire* of immutable origin. Maintaining the dynamic of language acquisition is maintaining the *nomadic dynamic of translation*, the continual move towards and away from origins. As Michel Le Bris notes:

> il faut une première perte de soi pour pouvoir vivre avec autrui. Et c'est ce qu'il y a de meilleur dans l'élan voyageur. On n'entre en humanité que par

l'expérience du passage à l'autre. Ce qui ne signifie pas que l'on ne puisse pas se sentir en même temps profondément breton, par exemple, pour ne parler que de moi.[108]

A happy homophone allows James Clifford to see all roots as involving routes. He seeks to destabilise the categories of travelling and dwelling and calls for 'a comparative cultural studies approach to specific histories, tactics, everyday practices of dwelling and traveling: traveling-in-dwelling, dwelling-in-traveling'.[109] One locus of such a comparative cultural studies approach might be departments of modern languages and centres of translation studies. In the disciplinary objectives that departments of modern languages have set themselves over the last two centuries, when most of these departments have come into existence, there is a distinct sense of the residue of the Grand Tour or the autonomous language strategy of empire. Modern language departments prepared young gentlemen and later young women for service abroad as diplomats, merchants, missionaries or pedagogues. An integrative approach to the language, literature and culture of the foreign country was justified at home by the vocational alibi of foreign diplomacy, trade and proselytism. These departments of French, German, Italian or Oriental languages 'dwelt' in a particular country but they were perpetually 'travelling' through scholarship, academic contacts and student visits elsewhere. This may indeed have been their principal handicap in terms of active participation in the intellectual life of the country in which these departments dwelled. Historians, economists, philosophers, sociologists, psychoanalysts and theologians have variously marked the public intellectual life of many countries in the West, but what of scholars in modern language departments? The specialists in the language and literature of a particular country will appear in the public fora of that country (English literature professors on British television, Irish language professors on Irish radio), but how many modern language scholars ever appear in the public eye unless there is a very specific issue directly relating to their specialist area? There would appear to be a problem of category definition. How are modern language departments and, more recently, translation centres to be defined, given that they imply a travelling-in-dwelling? This relative weakness of public identity could be seen in the light of a more recent reflection on travel as a source of disciplinary strength. The long experience of these departments in movement across cultures and borders and languages would appear to equip them ideally for the task of the comparative cultural studies that Clifford envisages – particularly because one of the principal advantages of foreign language acquisition is that it allows for that other element of Clifford's intellectual project, dwelling-in-travelling, the vertical travel of the extended sojourn in the country of the language being learned. If the focus in the past has been very firmly on an integrative, assimilationist approach to the foreign language and culture, with little or no cognisance taken of the native culture or language of the student, it is arguably by a greater attention to the in-between, to the translation dynamic of foreign-language acquisition, that modern language departments and centres for translation studies can have an impact not just on the countries to which their students or graduates are sent but also on the intellectual life of the countries in which they dwell. If it is now accepted that cultures do travel, that all roots lead to routes, then the foreign-language nomads may find that they have finally come home.

Chapter Five

FINAL FRONTIERS

At the age of twelve, Rydra Wong knew seven earth languages and could make herself understood in five extra-terrestrial tongues. Rydra Wong, the heroine of Samuel Delaney's science fiction novel, *Babel-17*, comes from a family of communicators.[1] Her father was a communications engineer at Stellarcenter X-11-B and her mother a translator at the Court of the Outer Worlds. Her eponymous mission is to try and translate Babel-17, a language that is posing a serious threat to the defence systems of the Alliance. Wong is also a poet and her poetry is appreciated both by those who live in the region of the Alliance and those who live in the realm of the Invaders. Further evidence of her analog or in-between status is that she does not fully belong to either of the two main classes in the Alliance, 'customs' or 'transport'. Wong eventually untangles the linguistic mysteries of Babel-17 and her successful translation of the language saves the Alliance from potential destruction.

Octospiders, Babel fish and the Holy Spirit

The translator as saviour is a recurrent idea in the travel fictions of the future. In *Rama Revealed* by Arthur C. Clarke and Gentry Lee, two of the female characters, Ellie and Eponine, are kidnapped by the octospiders. The octospiders communicate using colours and Ellie and Eponine learn the language of the octospiders in captivity. Ellie is particularly proficient in the language but, when she is returned to the group of humans, it transpires that her ability is no accident. Before her birth, Ellie tells her father, Richard, he had been taken by the octospiders and, unbeknownst to him, had been the subject of an experiment: 'What they attempted to do was to change the chromosomes in your sperm so that your offspring would have both expanded language capability and greater visual resolution of colours. In short, they tried to engineer me genetically . . . so I would be able to communicate with them without difficulty.'[2] Ellie admits to her astonished parents that she is, therefore, 'some kind of hybrid'. Ellie's translation abilities prove crucial later in the novel when relationships with the octospiders become increasingly strained. In the final film of the original *Star Wars* trilogy, *The Return of the Jedi*, it is C-3PO, the protocol droid whose language ability encompasses a modest six million forms of communication, who is deified by the Ewoks on account of his knowledge of their language. The Ewoks prove to be crucial allies in the final showdown between the rebels and the Empire's troops. The gold-coloured droid with its shambling gait and patrician distractedness is markedly different from the brutal machismo of the innumerable robocops that fill science fiction films with their staccato imperatives. It is the fretful figure of fun, working the in-between terrain of translation, who proves ultimately to be of more consequence than the traditional male heroes, Hans Solo and Luke Skywalker. Many more examples might be cited of the translator-as-mediator/deliverer in science fiction novels and films.[3] What is important from the point of view of the present study is that science fiction, which almost invariably takes the form of a travel narrative if only because it involves time-travel into the future, when it does pay attention to the phenomenon of translation and has the translation done by a human or near-equivalent (droid), portrays the translator as a necessarily hybrid creature.[4] The hybridity allows for communication to take place in the journey to other places and times and often proves a more effective means of survival than the monoglossic rhetoric of the translator's fellow beings. Yet, the hybridity that promises rescue is often deeply suspect. In *Rama Revealed*, Ellie's husband Robert is deeply troubled by his wife's report of the octospider experiments on his father-in-law:

> 'How can you be so calm about discovering that you're a hybrid?' he said to Ellie. 'Don't you understand what it means? When the octospiders altered your DNA to improve visual resolution and to make learning their language easier, they tampered with a robust genetic code that has evolved naturally over millions of years. Who knows what disease susceptibilities, infirmities or even negative changes in fertility may show up in you or subsequent generations?'[5]

Rydra Wong's most formidable opponent, the 'Butcher', also turns out to be a hybrid creature. Working for the Alliance, the Butcher's father, Baron Ver Dorco, creates a new generation of android spies, the TW-55. Experts in polyidentity, they can adapt to situations at will and are assisted in their chameleon task by intralingual translation abilities:

> TW-55 has twelve hours' worth of episodes in fourteen different dialects, accents, or jargons concerning sexual conquests, gambling experiences, fisticuff encounters, and humorous anecdotes of semi-illegal enterprises, all of which failed miserably.[6]

When one of the TW-55s is captured by the Invaders and programmed with the language Babel-17, he turns out to be a formidable saboteur precisely because of the carefully designed duplicity in his original make-up. Rydra Wong's capacity to perfectly simulate conversation in other languages is darkly mirrored by the destructive mimesis of the Butcher. In *Rama Revealed*, Robert's outburst is a familiar articulation of unease at the presence of the Other, particularly at the point of origin (seen here in uniquely patriarchal terms as Richard's sperm), and Ellie's translation abilities are not only evidence of travel elsewhere (even if under coercion) but are a constant reminder of her mixed otherness.

If Ellie is partly the result of non-human intervention, Rydra Wong's activities point to a crucial link between translation and humanity. When she describes the nature of Babel-17 to her colleagues, she claims that 'most of its words carry more information about things they refer to than any four or five languages that I know put together, and in less space'.[7] Her claim is not unusual. Alien languages are commonly represented as more economical, mathematical and logical than human languages – witness the cautious syntax of Dr Spock in *Star Trek*. These languages are bearers of pure equivalence, distinct from the allusive, ambiguous state of human speech that requires careful translation. What defines speech as human is in a sense the *translation residue*, the obstacle to simple lexical substitution or syntactic manipulation that requires active, interpretive intervention. Indeed, the search for perfect languages has often been expressed as a nostalgia for the language of Eden, for the prelapsarian, non-human (inhuman?) paradise of the *lingua adamica* where language existed in isomorphism with the divinely created world and where language was One not Many.[8] Translation problems are evidence of a fallen state but this state is the defining moment of the emergence of a mortal humanity, the Original Sin that is the necessary sin against origins if humans are to journey into separateness. Automatic translation is a familiar narrative device in science fiction for dealing with the problems posed by the residues of translation, from the Babel fish in the *Hitch-Hiker's Guide to the Galaxy* to the Translator in *Rama Revealed* to the Universal Translator in *Star Trek: The Next Generation*. However, if automatic translation solves a narrative problem - how do characters (and by extension the reader) know what the aliens are saying? – it is not without its difficulties. The difficulties are both technical and human.

Richard, who constructs the 'translator' in *Rama Revealed* for the automatic translation of the octospider language, is by his own admission a very poor linguist. In a classic gender division of communicative labour, he tells his daughter that her 'mother is the linguist in the family'.[9] However, Richard is helped in his work on the translation device by an octospider, Hercules. The octospider language is made up of sixty-four different colours. Fifty-one of these function alphabetically; the other thirteen are classed as 'clarifiers', that is, they specify tenses, comparatives, superlatives or are used as counters. Richard soon discovers that automatic translation is anything but automatic and has considerable difficulty converting octospider colour patterns into recognisable English sentences. In a discussion of Richard's problems, Ellie argues that octospider language is fundamentally different from human language because "'Everything is specified and quantified, to minimise the possibility of misunderstanding. There is no subtlety or nuance.'" Hercules confesses to finding two aspects of human language especially problematic: 'One is lack of precise specification, which leads to a massive vocabulary. The other is your use of indirectness to communicate . . . I still have trouble understanding Max because often what he says is literally not what he means.'[10] Thus, like Babel-17 and many other examples of xenoglossia, octospider language is the perfect realisation of the aspiration to mathematically based universal languages that marked the eighteenth century.[11] Notwithstanding the resistance of natural language to his ambitions, Richard perseveres in his task and eventually produces a reasonable working model of an automatic translation device (though the details are tellingly vague). Interestingly, he does not justify the construction of the 'translator' on the grounds of technocratic ostentation but human harmony. Hercules wonders why Richard is expending time and effort on producing the 'translator' when Ellie and Nicole already have a good understanding of the language and can interpret. Richard claims he was initially attracted by the technical challenge and a desire to understand the octospider language. However, he and his wife Nicole felt that the 'translator' was increasingly important because:

> our human clan here in Emerald City is dividing into two groups. Ellie, Nicole and I have made our life more interesting because of our increasing interactions with your species. The rest of the humans, including the children, remain essentially isolated. Eventually if the others don't have some way of communicating with you, they will become dissatisfied and/or unhappy. A good automatic translator is the key that will open up their lives here.[12]

For Richard and Nicole, the automatic translator is liberating in a way that the human translator is not. Where knowledge is a scarce resource, the knowledgeable exercise power and power creates resentment. The solution proposed by Richard is an interesting echo of the move we signalled for the travel guide in Chapter 3, the shift from heteronomy to autonomy. Heteronomous dependency on interpreters leads to a concentration of communicative power in a small number of people and to the alienation of the majority. The aim of Richard's device is primarily to restore communicative autonomy to the other humans in Emerald City and thus to avoid future conflict. The ready evacuation of translators by technology may not, however, bring the beatitude of understanding and tolerance to which Richard aspires.

In *The Hitch-Hiker's Guide to the Galaxy*, Arthur Dent finds himself aboard a Vogon spaceship after planet Earth has been destroyed to make way for a hyperspace bypass. Ford Prefect, an extra-terrestrial friend, slaps a Babel fish into Arthur Dent's ear so that he can understand the unchivalrous welcome of the Vogons. Arthur Dent looks up 'Babel fish' in the eponymous *Hitch-Hiker's Guide to the Galaxy* where he reads that the 'Babel fish is small, yellow and leech-like, and probably the oddest thing in the universe.' After a pseudo-scientific description of its operation, Dent learns that 'if you stick a Babel fish in your ear you can instantly understand anything said to you in any form of language'. However, transparency has not resulted in felicity. The entry for the Babel fish concludes unhappily: 'the poor Babel fish, by effectively removing all barriers to communication between different races and cultures, has caused more and bloodier wars than anything else in the history of creation.'[13] The galactic traveller's aid has had baleful and unforeseen consequences. Though it is normally incommunicativeness that is interpreted as hostility in fictional encounters with aliens (if we can't understand them their intentions must be unfriendly), Douglas Adams appears to offer the apparent paradox of communicativeness as a source of enmity. However, the paradox is only apparent and human history has often borne out the bleak conclusion of the entry for Babel fish in the *Hitch-Hiker's Guide*. As David Crystal observes, 'the use of a single language by a community is no guarantee of social harmony or mutual understanding, as has been repeatedly seen in world history (e.g. the American Civil War, the Spanish Civil War, the Vietnam War, former Yugoslavia, contemporary Northern Ireland).'[14] Translation, as we saw in Chapter 1, does not end with language difference. The complexity of intralingual translation shows the considerable potential for tension and discord along the faultlines of race, class, gender and ethnic difference within any one language. Although polyglossia gives way to heteroglossia in the starship *Enterprise* – ethnic origin indicated not by different languages but by different accents in one language (English) – tensions still run high among crew members in different episodes. In *Henry V*, Macmorris, Fluellen, Gower and Jamy, the Irish, Welsh, English and Scottish soldiers respectively, though ostensibly united in Henry's army by the English language, repeatedly quarrel over questions of meaning and intent in their shared idiom.[15] From Shakespeare to *Star Trek* to the linguistic utopia of automatic translation, language barriers may be not so much removed as displaced.

There is a further dimension to the Babel fish's dark legacy that can be linked to the Babel myth itself and the Pentecostal resolution of the *confusio linguarum* in the New Testament. The scene is described in Acts 2.1–11 in which the apostles are gathered together in a room on the day of the Pentecost. The sound of a 'rushing mighty wind' filled the room and 'there appeared unto them cloven tongues like as of fire'; filled with the Holy Spirit, the apostles began to speak in other tongues so that the polyglot crowd who were drawn to the spectacle 'were confounded, because that every man heard them [the apostles] speak in his own language'. The day of the Pentecost undoes the division of Babel through the gift of glossolalia. In her essay, 'The Curse and Blessing of Babel; or, Looking Back on Universalisms', Aleida Assmann sees the Pentecost as a radical break with the representation of language(s) initiated at Babel:

> With the linguistic fall at Babel language received its materiality. A language that is not understood turns into a dense mass of sounds. It is reduced to external noise, to dross or impenetrable materiality. Its very opposite is the language spoken at Jerusalem. This language is sheer immateriality, transparency, immediacy. Its materiality is evaporated.[16]

Unlike the Jewish tradition with its attention to the primacy of the letter of the law, the Christian tradition of the Holy Spirit guarantees a truth beyond language. The link with the materiality of language is severed and language and writing become mere conventional sign systems that express a spiritual core of meaning. Assmann argues that the idea of 'a mystic, pneumatic unity of the faith "in" the very variety of natural languages was the rock (to use an inappropriate metaphor) on which the institution of mission was founded.'[17] The message not the medium becomes the defining principle of Christianity, and if the story of Babel is a myth of diversification, 'the story of Jerusalem is a myth not of unity (which is not to be restored) but of universalization as it is to be achieved through the languages and the course of history.'[18] A transparent as opposed to a material concept of language lends itself more readily to proselytism, as truth is no longer felt to be bounded by its material expression. Reason and Nature would replace the Holy Spirit in secular Enlightenment representations of the notion of truth beyond language. The historical association of Christian proselytism with colonial adventure, and of the 'religion' of progress with imperialist expansion, shows the dangers of pneumatic depreciation of the materiality of language. We are close here to a variant of the pathological universalism described in Chapter 3. When you can 'instantly understand anything said to you in any form of language', the temptation may be not so much to engage with the Other as to expand the Self. When the materiality of language is considered to be a secondary or even (through divine or technological intervention) non-existent obstacle, then there is little to check the relentless expansion of Self as a carrier of Truth and/or Progress. In this context, Goethe's axiom that 'The most beautiful metempsychosis is the one in which we recognise ourselves in the shape of the other' is more alarming than reassuring.[19] The immediacy and transparency of the paradigms of automatic translation invite the projection of the self onto the screen of the other. Language is no longer a sufficient reason for failure to welcome the gospel of revelation or emancipation, so other means of persuasion need to be employed to effect coercive fusion, hence the ever-present possibility of 'more and bloodier wars'.

Bodies, territoriality, metaphor

For Robert, as we saw above, the incorporation of octospider elements into the human genome has all the potential of monstrous miscegenation. Rosa Braidotti in *Nomadic Subjects* offers a definition of monsters that makes Robert's fears explicit and that could apply equally well to the nomadic subject of translation:

> Monsters are human beings who are born with congenital malformations of their bodily organism. They also represent the in between, the mixed, the ambivalent as implied in the ancient Greek root of the word *monsters*, *teras*, which means both horrible and wonderful, object of aberration and adoration.[20]

Braidotti's image of the monster begins with the corporeal, the Hunchback and Cyclops of fairytale and myth. The body is important to any discussion of travel, language and translation in that travel is considered typically to involve physical displacement. Nicolas Bouvier comments on this physical investment in travel:

> Il faut qu'il y ait un équilibre entre le monde physique et le monde intellectuel, qui s'est vite établi chez moi puisque très tôt, à chaque fois que je pouvais, je partais. Ça, c'était la découverte physique, charnelle, musicale, vocale du monde. Ce que j'appelle la connaissance par la plante des pieds.[21]

This is not a strict condition. Users surf the Net, readers read travel accounts, viewers watch holiday programmes, friends hear from other friends tales of foreign marvels and mishaps; all these activities involve 'travel' that does not demand departure from the proverbial armchair. Of course, it could be argued that, in most of these cases, there has been prior physical displacement and that what the book, programme or tale provides is the vicarious experience of travel – secondary, as opposed to primary, travelling. The awareness of the physicality or the embodied nature of travel will greatly depend on the mode of travel. Jacques Lacarrière begins his account of his two-month walking trip through France with a loving evocation of his feet. In *Un voyage en Océanie*, an island-hopping tour of the South Pacific, Jean-Claude Guillebaud makes no mention of physical fatigue, discomfort or limits, travelling being mainly done by plane and car.[22] Wilderness hikes and organised sightseeing are at different ends of a scale of physical exertion, which can become an end in itself as in orienteering, but even where a minimum of physical effort is involved in getting from one point to the other, the intersemiotic dimension to travelling means that there will be sensory impressions that signal elsewhere.[23] The traveller is an *embodied* subject. Indeed, a difficulty of the genre of travel writing is finding a language that is adequate to the domain of physical sensation. The disappointment of the holiday snap is the disenchantment with the disembodied residue of the three-dimensional physical experience of being-in-another-world ('If only you'd been there!'). If the traveller is a figure of the in-between, it is in part because languages and cultures physically meet in, are inscribed at some level on, the body of the traveller. It is the same body that receives the different experiences. This embodiment of travel can be usefully related to the increasing emphasis in more recent translation theory on the importance of the translator as human subject. Edwin Gentzler, for example, has argued that 'most systemic or structuralist methodologies fail at the task of linking human agency to historical change'.[24] In developing an Aristotelian model of multiple causality for translation, Anthony Pym sees human translators as the efficient cause of translation. They are the intersections between cultures. Rather than see the translators as the discursive product of their translations or as professional functionaries, Pym sees translators as primarily *embodied* beings. In his discussion of the work of Moses Mendelssohn who translated into both Hebrew and German, Pym asks if Mendelssohn should be seen as belonging to a subculture of Hebrew or a subculture of German or to both at the same time but in different places. It might be argued from a systemic viewpoint that Mendelssohn simply changed subculture every time he changed languages, but Pym demurs:

> if he [Mendelssohn] had a physical body, as most of us admit to, the different languages and cultures would surely be brought physically together in the one place and time. They would be together in a minimal interculture. Hence the importance I have attached to translators who have bodies. Their material existence gives basic substance to interculturality.[25]

The embodied translator, then, is both a source of nomadic potential (s/he can get up and go) and the incarnation of the in-between, of the multiple intersections produced by the languages and cultures s/he has encountered. There is a further dimension to the embodied translator-nomad that concerns feminist responses to the removal of the subject from theory. Caren Kaplan describes the efforts made by Euro-American theorists to account for differences between women 'without losing the intrinsic basis of materialist feminist analysis: the female body, the lived experience of female bodies in a masculinist world, and the shared elements that analysis of female life might bring to the fore'.[26] This insistence on the materialist basis of the body leads to feminist scepticism about the eagerness in many strains of postmodernism to expel the subject from the citadel of thought.

The political scientist Nancy Hartsock claims that the postmodern view that truth and knowledge are contingent and multiple is a truth claim in itself and that the ontological status of the subject is undermined at the very time that women and non-Western peoples have begun to claim themselves as subjects.[27] If the postmodernist critique of a centred, unitary, male Cartesian subject has allowed others traditionally excluded from discourse to feature in analysis, the danger, as Mascia-Lees, Sharpe and Cohen point out, is that postmodern writing 'may erase difference, implying that all stories are really about one experience: the decentring and fragmentation that is currently the experience of Western white males'.[28] The erasure of difference can lie behind a celebration of 'polyvocality' that evacuates power in the name of plurality:

> If the postmodernist emphasis on multivocality leads to a denial of the continued existence of a hierarchy of discourse, the material and historical links between cultures can be ignored, with all voices becoming equal, each telling only an individualized story. Then the history of the colonial, for example, can be read as independent of that of the colonizer. Such readings ignore or obscure exploitation and power differentials and, therefore, offer no ground to fight oppression and effect change.[29]

Translators as embodied subjects are not only points of intersection of language, culture and textual and oral memory, they are also implicated in hierarchies of discourse and power relations.[30] It is their very physicality that makes them vulnerable to exploitation, persecution and manipulation. You may have to get up and go not so much to discover the charms of another culture as to flee for your life. The history of interpreting in the early colonial period has many instances of indigenes being forcibly moved to the imperial centres so that they could learn imperial languages and return to work as interpreters.[31] Kidnap is an extreme form of physical appropriation of the translator's body but hunger, fear and pain have been variously used to situate translators at subordinate points in networks of power. If bodies make translators vulnerable, they also ground their resistance to ill-treatment and provide a material basis not only for the interculturality to which Pym alludes, but for the translator to speak as an active subject of change rather than as a passive agent of discursive function.

The subject that we are describing here is not to be confused with the serial individualism of modernity. Michel Maffesoli has argued that individualist ideology is the '"territorialisation" par excellence de la modernité'.[32] If the modern state has been obsessed with observation, control and the regulation of the circulation of people and goods within and at its boundaries, the individual of modernity has become 'une sorte de prison morale, une sorte de petite institution sécurisante, une forteresse où, par le biais de l'éducation, de la carrière professionnelle, d'une identité typée, l'on s'enferme durablement.'[33] The definition of territoriality in this instance is the space of exclusion, of immigration control, whether at the level of the state or the individual. Where does this definition leave the translator? Must translators belong to one culture, two, three or more cultures (depending on the number of their working languages), to an interculture or no culture at all? What, in other words, does the notion of territoriality mean to a translator? Discussing the situation in Eastern Europe in *Le Vertige de Babel*, Pascal Bruckner claims that problems arise not from the excessive importance of national boundaries or limits but from their uncertainty:

> Contrairement à un cliché trop répandu, ce n'est pas la sacralisation des frontières mais au contraire leur incertitude qui a été le vrai malheur des peuples, surtout d'Europe orientale, ballottés au gré des guerres et des invasions d'une tutelle à une autre. La grande saveur des frontières, une fois reconnues et garanties, c'est qu'on peut les franchir, jouer à leurs marges, exercice autrement plus exaltant que leur abolition pure et simple. Seules les conquérants rêvent d'effacer les frontières, surtout celles des autres.[34]

Bruckner's contention that borders allow for all manner of transgressive possibility is part of a larger argument in which he challenges the pseudo-internationalism that is substituted for genuine cosmopolitanism. Jetting across continents and time-zones and communicating in the *lingua franca* of simple English does not make one cosmopolitan: 'Transiter d'une civilisation à l'autre est l'équivalent d'une mue, d'une métamorphose qui implique peine et travail, et n'a rien à voir avec le glissement feutré du *jet* reliant tous les points de la planète.'[35] The labour involved in the acquisition of a foreign language is added to, in the case of the translator, by the need to become fully proficient in his/her mother tongue and culture. As Bruckner points out, 'Aller vers les autres implique donc une patrie, une mémoire qu'il faut cultiver (même si on les relativise): je n'accorde l'hospitalité à l'étranger qu'à partir d'un sol où je peux l'accueillir.'[36] Thus, translators operate from territories, and conventional wisdom has it that this territory is the territory of the mother-tongue that allows translators to be *au fait* with the linguistic evolution and cultural changes in their target language(s), assuming that their mother-tongue is their target language.

However, is this notion of territory adequate to the experience of many translators? For instance, a clear majority of the professional members of the national translators' association based in Ireland are foreign nationals.[37] Outside the English-speaking world, and in particular in countries that in world terms use 'minority' languages, non-mother-tongue translation is widespread. Translators who return to their native country and language frequently maintain contact with the country or countries of their source languages if only because the risk of linguistic and cultural obsolescence is a real one. So we have three territorial configurations: firstly, translators who live abroad but translate into their mother-tongue; secondly, translators who live at home but translate into a language that is not their mother-tongue; and thirdly, translators who live at home, translate into their mother-tongue but frequently go abroad so as not to neglect their source languages. In none of these cases is there a nativist, unmediated relationship to territory. There is a further complication in the case of languages where the language does not equate invariably with one specific national culture. An Irish, English, American or Australian translator may have English as their mother-tongue but native culture for each of these translators is going to be decidedly different: the target culture of English is not homogenous, even if for economic reasons one particular variety of that culture may be dominant. Therefore, any formulation of the 'sol', ground or territory for translators must encompass a number of disparate formations. One of the configurations is arguably the notion of a *translation diaspora*. Though in emphasising the contribution of translators to national languages and national cultures, translation histories will give the impression of a national, territorial base for translation activity, the activities of many groups of translators throughout history show that they have typically operated away from home. In the Irish case, the wandering monks or *peregrini* of the seventh to ninth centuries or the Franciscans based in Louvain in the Spanish Netherlands in the seventeenth century are classic examples of translators who were based outside their country but who frequently maintained contacts with their language and culture of origin.[38] As Clifford observes, 'The empowering paradox of diaspora is that dwelling *here* assumes a solidarity and a connection *there*' (his emphasis).[39] The 'there' of Clifford's paradox can be seen not as a stable centre of origin but as a centre that is in its turn destabilised by translated material that comes into the culture via its diaspora. The possibility of a notion of tradition for a translation diaspora, a basis for a historical awareness, is suggested by Paul Gilroy when he affirms that tradition can become a way of 'conceptualizing fragile communicative relationships across time and space that are the basis not of diaspora identities but of diaspora identifications'.[40] A function of language and translation is precisely that of sustaining communicative relationships across time and space and the existence of translators as cosmopolitan intermediaries in a translation diaspora points once again to the nomadic basis of 'sedentary' national cultures.

Maffesoli posits the nomadic as a way of overcoming the cult of monadic autonomy in modern social life with its contention that individuals are laws unto themselves, a thesis that is profoundly negative in its social consequences. On the contrary,

> lorsque l'errant transgresse les frontières, il en appelle, d'une manière peut-être non consciente à une sorte de "hétéronomie": la loi vient de l'autre, on n'existe qu'en fonction de l'autre, ce qui redonne au corps social sa densité et sa signification concrète.[41]

The nomad, though typically represented as marginal, destructive or anarchic, articulates an important principle of social cohesion, the necessary open-endedness of relationships if societies are to constitute and renew themselves. Furthermore, and this applies notably to translators, if we accept the necessity of nomadism for the establishment and renewal of communities, then Maffesoli's concept of *'distance reliée'* – relationships established over distances – shows translation as a nomadic practice that not only creates relationships of exchange, contact or influence over distances of space and time but also links translators themselves, by virtue of the *distance reliée*, to target and/or source cultures through their nomadic coming and going. From a nomadic perspective Maffesoli sees the need for a notion of the *'territoire flottant'*. This floating territory is akin to Clifford's idea of roots being deeply routed or Rojek and Urry's thesis that all cultures are at some level travelling cultures. If we are to see translators as inhabitants of this floating territory, this is not to argue that translators are feckless, footloose and deracinated but that translators should not be seen as axiomatically 'belonging to one culture or the other'.[42] Translators can indeed strongly identify with their native language and culture but by virtue of having experienced another language or culture they have become, to use a term from Chapter 2, changelings. The dialectic of proximity and distance is the lot of the returned native, the native who can no longer experience language and culture in the same way as the homebody. In the case of all three of the territorial configurations described above, the translators are floating in an *entre-deux* (home/away, source language/target language, mother-tongue/non mother-tongue) and they are not reducible to any one of the poles of exchange. Again, the idea of pulsation that we discussed in Chapter 4 appears to capture the movement of translators in very different contexts without needing to have recourse to binary reductionism.

This very mobility and flexibility of translators that permits the circulation of goods, people and ideas in human society accounts for their foundational influence in different cultures, but it may also paradoxically account for their invisibility and not only for reasons of the distrust of the hybrid that we noted in science fiction representations of translators. In the last chapter we discussed Georg Simmel's essay on money with respect to translation and the teleological chain. There is another observation of Simmel's regarding money that is pertinent to our analysis here. Simmel notes that one of the salient features of money is that it is the intersecting point for a large number of ends. Money can be used to do all kinds of different things and this polyvalency produces an absence of distinct value:

> Just as very versatile people, active in a great many directions, easily give the impression of a certain lack of character, a lack of any definite coloration, which is more appropriate to a one-sided and pronounced nature, so a kind of psychological interference effect also enters in the

case of money, because the qualitative plenitude of the ends that are gathered together in it place it somehow between all qualities, and thereby deprive it of any specific psychological coloration, which always possesses a somewhat one-sided trait.[43]

Translators are by professional necessity 'very versatile people' and it is interesting to speculate whether the protean nature of their work, the use of translation for very different ends – from the scientific to the commercial to the literary and political – leads to the absence of coloration to which Simmel refers. Thus, though they are important agents of circulation and openness and renewal in society, translators (who occupy in-between spaces, and are therefore not 'one-sided', and who, in addition, tend to work in many different areas, particularly in smaller markets) do not have the distinctive 'coloration' of those who are less nomadic and multifarious in their activities.

If translators and travellers engage in a dialogue with languages and cultures, Karlheinz Stierle reminds us that, 'In every dialogue, there is an interplay between distance and closeness, difference and resemblance, which reminds us of the structure of metaphor. In metaphor two poles have to work together in order to bridge a semantic gap.'[44] The importance of metaphor for travel writing can hardly be overstated. The word itself in its Greek origins implies carrying, movement or displacement and, as Michel de Certeau has pointed out, it is still used in modern Greek by removal companies.[45] As writing is not reality, the images of metaphors are a way of visualising the real, *a fortiori* when the reality is foreign to the reader. In addition, metaphors through the pairing of the familiar and the alien allow travel writers to introduce different kinds of heterogenous material into their texts. Christine Montalbetti in *Le Voyage, le monde et la bibliothèque* sees metaphor as a way of enabling travel writers to overcome the fundamental gap between the library and the world. She points out that, like fiction in general, metaphor implies a willing suspension of disbelief as loves are obviously not red roses unless the poet is a flower fetishist and hallucinates. More generally Montalbetti claims:

> la notion de *transport*, qui fonde la structure de la métaphore dans la définition aristotélicienne, contamine sa lecture: comme la figure opère un *déplacement*, le lecteur se trouve *transporté* d'un champ à un autre, selon une dynamique du même type que celle qui fonde la lecture de la fiction, comme elle de l'ordre de la substitution d'espaces, et de *l'échappée*; . . .[46]
> (her emphasis)

Metaphors are frequently viewed in translation studies as a problem to be overcome rather than a process to be analysed. Given the prevalence of metaphor in everyday discourse, most translators do indeed have to deal with the very real problem of transferring metaphor from one language to the other. However, there is a relationship between translation, metaphor and travel that goes beyond the incidence of free and fixed modulation in translation practice. Metaphor, like play, is paradoxical. It links two disparate semantic fields that are not normally linked. The metaphor depends for its dramatic effect on the two notions or images remaining separate while they must, at the same time, be joined together if the metaphor is to make any sense. Through its paradoxical status, metaphor, like play, allows the unlikely, or in some cases the impossible to happen. James Carse argues that, in joining like to unlike, metaphor is emblematic of all language: 'At its root, all language has the character of metaphor, because no matter what it intends to be about it remains language and remains absolutely unlike whatever it is about.'[47] If Carse is expressing here the similarities between the arbitrary nature of signifiers in language and the operations of metaphor, it is interesting to note the attention drawn to the presence/absence feature of language. Metaphor draws our attention to what is not there, to unlikely or surprising associations, which most of the time are absent in the reader's and indeed, presumably, the writer's mind. Much as play activities are found acceptable because they are framed as play, metaphorical statements would be deemed nonsensical if they were taken literally, if metaphorical interpretive procedures were not applied.

Arthur Koestler's distinction between association and bisociation offers a suggestive link between metaphor and translation that can ultimately be related to travel or the nomadic. Koestler advances the thesis that, 'associative routine means thinking according to a given set of rules on a single plane, as it were. The bisociative act means combining two different sets of rules, to live on several planes at once.'[48] Bisociative thinking, by combining two previously unrelated areas in a new synthesis, both typifies the way original insights emerge and demonstrates the metaphorical nature of inventive thought. By virtue of its role in preparing humans to create possible frames for unlikely situations, travel prepares the way for metaphor and discovery. In the travel text, part of the enjoyment is found in the sense of revelation that comes from the association of the like and the unlike in metaphor, pointing to the cognitive possibilities of travel writing. Like metaphor, translation joins together the like and the unlike, two disparate languages. The languages are joined, which is why the translation makes sense, but they are at the same time separate, for translations imply a distinct original. Furthermore, the bisociative quality of metaphor is present also in the translator's constant movement between different languages and cultures. The translator must, by definition, operate on two or more planes at any given time. The tangible expression for translators of this perpetual commerce is what Koestler calls the 'A-ha!' experience. This occurs when the translator is translating a text and comes across a word or often an expression for which there is no immediately obvious translation.

Minutes, hours, days can be spent searching for an appropriate equivalent and then, all of a sudden, the *mot juste* appears and there is the sudden release of discovery. It is arguably this bisociative process that is being alluded to in Romantic and Hermeneutic theories of the creative 'energy' of translation.

Flâneur, flâneuse and taking a hint

When the search for equivalents takes time, it is usually because the purposeful exploration of translation solutions has proved fruitless. The translator has to move away from the straight and narrow paths of conventional equivalence to wider horizons of possibility. The translator, in the tradition of Baudelaire, Simmel, Benjamin and Bauman, becomes a *flâneur*. The necessary backdrop for the urban strolling described by writers and critics is the city, and it also the city that Anthony Pym posits as the intercultural space *par excellence* for modern translators: 'cities, especially the larger cities, of our day, are now the privileged places for cultural intersections.'[49] For the *flâneur*, the city provided an exemplary space for seeking out various forms of otherness. In Eamonn Slater's words: 'the quest for different ways, different ideas, different peoples and different cultures was done mainly by walking about, without any clear purpose, but with an openness, an availability to whatever came the way of the stroller.'[50] This sense of openness and temporary abandonment of immediate purposefulness is the precondition for the element of creative, bisociative thinking in translation practice. Indeed, it could be argued that to see the translator as *flâneur* is to emphasise the epistemic as opposed to the solely instrumental function of translation. Translation is routinely defended on the grounds that it promotes understanding between peoples and cultures, facilitates trade and accelerates the exchange of ideas. In all these instances, translation is lauded because it is the instrument of *something else*: cultural understanding, trade, ideas. However, to present translation as at some level involving the inventive openness of the alert urban stroller suggests that the epistemic value of translation can lie *within* translation itself and does not always have to be sought externally.

Modernity's *flâneurs* were not only to be found on the streets of Paris, they were also to be found on the divans of Vienna. The classic psychoanalytic notions of free association and floating attention are strolls through the conscious and unconscious mind that explore the inner otherness of self and that yield, in the best of cases, the bisociative insights of interpretation. In this context, it is interesting to relate Adam Phillips' discussion of the phenomenon of hinting to the teaching and apprenticeship of translation. In his collection of essays *The Beast in the Nursery* Phillips asks the question as to why people come to psychoanalysis in the first place:

> People come for psychoanalysis when they are feeling undernourished;
> and this is either – depending on one's psychoanalytic preferences –
> because what they have been given wasn't good enough, so they couldn't
> do enough with it; or because there is something wrong with their capac-
> ity for transformation. In James's terms, they are the failed artists of their
> own lives.[51]

What is important is not so much what we are given (children do not
choose their parents) as what we do with what we are given. Our appetite
for life is related to our capacity for transformation. However, change that
occurs under coercion becomes not so much transformation as (dis)simula-
tion. Philips makes a distinction between an order and a hint, 'An order, in
some fundamental sense, can only be accepted or rejected; it cannot like a
hint be easily used.'[52] A good hint is always unintentional and a calculated
hint is something of a contradiction in terms. In dreams, reality functions
more as a hint than an instruction or an order, thus allowing dreamers to
effect their own work of transformation. Similarly, analysts by offering hints
rather than orders (or orders disguised as hints) undo 'the patient's habitual
defensive associations in the service of spontaneous recombinations. Loose
ends become newer beginnings.'[53]

If hints are essential factors in the transformative work of infant and
adult life, what are the implications for teaching? In a 1950 lecture given to
students of psychology and social work entitled, 'Yes, but how do we know
it's true?', D.W. Winnicott claims that there are two stages in the learning of
psychology. The first stage is when psychology is learned like any other
subject. The second stage is when the student realises that psychology is
not like any other subject and that it cannot be learned the same way: 'It
has to be felt as real, or else it is irritating, or even maddening.'[54] The first
stage is what Freud calls identification and Winnicott compliance, where
the student is primarily complying with the teacher's and the culture's
expectations, imitating someone who knows these things. In the second
stage, which corresponds to dream-work for Freud and object-usage for
Winnicott, the students find those bits and pieces of knowledge that are felt
to have real meaning. The subject is radically recontextualised to produce
personal significance for the student. This may involve sustained criticism
to see what survives the attack or the teaching may be the dream-day
where the student unwittingly selects material to be transformed in that
night's dreaming. Philips draws the following conclusion from Winnicott's
observations:

> One is that people can learn but that they can't be taught; or, at least, they
> can't be taught anything of real significance. And this is partly because no
> one – neither student nor teacher – can ever know beforehand exactly what

is of personal significance; that is, exactly what a person will find significant, select out to dream with, to remember or to forget; to work on.[55]

Therefore, just as a good interpretation is one that is not intended as a
hint by the analyst but is taken as one by the patient, 'the best kind of teaching . . . is all hinting'.[56]

Is the learning of translation comparable to the learning of psychology as
presented by Winnicott? Is there a sense in which translation students can
learn but cannot be taught? The proposition appears heretical and would set
to nought the considerable investment of time and effort in translation pedagogy in recent decades. However, it is possible to argue that the notion of
'hinting' has a certain applicability to the teaching of translation. A common
problem in translation pedagogy is progression. How do you structure a
course so that both the teacher and student have the impression that they
are making progress in their learning, advancing from the relatively easy to
the progressively more difficult? Mona Baker and Jean Delisle, for example,
in their respective textbooks, offer a comprehensive coverage of the main
problems encountered by translators in translating texts. The problems are
presented in discrete sections and chapters, which makes perfect sense from
the point of view of clarity of exposition.[57] The difficulty arises when authentic texts are used, because it is a common feature of texts to present many
translation problems all at once rather than in pedagogic isolation. The
teacher can of course decide to stress one particular aspect of translation
practice, such as the translation of idiom, one week and to concentrate on
the translation of relative clauses the next, but the profusion of textual detail
with its plethora of translation difficulties can often obscure the momentary
emphasis on one particular problem. The frustration that results can lead to
pressure for the kind of solution identified in the first stage of Winnicott's
psychology learning experience. The equivalent first stage in translation
teaching would be imitation, where the student 'imitates' the teacher's fair
copy which is seen as the correct, legitimate translation. Even where the
teacher does not have a physical fair copy, in the classroom, a 'virtual' fair
copy will be pieced together by the students through collating the teacher's
explicit or implicit preferences for particular translation solutions. The difficulty with this first stage where the student acts like one who knows is that
it ultimately becomes 'irritating, or even maddening', because the translation activity is not felt as real, it is not the student who is 'really' doing the
translating. It is only by a successful transition to the second stage that
students begin to see what in translation practice is significant for them,
what 'really' works. One approach is to adopt Winnicott's notion of 'object-
usage' and attack the translation object to see what resists. Thus,
translations produced by translators other than the teacher (for reasons of
the internal power dynamic) or produced by other classmates and presented

anonymously for group discussion can be the objects of a liberating critique. The other element of second-stage learning is by definition difficult to articulate in programmatic terms: this is the element of 'hinting' in translation pedagogy. This element becomes clearer perhaps if we link it to the nomadic and see the object of translator education as the formation of the translator as *flâneur*, the encouragement of floating attention, an open-ended, inquisitive attentiveness that explores affinities as against forcing relations. As we have already noted, a calculated hint is a contradiction in terms but it is possible to argue that, for example, more extensive use of parallel texts, corpora and translation autobiography, as well as a teaching practice that favours questions (genuine ones, not disguised orders) over prescriptions, can favour a learning style that allows students to transform the contact hours in the translation classroom into a dream of understanding rather than a nightmare of incomprehension. Progression in this nomadic perspective on teaching is as much about *digression* as *progression*. There will be a certain amount of wandering, the student will feel anxious or lost and hanker after the guide book of the fair copy, but disorientation is the necessary prelude to any experience of authentic discovery.

The figuration of the *flâneur* is never innocent. Eeva Jokinen and Soile Veijola stress the gendered nature of many representations of the *flâneur* and argue, 'A flâneur is a man, by definition, or a woman dressed as a man. Women, instead, are part of the spectacle – flâneuring – among the curiosities of the flâneur's interest.'[58] Thus, the most prominent female city-dwellers are prostitutes, widows, old ladies, murder victims, lesbians and passing, unknown women. Window-shopping as a seemingly purposeful activity does not, for example, qualify as genuine flâneuring.[59] Jokinen and Veijola take four nomadic figures presented by Zygmunt Bauman as emblematic of postmodernity – the stroller, vagabond, tourist and player – and translate them into other figures to make their sexed nature explicit.[60] The stroller is reconfigured as the paparazzo, the vagabond as the homeless drunk, the tourist as the sextourist and the player as the womaniser. According to the two Finnish scholars, 'when the sexed nature of these social figures is rendered explicit, the illusion that they represent humanity in general is destroyed; the universal "post-modern self", which we found presupposed in Bauman's original gallery, is shattered.'[61] As a corrective to the predominantly male representations of the nomad, stranger and adventurer, they offer the figures of the babysitter and the au-pair. The babysitter experiences a dwelling-in-travelling that has a markedly intersemiotic element and is expressed metaphorically, 'She is in a familiar surrounding (we all know a home, don't we?). At the same time she does not know where the salt is. She usually knows the language but the baby does not. Nevertheless, they have a language, that of touching, singing, caressing. The metaphor of babysitting unites and separates, as all good metaphors do.'[62] Babies can be minded, of course, further away from home, and often one of the only ways for an adolescent girl or a young woman to get on the road is to work abroad as an au-pair, thus experiencing another form of dwelling-in-travelling. Significantly, the work of the au-pair often involves dwelling temporarily in another language: 'The au-pair enters – not only a foreign culture, a foreign locality, a foreign family, but also – a foreign language. In more than one sense, she has left all her homes/houses, in order to enter a totally strange symbolic order, a configuration of a foreign culture/language/household.'[63] One of the tasks of the au-pair is often to establish herself as a subject in the new language, if only to have some control over the situation in which she finds herself. The au-pair classically embodies the between-subject, engaged in constant translation between home and away, source culture and target culture, source language and target language. Many female students indeed work as au-pairs either before or during their translation studies. As we saw in Chapter 2, the predominantly female student body in translation schools in many Western countries points up the importance of the au-pair as a nomadic figure of translation. Contrary to the traditional gender bias with respect to grammatical number in Romance languages, the translator as *flâneuse* is a more all-encompassing figure of nomadic practice than the *flâneur* and is closer to the current realities of the modern translation profession.

Reciprocity, the third culture and cybertravel

The au-pair may need the foreign language as a basic survival skill but does anybody else? Is the insistent equation between language, culture and identity a reactionary throwback to Fichtean cultural nationalism and the catalogue of horrors generated by pathologies of difference over the last century? Are travellers better off ignoring the claims of languages and making do with a global *lingua franca* like English, which, if not the perfect language of the philosophers, at least allows people from different linguistic and cultural backgrounds to speak to each other? In an earlier period of linguistic debate, a standard defence of individual languages was to invoke linguistic relativism or the Sapir-Whorf hypothesis and argue that languages divide up realities in different ways and that languages determine the way their speakers think about the world.[64] The Eskimos with their innumerable words for snow were routinely held up as bearing eloquent lexical witness to the truth of the hypothesis. Few linguists, however, would defend the hypothesis in its strong form today and Geoffrey Pullum has revealed that even the Eskimo example is deeply flawed. Some more excitable linguistic commentators had attributed up to 400 words for snow to the Eskimo languages but Pullum demonstrates that there are only two relevant roots for snow in the air and snow on the ground listed in an authoritative Innuit dictionary and the other words are derived from these roots in much the same way as compound words are generated in English.[65] John Edwards voices the more usual consensus among linguists now when he claims 'that a "weak form" of the Sapir-Whorf hypothesis – that language influences our *customary* way of thinking – is both reasonable and unsurprising' (his emphasis).[66] Even in its weaker form, then, language can be accounted important in that, as Edwards' adjective suggests, language will affect the way its speakers usually view the world. The force of relativism can be felt in the problems that immediately arise in even the most apparently straightforward translations between languages, no matter how close they are. There is a sense, however, in which language knowledge is more than simply a question of world view. If languages are held to be, in part, constitutive of identity, then a failure to acknowledge this fact diminishes the specific presence of the speakers of the language. Writing on an exhibition staged in the Museum of Mankind in London which dealt with the theme of continuity and change in the New Guinea Highlands, James Clifford discusses different views of the nature of the relationship between the museum staff and the New Guinea highlanders as a result of the museum having purchased various objects from the highlanders. For the Melanesians, the purpose of payment is not to be quits but to stay in relation, to maintain a continuing relation of indebtedness. This is their understanding of reciprocity. Thus, as Clifford points out, 'A capitalist ideology of exchange posits individual transactions between partners who are free to engage or disengage; a Melanesian model may see ongoing relationships in which the wealthier partner is under a continuing obligation to share.' Understanding of reciprocity differs but, for Clifford, reciprocity 'is itself a translation term linking quite different regimes of power and relationality'.[67]

Though Clifford does not say this, one could go further and argue that reciprocity is not so much a translation 'term' as something inherent in the practice of translation itself. Translation as reciprocity takes two forms, autotranslation and heteronymous translation. In the case of auto-translation, speakers of a language translate themselves into the language of the other. Respect for the identity of the other, the demonstration of an express wish to celebrate specificity, involves learning the language of the host or travelee. The desire for reciprocity is articulated at its most basic level in the scattering of greetings in foreign languages that preface guide books. Heteronymous translation is translation that is provided by an intermediary in the form of an interpreter. Here the demands of difference and communication are reconciled. The employment of the interpreter is an acknowledgement of the right to a separate existence of another language and the speakers' entitlement to monoglossia, if that is their individual or collective choice. When Hugh O'Neill, the Gaelic Irish leader, went to London to negotiate with Elizabeth I he brought an interpreter, not because he could not speak English (he could) but because the presence of an interpreter implied that both languages, Irish and English, had equal cultural and political status. Both these forms of reciprocity can link different regimes of power and relationality, as we have seen in earlier chapters. Heteronymous translation offers considerable potential for obstruction, manipulation and misunderstanding, fears that have notably been articulated in the metaphorical and sometimes indeed literal arraignment of translators for high and low treason. Auto-translation has been widely practised not only as a tribute to the holiness of particulars but as a professional alibi for unscrupulous informers, proselytisers and traders, who see language as a strategy for expropriation rather than a pact of mutual respect. Reciprocity is always bounded then by the relationships of power that obtain between cultures at any given moment, but the demand for and acknowledgement of *symmetrical reciprocity* is arguably a powerful motive for the continued value and existence of translation and language learning in a mobile world.

The difficulty is that reciprocity, of course, is differently interpreted by the various actors in linguistic and cultural exchange. Anthony Pym, drawing on the work of Robert O. Keohane, argues that one of the functions of a 'regime' (the implicit or explicit principles, norms, rules and decision-making procedures that are shared by a group of states in international relations) is to 'control the transaction costs involved in the transfer of information'. If the transaction costs are high, the regime will not be very effective and few negotiations will take place. On the other hand, 'if the transaction costs are extremely low, we are likely to form unstable transitory alliances between any number of cultures; none of our relations will develop strong patterns; the regime will fail to build up the relations of trust or predictability required for cooperation.'[68] Translation is a transaction cost and Pym sees the parabolic rise and fall of translation activity at different times in different cultures as pointing to the unsustainable long-term cost of translation. Translation is understood here as heteronymous rather than auto-translation. The perennial difficulty in relations between nations is that transaction costs are not all equally determined by the parties to a relationship. In other words, dominant languages will see no reason to increase transaction costs by having recourse to translation (of the auto- or heteronymous variety) and weaker, lesser-used or minority languages will not have the political or economic power to insist on reciprocity. While ethnic groups or nations may enter into relationships because they need to be part of a telecommunications network or to fly their planes safely or to have access to a clean water supply, this does not necessarily mean that they willingly renounce the right to use their own language. They often have no choice in the matter. In addition, writers, linguists and cultural activists may see the relationship between language and culture and translation as important, but this point of view need not necessarily be shared by specialists in other disciplines who sit at negotiating tables. Particularly in view of the fact that the very notion of 'costs' is frequently understood in strictly economic and utilitarian terms (and the strong are frequently reluctant to bear the linguistic costs of the weak), instrumental pragmatism rather than any symmetrical reciprocity will guide policy decisions with respect to language and translation.

The parallel with the position of minority languages within nation-states is revealing in this respect. The dominant language and its expansion will appear natural while the intervention of the state to protect a weaker language is often presented as unnatural. The efforts of states to actively promote languages in a minority position is equally derided by the Left (the unacceptable face of ethnic nationalism) and the Right (a waste of taxpayers' money). Underlying both positions is a deeply conservative commitment to the rightness of pragmatic materialism. In this vision of things, material circumstances are immutable – for example, in the Irish case, the Irish changed language for material reasons because 'there is no doubt English was . . . the language of survival and social advancement'[69] – and any attempt to counter the implacable logic of this materialist monoglossia is seen as either another example of the interventionist monstrosity of central government (Right) or a further example of suspect bourgeois idealism (Left). In intercultural relations, one person's transaction cost is another's cultural entitlement and when social costs are ignored, as they frequently are in narrower versions of accountancy and budgetary practice, translation and/or language acquisition will be seen as a wasteful superfluity by the culturally and linguistically powerful. High transaction costs may be described as inefficient but, as the writer and broadcaster Charles Handy has pointed out, 'Efficiency calculations are ring-fenced, confined to the economics of the particular unit; they are local and partial, which leaves society in general to pay for the unintended outcomes.'[70] Even if there is an awareness of the dangers of excessively low transaction costs for the establishment of trust and predictability, the awareness may result in a version of intercultural studies that is largely language-free (as is evident in certain North American 'intercultural communication' programmes). Intercultural studies in this perspective becomes a checklist of cultural differences (when you should take off your shoes in Japan, why you shouldn't offer chrysanthemums to your hosts at a French dinner-party), cross-border rules of etiquette, that see reciprocity as cultural sensitivity independent of language. Though such sensitivity is obviously desirable, even necessary, a notion of reciprocity which does not extend to the other, where possible, the basic courtesy of language difference appears greatly diminished.[71]

In the educational programme outlined in *Le Tiers-Instruit*, Michel Serres sees the equal importance of the humanities and sciences in producing the 'third' person, an educated human being. Despite the stated intent of educational systems throughout the world to attend to these dual areas of knowledge, the renowned physicist Murray Gell-Man articulated a familiar cultural schism when he claimed:

> there are people in the arts and humanities – conceivably, even in some social sciences – who are proud of knowing very little about science and technology, or about mathematics. The opposite phenomenon is very rare. You may occasionally find a scientist who is ignorant of Shakespeare, but you will never find a scientist who is *proud* of being ignorant of Shakespeare.[72] (his emphasis)

A translator who is 'proud of knowing very little about science and technology' is not likely to get very much work in the modern world. An English-language translator who was 'ignorant of Shakespeare' would find that whole areas of idiomatic resource and cultural allusion in the language were off-bounds. When 'intercultural studies' is invoked in translation studies, the term is almost invariably used to describe an interaction between languages and ethnic or national cultures. However, it is also possible to see translation studies as another form of intercultural studies in the sense of bridging the gap between the two cultures of science and the arts/humanities. The music critic and archaeologist Jamie James has denounced this gap as evidence of the 'psychotic bifurcation in our civilisation' and claims that 'In this era of over-specialization, what passes for a Renaissance man is a biologist who goes to the opera twice a year, or a poet who uses the laws of planetary motion as a metaphor for love.'[73] The translator is not only a nomad between ethnic/national cultures but s/he is also a traveller between disciplinary cultures. Curiously, this aspect of translation studies is underplayed and often indeed (though not always) writing on translation studies can reflect the 'two cultures' rift, with theoreticians choosing to dwell exclusively on the problems of either 'literary' or 'technical' translation, a division that is also mirrored in national translators' associations and the organisation of panels at translation conferences. Translation involves working with language and texts and is thus firmly anchored in the humanities but much of the material that is translated by translators, when not of a commercial nature, is scientific and technical and thus requires an understanding of fundamental scientific concepts. Translators can, and indeed many do, specialise but specialisation is a function of the size of the market and many translators will find themselves at some stage in their career translating a wide variety of texts, particularly in smaller markets or lesser-used languages. Thus, their work is conspicuously intercultural in an age of (disciplinary) monocultural specialisation. In many respects, the translator has the omnivorous passions of the traveller. The travel account as a digressive genre is characterised by the extreme eclecticism of the narrative focus. Bill Bryson comments on British food, politics, town planning, public transport, weather forecasts, language, and these are but some of the topics. Jacques Lacarrière discusses, among other subjects, the massacre of animals on French roads, the sex life of slugs, the uncharted immensity of French rural vocabulary and why Jesus should appear in modern iconography as a car mechanic not a shepherd. The capaciousness of the travel book makes it a deeply attractive form of expression for writers animated by an intense curiosity in the variousness of human knowledge and experience. Nicolas Bouvier has described the pleasures of this curiosity that informs his own travel writing:

> Depuis la toute petite enfance, j'ai une fringale de connaissances disparates et un peu tizganes. Je chéris ce qu'on appelle la culture générale et je me bricole de petits morceaux de savoir comme on ramasserait les morceaux épars d'une mosaïque détruite, partout où je peux, sans esprit de système. Et je vois ces choses se mettre en place, d'une façon mystérieuse, comme à l'intérieur d'une sphère où tout conspirerait à achever une sorte d'ensemble harmonique, polyphonique.[74]

The translator and the interpreter, moving between disciplines, between the allusive language of general culture and the hermetic sublanguages of specialisms, are practitioners in a sense of the encyclopedic culture of travel, of a *third culture* that is inclusive not only of the classic polarities of the humanities and sciences but of many other areas of human enquiry. In an era of disciplinary parochialism, the third wo/man as translator or travel writer is valuable as a nomad bringing us the news from elsewhere. This specificity grounded in diversity should be cherished and it seems an impoverishment for translator training institutions to concentrate exclusively on one kind of translation, with students doing only technical/commercial translation and no literary translation, or vice-versa. The risks of superficiality and dilettantism are, of course, real in a more ambitious vision of translator education but it would be deeply regrettable if translation studies were to abandon the nomadic adventurousness of their calling. In addition, there is a sense in which late modernity, while driven by the evangel of specialisation, is also pre-eminently a period of the relative decline of what were seen as stable, permanent institutions – the Fordist factory, the nuclear family, the nation-state – and of the rise of looser, more flexible relationships between individuals and institutions. Change is nothing new, of course, and adaptation to changing developmental conditions rather than the observance of uniform and unchanging forms of behaviour has been a general characteristic of modernity. However, the experience of recent decades, as we saw in Chapter 4, has been an acceleration in the rate of change. McKinsey, the consulting firm, estimate that the speed of data transmission will have increased by a factor of 45 by the year 2005.[75] The rapid circulation of goods, people and ideas that is the hallmark of the new 'economy of signs and spaces' (Urry and Lash) underlines the increased importance of adaptive skills in a rapidly changing environment. In the 'The Pivotal Status of the Translator's Habitus', Daniel Simeoni stresses the importance of the adaptive faculty in any definition of the translatorial habitus. Simeoni claims that, unlike European writers in the seventeenth and eighteenth centuries, 'most translators currently practice their trade in highly differentiated societies where clients, tasks and contracts tend to be widely contrasted.' He then asks whether the elusive faculty of translating today could 'primarily be one of *adjusting* to different types of norms, making the most of them under widely varying circumstances' (his emphasis), and whether the cognitive specificity of a translating faculty could have 'less to do with language and verbalisation than with social cognition and sensitivity, interaction with the outside world and beyond that, perhaps, adaptive movement, or motor control?'[76] Though in our third culture model, 'language and verbalisation' remain crucial elements of the translator's hybridity, Simeoni's emphasis on adaptive movement allows us to see the translator as a strikingly representative figure of late modernity. In a world of flexible accumulation, time-to-market procedures and lean production, the cognitive specificity of the translation faculty underlined by Simeoni means that translators rather than being valuable heirlooms of a vanishing craft industry have the epistemic and ontological flexibility of independent travellers who must adapt to all manner of different peoples, places, languages and cultures and are thus at 'home' in a globalised age.[77]

Des Esseintes in Joris-Karl Huysmans's *À rebours* (1884) asked the famous question as to why it was necessary to travel at all when one could travel quite magnificently seated on a chair.[78] Xavier de Maistre almost a century earlier has the narrator of *Voyage autour de ma chambre* (1794) embark on a forty-two-day journey around his bedroom. The narrator notes that it is both 'utile et agréable d'avoir une âme dégagée de la matière'.[79] Freed from the physical limits of the body, the soul can travel endlessly in imaginative fancy, assisted in this sedentary odyssey by the dream-days of a good library. Des Esseintes and de Maistre's narrator in their disruptive ironies anticipate the nomadic reconfiguration of the digital age. William J. Mitchell, professor of architecture and media arts and sciences at MIT, describes himself in *City of Bits: Space, Place and the Infobahn* as follows: 'My name is wjm@mit.edu (though I have many aliases), and I am an electronic *flâneur*. I hang out on the network.'[80] The Internet (or Net) with its world-wide computer network is saturated with the metaphors of movement and travel: surfing; information superhighway; infobahn; infonauts; (Netscape) navigators; the electronic frontier. The purple prose of cyberhype is the visionary rhetoric of the pilgrim brethren. Mitch Kapor and John Perry Barlow note that,

> In its present condition, cyberspace is a frontier region, populated by the few hardy technologists who can tolerate the austerity of its savage

computer interfaces, incompatible communication protocols, proprietary
barricades, cultural and legal ambiguities, and general lack of useful maps
or metaphors.[81]

Surfing on the Net then would appear to be the magnificent travel
announced by Des Esseintes. Going away no longer involves going out.
News, entertainment, education, work, shopping, come to the home via the
Net and the 'domestic living room is emerging as a major site at which digi-
tally displaced activities are recombining and regrounding themselves in the
physical world.'[82] This is de Maistre's *chambre* as the interface between
bodies and bits, a site for electronic flâneuring or 'browsing' (an echo here of
text and movement).

The paradox is that the increased velocity of the modern age, the acceleration of movement, leads to more and more advanced degrees of inertia.
The passenger seated in a train, a car, an airplane, the cosmonaut or astro-
naut strapped to his/her seat in a rocket or space shuttle, is going faster and
faster but is moving less and less. Alain Borer claims that, in the age of
Armstrong, 'la figure du voyageur est désormais l'immobilité.'[83] Walking on
the moon is an ironic postscript to the evolution of travel, a reminder of how
extreme movement leads to the cessation of movement. For Paul Virilio, the
audiovisual vehicle is the ultimate vehicle, the static vehicle that will at last
'bring about the victory of sedentariness'.[84] From the television to the
computer and the Net, the telematics revolution means that everything will
happen to us without our even having to set out. Virilio conflates the chair of
Des Esseintes and the bedroom of de Maistre in his image of a sedentary
future. He details the interactive dwelling:

> this residential cell that has left the extension of the habitat behind it and
> whose most important piece of furniture is the *seat*, the ergonomic arm-
> chair of the handicapped's motor and – who knows? – the bed, a canopy
> bed for the infirm voyeur, a divan for being dreamt of without dreaming, a
> bench for being circulated without circulating.[85]

The picture of the residential cell does not tally with the fact that more and
more people than ever before on the planet are on the move (even if, to get
from one location to the other, they are often immobile). Tourism is fast
becoming the world's largest item of trade, and mobility as much as
immobility is the watchword of our age, as we have seen throughout this
book. The forms of travel are as various as its destinations and there are
any number of ways to experience the sensation of travel, from hitch-hiking
to Net surfing. Thus, it may be more useful to think of virtual travel on the
Net not as a substitute for real travel, the logical *telos* of nomadic
(post)modernity, but as another form of travel, a form that has particular
importance for the history of travel because of its insistent nomadic self-
presentation.

How does this new form of travel that we might term for the sake of convenience 'cybertravel' relate to issues that we have raised concerning language, translation and travel? A salient difference between cybertravel and forms of travel previously discussed is the disembodied nature of the cybertraveller. William J. Mitchell's e-mail address specifies virtual but not real location. The message comes with an address but the address does not tell you whether the message was sent while the author was in bed, in the office, on a transatlantic plane or in the snug of a Dublin bar (using a mobile phone). The location of the author is in a real sense indeterminate. However, it is not only the physical location of the sender that is difficult to determine, it is also his/her identity, the potential subversiveness of the 'many aliases' to which Mitchell refers. The potential for disguise is particularly apparent in software constructions known as MUDs, originally Multi-User Dungeons, latterly defined as, Multiple-User Domains. They provide the settings for online, interactive role-playing games where each player constructs an online persona by choosing a name and writing a description of themselves that can be seen by the other players that they encounter. In one example of a MUD, LucasFilm's *Habitat*, it was established that at any given time approximately 15 per cent of the players were engaged in cross-dressing or crossgender behaviour. For Allucquère Roseanne Stone, the 'virtual age' that has succeeded the mechanical age is not so much about virtual reality as about the changing relationship between the self and the body and between the individual and the group in the social spaces of computer networks: 'I characterize this relationship as virtual because the accustomed facticity of human bodies is changing.'[86] If the self is no longer defined by the physical body in physical space, then virtual space allows for a multiplication of selves, and the 'multiple' being for Stone is the socialiser within computer networks, 'a being warranted to, but outside of, a single physical body.'[87] Networks, then, allow for a displacement from a familiar self that is profoundly therapeutic: 'The technosocial space of virtual systems, with its irruptive ludic quality and its potential for experimentation and emergence, is a domain of nontraumatic multiplicity.'[88]

It is significant that, though the cybertraveller is disembodied, the virtual space of computer networks replicates the traditional functions of travel and travel literature. From Odysseus returning to Ithaca to Isabelle Eberhardt travelling through North Africa, disguise has been a part of the panoply of travel. Changing your clothes, your hair, your skin, learning a language, acquiring an accent, altering your habits – these have figured as means used by travellers to try out different personalities, experience different (and familiar situations) from another point of view. The difference is, of course, that in real travel the body itself is the site of the personality change, whereas in virtual travel personalities can be adopted or abandoned without any visible alteration to the body. In this respect, however, virtual or

cybertravel is like travel literature. In the more personal, subjective narrative of the sentimental traveller as opposed to the more objectifying
narrative of the manners-and-customs traveller, the reader was invited to
enter into complicity with the traveller.[89] The reader identifies with the
narrator of the travel account and mentally travels with the narrator *as if*
s/he were on the same journey, as if s/he were that traveller in
Afghanistan, Cork or Madagascar. Reading travel narratives is an experiment in multiple personality, made possible by a ludic *as if* quality that
characterises fiction generally and is translated in travel literature into the
narrative devices (first-person narration, dialogue, dramatic juxtaposition,
characterisation and so on) that are employed to sustain the reader's interest and facilitate identification with the narrator. It could be argued that,
whereas MUD personalities are constructed, the place of the reader is a
given in travel narratives. However, this is to ignore the active labour of
empathy, projection and identification involved in reading travel accounts
and also the extent to which in the case of multiple player games, for
example, experiment with personality is powerfully determined by intertextual constraints (characters from films, comic strips, video games, literature
itself). Thus, 'the technosocial spaces of virtual systems' are distinctive in
allowing for a form of disembodied travel but travel myths and travel
writing have long offered listeners/readers a domain of 'nontraumatic
multiplicity'.

Mitchell observes that, as bandwidth expands and computers become
even more powerful, cyberspace places will look, sound and feel more real-
istic. They will become more obviously multisensory. In the future,

> Robotic effectors combined with audio and video sensors will provide
> telepresence. Intelligent exoskeletal devices (data gloves, data suits,
> robotic prostheses, intelligent second skins, and the like) will both sense
> gestures and serve as output devices by exerting controlled forces and
> pressures.[90]

It will be possible to initiate a conversation by shaking hands at a distance
and say goodnight to a child by transmitting a kiss across continents. In this
version of virtual connectivity, the body is engaged but distant, the teleac-
tors are Simmel's Strangers, caught between corporeal proximity and
distance. If this multisensory technology develops to the degree envisioned
by Mitchell, then there will be a distinct intersemiotic dimension to cybertravel where the sensuous geographies of elsewhere will be replicated in
cyberspace. The multisensory reconstruction of Away at Home is already
apparent in large shopping centres and malls in the West where 'ethnic'
shops and restaurants try to recreate the sensation of being in the foreign
country through sound (music, backstage employees speaking ethnic
language), taste (food, drink), sight (posters, postcards, video clips), touch

(food, ethnic fabrics) and smell (plants, oils, joss sticks, food). After the Irish theme pubs from Tallinn to Tokyo comes the Irish Pub on the Net. When these virtual pubs become multisensory experiences, then cybertravel will have entered a dimension that will unsettle conventional notions of home. The travel writer Pico Iyer notes that, 'As time goes on I try to find ways of formulating how to define home and how to choose between the different locations I have known. I think of it as something that propels you away from it.'[91] The potential for being propelled away from home while still remaining physically inside it is sketched out by the new technologies of virtual reality, but whether human bodies will be happy to surrender real for virtual geography is another matter.

The relationship between translation, speed and technology was discussed in the last chapter, but what of the role of language and translation in the new 'bitsphere', the worldwide electronically mediated environment in which networks are everywhere and where 'most of the objects that function within it (at every scale from nano to global) have intelligence and telecommunications capabilities'?[92] How will language and translation figure in cybertravel as opposed to the forms of travel examined in the first three chapters of this book? Comments can, of course, only be speculative. A predictable future is no longer a future, only an extension of the present. Going beyond the obvious necessity for multilingual web development and the impact of this development on the localisation industry and the much greater use of machine translation, there are two areas of potential change that merit brief comment. The first of these is the development of software surrogates or semi-autonomous software agents that are deputed to perform various tasks for the computer user such as filtering e-mail, scanning news services, consulting databases. Steve G. Weinberg describes these applications that would allow, for example, a client while away from his/her computer to perform a specialised database search, as '"applets"'. He claims, 'Applets will begin to resemble agents – nomadic programs sent out to find and gather information.'[93] Mitchell, for his part, argues, 'While the Net disembodies human subjects, it can artificially embody these software go-betweens.'[94] It is significant that familiar metaphors recur here of nomadic subjects and go-betweens. There is no reason to believe that these applets might not at some stage act as translators, finding material in the foreign language and translating it into the target language of the user, functioning in effect as a heteronymous translation aid for the cybertraveller. As voice recognition, speech synthesis and automatic interpreting systems developed, the software agents might in time function as interpreters. The fact that these developments may be a long way off, given the scale of the problems that remain to be surmounted, is not particularly relevant. Human translators and interpreters will still be busy catering for the real and virtual (web pages) needs of travellers for many years to come but their cyber equivalents will in all likelihood be a part of our new millennium. Just as viruses, however, have thwarted the best efforts of system designers to construct secure, stable computer environments, suitably skilled hackers will doubtless find their own way to exploit the doubleness of the 'go-betweens' and program resistant or subversive software (double) agents. A second arena of change will be the setting for our translation *flâneuse*. If the city has classically drawn in translators from the periphery to service the centre and translators have often felt at 'home' in the intercultural spaces of large, cosmopolitan cities, the technosocial space of computer networks may emerge as the new locus of translation communities. Already, these groups have begun to cluster around newsgroups, bulletin boards, formal and informal e-mail lists and the occasional on-line conference, but these contacts can only increase and intensify over time.[95] The Net has obvious instrumental advantages for translators in terms of accessing information, advertising services, overcoming geographical peripherality, and being itself a potential source of localisation employment. However, its more enduring importance may turn out to be as a site for the constitution of new virtual communities of translators who will be the cyberspace equivalents of what once constituted the translation hubs of Toledo, Louvain or Paris. Of course, the genuine 'interculturality' of these communities will depend, in part, on the extent to which Anglo-American language and culture does or does not act as an hegemonic force but also on questions of access. Just as cities traditionally have their social geographies of poverty and privilege, and certain areas are 'no-go' areas for the rich (fear of being robbed) and for the poor (fear of police harassment), the 'bitsphere' will have its own problems of access, commercialisation of networks and exclusion zones. When only 3 per cent of the world's population have access to a personal computer, many of the world's translators will find themselves *extra-muros*, forbidden by economic disadvantage from strolling through the 'capital of the twenty-first century', the City of Bits.[96]

The patterns of exclusion that increasingly characterise cities, virtual or otherwise, are maps of fear. Richard Sennett logs the consequences of enclosed indifference:

> A city ought to be a school for learning how to lead a centred life. Through exposure to others, we might learn how to weigh what is important and what is not. We need to see differences on the streets or in other people neither as threats nor as sentimental invitations, rather as necessary visions. They are necessary for us to learn how to navigate life with balance, both individually and collectively.[97]

In our journey through the chapters of this book we have tried to describe and measure the impact of linguistic exposure to others, how we learn or sometimes refuse to learn from our travels in a world of language(s).

Differences of language are indeed often seen as either the polyglot threat of immigration or as the sentimental invitation of a facile exoticism. Only more rarely are the exposure to language through travel and the accompanying practices of translation seen as the necessary vision of what might constitute our humanity in late modernity. The central argument of the work has been that the traveller as translator and the translator as traveller have much to teach us about learning to navigate a life on a post-Babelian planet.

The City of God may be virtual but our human cities remain shockingly alive in their plurality of sight and speech. It is a Thursday in November and the city of Stockholm is drenched in brightness. Water and bridges and the faded ochres of Venice on wood and stone. There is Swedish on the streets and in the shops. Two of my companions speak Dutch, the third is a Norwegian translator. The variousness of the world seems inexhaustible on a morning like this and Babel a miracle of particulars. Kenneth White speaks of the geopoetic adventure, the discovery of an elsewhere within and without. Here, in blanched sunlight, on the flagstones of a city fading to love-liness, languages and memory mingle in the sustained, enduring wonderwork of human geopoetics.

NOTES AND REFERENCES

Introduction: Floating Territories

1 Bram Stoker, *Dracula*, 1897, London, Dent, rpt. 1993, p. 20.
2 Roman Jakobson, 'On Linguistic Aspects of Translation', Rainer Schulte and John Biguenet, *Theories of Translation: An Anthology of Essays from Dryden to Derrida*, University of Chicago Press, 1992, pp. 144–51.
3 James Clifford, *Routes: Travel and Translation in the Late Twentieth Century*, London and Cambridge (Mass.), Harvard University Press, 1997.
4 Alan Bennett, 'What I Did in 1998', *London Review of Books*, vol. 20, no. 2, 21 January 1999, p. 3.
5 Zygmunt Bauman is particularly eloquent on the social stratification of a world where the prestigious, voluntary mobility of 'tourists' (film stars, singers, multi-national executives) contrasts with the suspect, enforced mobility of 'vagabonds' (economic refugees, asylum seekers, immigrants). See Zygmunt Bauman, *Globalization: The Human Consequences*, Cambridge, Polity, 1998, pp. 77-102.
6 Barbara Wilson, *Gaudí Afternoon*, Seattle, Seal Press, 1990, p. 3.

1: The Rambling House of Language

1 John Gibbons, *Tramping through Ireland*, London, Methuen, 1930, p. 1.
2 Gibbons, p. 6.
3 ibid., p. 12.
4 ibid., p. 18.
5 John Urry, *The Tourist Gaze*, London, Sage, 1990, pp. 1–15.
6 Paul Theroux, *The Kingdom by the Sea*, London, Penguin, 1984, p. 16.
7 Jacqueline Amati Mehler, Simona Argentieri and Jorge Canestri, *La Babel de l'inconscient: Langue maternelle, langues étrangères et psychanalyse*, tr. Maya Garboua, Paris, Presses Universitaires de France, 1994, p. 3.

   'Broadening the scope of our enquiry, admitting that it is possible to find an individual who really only speaks the mother tongue, "naturally" without interference from any other language, jargon or dialect, we must ask ourselves whether within the same language, in an apparently identical lexical, syntactic and grammatical context, every communication event, interpersonal or intrapsychic, does not always involve an unconscious act of "translation" and interpretation.'

8   Daniel Sibony, *Entre-Deux: L'origine en partage*, Paris, Seuil, 1991, p. 34.
    'This is the case for almost everybody: the father struggles with the
    language around him – the multiple language of the social order. The
    mother has her regretted origin (the house of her father, the time when she
    was a little girl, the time of her fantasy). And the child is always between
    two languages, not knowing which one to speak because each one is
    "impossible."'

9   Jonathan Raban, *Old Glory: An American Voyage*, London, Picador, 1986, p. 301.

10 Raban, *Old Glory*, p. 75.

11 Jonathan Raban, *Hunting Mister Heartbreak*, London, Picador, 1990, p. 144.

12 Paul Theroux, *The Kingdom by the Sea*, p. 214.

13 Bill Bryson, *Notes from a Small Island*, London, Black Swan, 1996.

14 Raban, *Heartbreak*, p. 229.

15 Raban, *Old Glory*, p. 386.

16 Roy Kerridge, *Jaunting through Ireland*, London, Michael Joseph, 1991, p. 315.

17 Bryson, *Notes*, pp. 342–3.

18 Theroux, *The Kingdom*, p. 224.

19 ibid., p. 224.

20 Edward Tylor, *Primitive Culture: Researches into the Development of Mythology,
    Philosophy, Religion, Language, Art and Customs*, London, 1871.

21 Theroux, *The Kingdom*, p. 263.

22 Charles Graves, *Ireland Revisited*, London, Hutchinson, 1949, p. 15.

23 Graves, p. 20.

24 ibid.

25 Bryson, *Notes*, p. 19.

26 Theroux, *The Kingdom*, p. 121.

27 Raban, *Heartbreak*, p. 128.

28 Raban, *Old Glory*, p. 312.

29 Raban, p. 317.

30 ibid., p. 319.

31 Georg Simmel, 'The Stranger', in Donald N. Levine, ed., *On Individuality and Social
    Forms*, University of Chicago Press, 1971, pp. 143–9.

32 Jonathan Raban, *Coasting*, London, Picador, 1986; Rosita Boland, *Sea Legs: Hitch-
    Hiking the Coast of Ireland Alone*, Dublin, New Island Books, 1992.

33 Benoît Mandelbrot, *The Fractal Geometry of Nature*, New York, Freeman, 1977.

34 James Gleick, *Chaos: Making a New Science*, London, Cardinal, 1987, p. 96.

35 Paul Fussell, *Abroad: British Literary Traveling Between the Wars*, New York, Oxford
    University Press, 1980.

36 For an account of the origins and history of anti-tourist discourse see James
    Buzard, *The Beaten Track: European Tourism, Literature and the Ways to 'Culture'
    1800–1918*, Oxford, Clarendon Press, 1993.

37 Boland, *Sea Legs*, p. 216.

38 Tim Robinson, *Stones of Aran: Labyrinth*, Dublin, Lilliput Press, 1995.

39 Theroux, *The Kingdom*, p. 29.

40 James Clifford, *Routes: Travel and Translation in the Late Twentieth Century*,
    London and Cambridge (Mass.), Harvard University Press, 1997, p. 204.

41 Raban, *Old Glory*, p. 461.

42 See Edgar Morin, *Penser l'Europe*, Paris, Gallimard, 1990, pp. 231–2.

43 Vertical travelling is defined here as *temporary* dwelling in travelling as distinct
    from the more permanent travelling implied by *residence*. It is necessary to make

the temporary/permanent distinction in order to retain the distinctiveness of travel itself. If everything is travel, nothing is travel.

44   Raban, *Old Glory*, p. 226.
45   Bryson, *Notes*, pp. 118–19.
46   Raban, *Heartbreak*, p. 91.
47   Amati Mehler, Argentieri, Canestri, *La Babel de l'inconscient*, p. 247.
      'Private language, infant language, the language of ideologies – sometimes explicit but more often than not hidden from the subject – language based on age and gender, must be considered as variables, not necessarily shared, even if one speaks the same language as a monolingual patient. Each analyst knows how many "translations" their own words and those of the patient need in order to become alike, to carry a shared meaning.'
48   Raban, *Old Glory*, p. 159.
49   Simmel, 'The Stranger', p. 145.
50   Chris Rojek and John Urry, 'Transformations of Travel and Theory', in Chris Rojek and John Urry, eds., *Touring Cultures: Transformations of Travel and Theory*, London, Routledge, 1997, p. 12.
51   Cited in John Edwards, *Multilingualism*, London, Penguin, 1995, p. 18.
52   Theroux, *The Kingdom*, p. 14.
53   Raban, *Heartbreak*, p. 272.
54   Diarmuid Ó Catháin, 'Ramblings', *Lixnaw 1995*, Lixnaw, Ceolann, 1995, p. 9.
55   Boland, *Sea Legs*, pp. 195–6.
56   Raban, *Heartbreak*, p. 327.
57   Walter J. Ong, *Orality and Literacy: The Technologizing of the Word*, London, Routledge, 1988, p. 142.
58   ibid., p. 148.
59   ibid., p. 149.
60   Wolf Lepenies, 'Translation's Role in National Identity', *Times Higher Education Supplement*, 2 October 1992.
61   Gibbons, *Tramping through Ireland*, p. 65.
62   Gibbons, *Tramping*, p. 66.
63   Bryson, *Notes*, p. 228.
64   Theroux, *The Kingdom*, p. 15.
65   Sibony, *Entre-Deux*, p. 57.
66   Raban, *Heartbreak*, pp. 318–19.
67   See Johannes Fabian, *Language and Colonial Power*, New York, Cambridge University Press, 1986.
68   Graves, *Ireland Revisited*, p. 9.
69   Eric Newby, *Round Ireland in Low Gear*, London, Viking, 1987, p. x.
70   Kerridge, *Jaunting*, p. 129.
71   Bryson, *Notes*, p. 258.
72   Johannes Fabian, *Time and the Other: How Anthropology Makes its Object*, New York, Columbia University Press, 1983, p. 35.
73   ibid., pp. 18–19.
74   Theroux, *The Kingdom*, p. 163.
75   Dinesh D'Souza, *The End of Racism: Principles for a Multiracial Society*, New York, Free Press, 1995, p. 122.
76   For further discussion of the situation of minority languages in translation see my 'The Cracked Looking Glass of Servants: Translation and Minority Languages in a Global Age', *The Translator*, vol. 4, no. 2, 1998, pp. 145–62; 'Altered States:

Translation and Minority Languages', *TTR*, vol. VIII, no. 1, 1995, pp. 85–103.

77 Raban, *Heartbreak*, p. 10.

78 Brian Friel, *Translations*, London, Faber & Faber, 1971.

79 George Steiner, 'An Exact Art' in his *No Passion Spent: Essays 1978–1996*, London, Faber and Faber, 1996, p. 194.

80 For a discussion of the problems of translating proper nouns for the media see the essays in Máirín Nic Eoin and Liam Mac Mathúna, *Ar Thóir an Fhocail Chruinn: Iriseoirí, Téarmeolaithe agus Fadhbanna an Aistriúcháin*, Dublin, Coiscéim, 1997. Sewell's translations are in Cathal Ó Searcaigh, *Out in the Open*, tr. Frank Sewell, Indreabhán, Cló Iar-Chonnachta, 1997.

81 Raban, *Heartbreak*, p. 8.

82 ibid., p. 60.

83 Eva Hoffman, *Lost in Translation*, London, Minerva, 1989, p. 105.

84 Edmund Spenser, *A View of the Present State of Ireland*, ed. W.L. Renwick, Oxford, Clarendon, 1970, pp. 155–6. The word 'sept' as Spenser uses it here corresponds roughly to 'clan' as Gaelic Ireland was a clan or lineage-based society (see Kenneth Nicholls, *Gaelic and Gaelicised Ireland in the Middle Ages*, Dublin, Gill & Macmillan, 1972). Sept is also used to refer to sub-divisions or subordinate family groupings within the clan.

85 Newby, *Round Ireland in Low Gear*, p. 263.

86 Bryson, *Notes*, p. 181.

87 Theroux, *The Kingdom*, p. 292.

88 Bryson, *Notes*, p. 181.

89 ibid., p. 25.

90 Theroux, *The Kingdom*, pp. 14–15.

91 John Thieme, 'Authorial Voice in V.S. Naipaul's *The Middle Passage*', in Philip Dodd, ed., *The Art of Travel: Essays on Travel Writing*, London, Frank Cass, 1982, p. 143.

92 The referent rarely disappears altogether, however, unless the person encountered is imaginary. It is a convention among travel writers to change personal names for understandable reasons of privacy. The name may be different but the person referred to exists or has existed. In the case of caricature, however, the referent is overshadowed by the connotations of the signified.

93 Boland, *Sea Legs*, p. 99.

94 For a discussion of some of the issues involved for anthropology and ethnology see James Clifford, 'Spatial Practices: Fieldwork, Travel, and the Disciplining of Anthropology' in his *Routes: Travel and Translation in the Late Twentieth Century*, Cambridge (Mass.), Harvard University Press, pp. 52–91. In the French tradition, Marc Augé has been notably active in promoting ethnological attention to the familiar, see Marc Augé, *La Traversée du Luxembourg*, Paris, Hachette, 1985, and Marc Augé, *Un ethnologue dans le métro*, Paris, Hachette, 1986.

95 Clifford, *Routes*, pp. 84–5.

96 Theroux, *The Kingdom*, p. 299.

97 Bill Bryson, *Mother Tongue: The English Language*, London, Penguin, 1991; Bill Bryson, *Made in America*, London, Secker & Warburg, 1994.

98 Bryson, *Notes*, p. 290.

99 Bruce Chatwin, 'Nomad Invasions', *What Am I Doing Here?*, London, Picador, 1990, pp. 216–29.

100 Mikhail Bakhtin, *The Dialogical Imagination*, Austin, University of Texas Press, 1981. For a recent discussion of Bakhtin's work see Tony Crowley, *Language in History*, London, Routledge, 1996.

101   Jacques Derrida, *Le monolinguisme de l'autre*, Paris, Galilée, 1996.
       '1. *We always speak only one language*. 2. *We never speak only one language.*'
102   Derrida, p. 47.
       'My language, the only one I hear myself speaking and that I understand
       myself to speak is the language of the other.'
103   ibid., pp. 110–11.
       'I say route and trace of return, because what makes a route different from
       a cleared path or a *via rupta* (its etymon), as *methodos* is different from *odos*,
       is repetition, return, reversibility, iterability, the possible iteration of the itin-
       erary. How is it possible that, given or learnt, this language should be
       experienced, explored, worked through, to be reinvented without itinerary
       or map, as the language of the other.'
104   Margaret Sabin, 'The Spectacle of Reality in *Sea and Sardinia*', Philip Dodd, ed.,
       The Art of Travel: Essays on Travel Writing, London, Frank Cass, 1982, pp. 85–6.
105   Fussell, *Abroad*, p. 48.
106   Gibbons, *Tramping through Ireland*, pp.32, 52.
107   Amati Mehler, Argentieri and Canestri, *La Babel de l'inconscient*, p. 244.
       'Anyone who has translated knows that within a language many choices
       are possible, theoretically equivalent but it is personal preferences, that
       characterise, in the final analysis, a style.'
108   Cited in Derrida, *Le monolinguisme*, p. 110: 'the essence of language is friendship
       and hospitality.'
109   Theroux, *The Kingdom*, p. 41.
110   Derrida, *Le monolinguisme de l'autre*, p. 32; Émile Benveniste, 'Hospitality', *Indo-
       European Language and Society*, tr. Elizabeth Palmer, London, Faber and Faber,
       1973, pp. 71-83.

2: The Changeling

1   Liam Ó Rinn, *Turus go Páras*, Dublin, Oifig Díolta Foilseacháin Rialtais, 1931, p. 95.
     'After three weeks spent rushing through the streets of Paris, in the heat of
     the day and the night, looking at every beautiful or wonderful or elegant
     thing I came across, my legs and eyes were sore and my mind and body
     weary. It also bothered me that I could not speak to the people easily and
     fluently, because I did not know enough of the language of the country.'
2   See Jenny Mezciems, '"Tis not to divert the Reader": Moral and Literary Determi-
     nants in Some Early Travel Narratives', in Philip Dodd, ed., *The Art of Travel:
     Essays on Travel Writing*, London, Frank Cass, 1982, pp. 2–16.
3   Robert Byron, *The Road to Oxiana*, 1937; London, Pan, 1981, p. 223–4.
4   Nicolas Bouvier, *L'usage du monde*, 1963; Paris, Payot, 1992, p. 136.
5   Dervla Murphy, *Muddling Through in Madagascar*, London, Century, 1986, pp.
     19–20.
6   Bruce Chatwin, *In Patagonia*, London, Picador, 1979, p. 26.
7   For a discussion of the problems and how translators can nonetheless try to over-
     come them see Javier Franco Aixelá, 'Culture-Specific Items in Translation', in
     Román Álvarez and M. Carmen-África Vidal, eds., *Translation, Power, Subversion*,
     Clevedon, Multilingual Matters, 1996, pp. 52–78.
8   Chatwin, *Patagonia*, p. 12.
9   For a discussion of translation and paradox in the context of theories of play and
     metaphor, see my 'Keeping One's Distance: Translation and the Play of Possibil-
     ity', *TTR*, vol. 8, no. 2, 1995, pp. 227–43.

10 Byron, *Oxiana*, p. 237.

11 Claudio Magris, *Danube: A Sentimental Journey from the Source to the Black Sea*, London, Collins Harvill, 1989, p. 306.

12 Erwing Stengel, 'On Learning a New Language', *International Journal of Psychoanalysis*, vol. 20, 1939, pp. 45–60.

13 Jacqueline Amati Mehler, Simona Argentieri and Jorge Canestri, *La Babel de l'inconscient: Langue maternelle, langues étrangères et psychanalyse*, tr. Maya Garboua, Paris, Presses Universitaires de France, 1994.
   'on the one hand, the difficulty of abandoning the universal narcissistic illusion that your own language is the best, the only one capable of expressing the complexity of life and of reflecting the truth: on the other hand, the feelings of shame, guilt, fear of ridicule and narcissistic hurt linked to the regression to primary processes necessitated by learning to understand and use a foreign language.'

14 Jonathan Raban, *Hunting Mr Heartbreak*, London, Picador, 1991, p. 337.

15 Lisa St Aubin de Terán, *Off the Rails: Memoirs of a Train Addict*, London, Sceptre, 1990, pp. 81–2.

16 H. Schutz, 'The Stranger: An Essay in Social Psychology', in A. Brodersen, ed., *Studies in Social Theory, Collected Papers II*, The Hague, Martinus Mjnoff, 1964, p. 95.

17 Schutz, 'The Stranger', p. 96.

18 Eva Hoffman, *Lost in Translation*, London, Minerva, 1991, p. 278.

19 Lisa St Aubin de Terán, *Off the Rails*, p. 84.

20 Úna Ní Mhaoileoin, *Turas go Túinis*, Baile Átha Cliath, Sáirséal agus Dill, 1969, pp. 26–7.
   'They have the same word as the Italians for house and cow and other things that you wouldn't be looking for at any rate, but I don't know the word they use for toilet. They don't understand gabinetto and when I asked them for a place to lavarsi le mani, they brought me there straight away, but there was nothing beside it! I'm afraid I'll have to make some room in my wee bag for a little dictionary.'

21 Henry James, *Italian Hours*, New York, Houghton Mifflin, 1909, pp. 165–6.

22 Byron, *Oxiana*, p. 129.

23 Jorge Semprun, *Adieu, vive clarté* . . ., Paris, Gallimard, 1998, p. 79.
   'I decided to eliminate as quickly as possible any trace of an accent from my French pronunciation: nobody ever again on hearing me speak would call me *Spaniard from a routed army*. To maintain my identity as a foreigner, to make this an internal, secret, founding and perplexing virtue, I will disappear into the anonymity of correct pronunciation.'

24 Jacques Derrida, *Le monolinguisme de l'autre*, Paris, Galilée, 1996, pp. 77, 78.
   'You entered French literature on condition you lost your accent.'
   'Accent points to a hand-to-hand struggle with language in general, it means more than accentuation. Its symptomatology invades writing.'

25 Julia Kristeva, *Étrangers à nous-mêmes*, Paris, Gallimard, 1988, p. 27.
   'You can become a virtuoso in the use of this new artifice, besides which it gives you a new body, just as wholly artificial and sublimated – some say sublime. You feel that the new language is your resurrection: new skin, new sex. But the illusion is shattered when for example you listen to a recording, and the sound of your voice comes back to you strange, from nowhere, closer to the mumbling of yore than to the code of the present.'

26 Daniel Sibony, *Entre-Deux: L'origine en partage*, Paris, Seuil, 1991, p. 40.

'one speaks the host language, the second language with an accent; the accent of the first language, its modulated music, the trace of awkwardness: unfortunate love of origin, neither wanted nor forsaken.'

27 Amati Mehler, Argentieri and Canestri, *La Babel de l'inconscient*, p. 148.

28 Hoffman, *Lost in Translation*, p. 209.

29 Ní Mhaoileoin, *Turas*, p. 215.

30 Liam Ó Rinn, *Turus*, p. 89.

'For my part, because I spoke English it was hard for me to convince him I was not English. Despite the fact that I denied this, he kept on speaking to me as if I were English.'

31 There are of course intralingual equivalents of this vagueness concerning origin. In the English-speaking world, when they are sufficiently far away from home, Canadians, US Americans, Australians, New Zealanders, the Scots, Welsh, English and Irish are not always told apart.

32 Magris, *Danube*, p. 225.

33 For a succint description of the phenomenon see David Crystal, *English as a Global Language*, Cambridge University Press, 1997.

34 Murphy, *Madagascar*, pp. 89–90.

35 David Harvey, *The Condition of Postmodernity*, Oxford, Blackwell, 1989.

36 Byron, *Road to Oxiana*, p. 98.

37 Chatwin, *Patagonia*, p. 171.

38 Ní Mhaoileoin, p. 199, pp. 242–3.

39 Murphy, *Madagascar*, p. 157.

40 Bouvier, *L'usage*, p. 30.

Imam, li vam navoštiti brk? - should I wax your moustache? - to which the appropriate reply was to immediately say:
Za volju Bozyu nemojte puštam tu modu kikošima - God be preserved! I leave that to the ladies.

41 Cited in ibid., p. 192.

42 Paul Fussell, *Abroad: British Literary Traveling Between the Wars*, New York, Oxford University Press, 1980, p. 47.

43 Lisa St Aubin de Terán, *Off the Rails*, p. 107.

44 ibid., p. 91.

45 For a discussion of these two contrasting notions of self in the context of translation, see Susan Ingram, 'Translation, Autobiography, Bilingualism', in Lynne Bowker, Michael Cronin, Dorothy Kenny and Jennifer Pearson, eds., *Unity in Diversity? Current Trends in Translation Studies*, Manchester, St Jerome, 1998, pp. 15–22.

46 St Aubin de Terán, *Off the Rails*, p. 89.

47 Byron, *Road to Oxiana*, p. 141.

48 Chatwin, *Patagonia*, pp. 128–31.

49 Byron, *Road to Oxiana*, p. 244.

50 Joseph Campbell, *The Masks of God: Primitive Mythology*, vol. 1, London, Souvenir Press, 1973.

51 Kate O'Brien, *My Ireland*, London, Batsford, 1962; Kate O'Brien, *Farewell Spain*, 1937; rpt. London, Virago, 1985.

52 O'Brien, *Farewell Spain*, p. 21.

53 Adam Phillips, 'Looking at Obstacles', in *On Kissing, Tickling and Being Bored: Psychoanalytic Essays on the Unexamined Life*, London, Faber and Faber, 1993, p. 88.

54 Phillips, *On Kissing*, p. 96.

55   Henry David Thoreau, *Walden*, Carl Bode, ed., *The Portable Thoreau*, London, Penguin, 1982, p. 352.
56   Thoreau, *Walden*, pp. 352–3.
57   ibid.
58   ibid.
59   Nicolas Bouvier, *L'Échappée belle: Éloge de quelques pérégrins*, Geneva, Métropolis, 1996, pp. 64–5.
    'Therefore it was in order to get away from this indifference and boredom that we were said to have begun this hopeless construction. If certain authors are to be believed, even this challenge was not enough to awaken humanity from its torpor and taciturnity. Looking closely at the painting of Pieter Brueghel, it certainly seemed to me that I could hear some cocks crowing and the carters' whips cracking in the wind, but no human voice. The tower is said to have been built in a deathly silence. Then God, who considered this waste with a sad smile, in his infinite mercy, reportedly created all the different languages, dialects and patois to reawaken a moribund curiosity.
    Our mind being more preoccupied with what it cannot understand than with what it has already understood, the Other that we ignored the day before had become all at once an enigmatic character, the object of speculation, study and interest.'
60   St Aubin de Terán, *Off the Rails*, p. 47.
61   Ní Mhaoileoin, *Turas*, pp. 126–7.
    'they have the same love for the country and for the language as they have for the bambini.'
62   ibid., p. 273.
63   ibid., p. 266.
    'they are amazingly serious.'
64   Byron, *Road to Oxiana*, pp. 274–5.
65   Stéphane Mallarmé, *Oeuvres complètes*, Paris, Gallimard, 1975, p. 975.
    'You almost never see a word as surely as from the outside, where we are; that is, from abroad.'
66   Hoffman, *Lost in Translation*, p. 170.
67   Bouvier, *L'usage*, p. 68.
    'Travel provides opportunities to give yourself a good shake but not – as was previously thought – freedom. It results in the experience of a kind of reduction. The traveller appears on a more modest scale, outside his normal environment and stripped of the thick packaging of habit. He is also more open to curiosity, intuition and love at first sight.'
68   See especially Mary Russell, *The Blessings of a Good Thick Skirt: Women Travellers and Their World*, London, Flamingo, 1994; Jane Robinson, *Wayward Women: A Guide to Women Travellers*, Oxford University Press, 1990; Dea Birkett and Sara Wheeler, eds., *Amazonians: The Penguin Book of Women's New Travel Writing*, London, Penguin, 1998.
69   Sherry Simon, *Gender in Translation*, London, Routledge, 1996; Luise von Flotow, *Translation and Gender: Translating in the 'Era of Feminism'*, Manchester, St Jerome, 1997.
70   Amati Mehler, Argentieri and Canestri, *La Babel de l'inconscient*, p. 79.
    'if for a boy anatomical difference from the mother can be a physiological trigger that leads to psychological differentiation, we believe, on the other

hand, in the case of a girl, morphological similarity can take on a regressive meaning as growth and the process of separation and individualisation leads to psychological difference from the mother but the acquisition of female identity means becoming corporeally like the mother, being imprisoned again and for good by this mother that you try desperately to get away from.'

71 Alice Kaplan, *French Lessons: A Memoir*, University of Chicago Press, 1993, pp. 140–1.

72 Darian Leader, *Why Do Women Write More Letters Than They Post?*, London, Faber and Faber, 1996, p. 6.

73 Sara Mills, *Discourses of Difference: An Analysis of Women's Travel Writing and Colonialism*, London, Routledge, 1991, p. 3.

74 O'Brien, *Farewell Spain*, p. 6. For a discussion of O'Brien and the sentimental imagination in travel writing see my 'Marvellous Travelling: Kate O'Brien's Travel Accounts', in Eibhear Walshe, ed., *Ordinary People Dancing: Essays on Kate O'Brien*, Cork University Press, 1993, pp. 137–49.

75 Jacques Lacarrière, *Chemin Faisant: Mille kilomètres à pied à travers la France*, Paris, Fayard, 1977, p. 80.
    'These brief conversations, these momentary exchanges of glances with strangers, I wish they would bring me further, that I could have a different kind of relationship with others, that I wasn't just someone passing through. But the very idea is absurd or mad. How could I myself live everybody's life, spend the time necessary to follow each separate existence, be myself and all the others at the same time? I would need several lives and bodies for that.'

76 Martha C. Nussbaum, 'Transcending Humanity', *Love's Knowledge: Essays on Philosophy and Literature*, Oxford University Press, 1990, p. 378.

77 Nussbaum, 'Transcending Humanity', p. 381.

78 Seamus Heaney, *Station Island*, London, Faber and Faber, 1984.

79 George Steiner, *Real Presences*, London, Faber and Faber, 1989, p. 69.

80 Adam Phillips, 'The Interested Party', in *The Beast in the Nursery*, London, Faber and Faber, 1998, p. 19.

81 Lawrence Venuti, *The Translator's Invisibility: A History of Translation*, London, Routledge, 1995.

82 Byron, *Road to Oxiana*, p. 124.

83 Tzvetan Todorov, *L'homme dépaysé*, Paris, Seuil, 1996, pp. 24–5.
    'His/her presence among the "natives" in turn has an unsettling effect. By upsetting their habits or disconcerting them by virtue of his opinions or behaviour, s/he can help some of the natives to begin to experience the same detachment from what they have taken for granted, a path of exploration and wonder.'

84 Edwin Gentzler, 'Translation, Counter-Culture, and *The Fifties* in the USA', in Álvarez and Vidal, *Translation, Power, Subversion*, pp. 116–37.

85 Nicolas Bouvier, *Routes et Déroutes: Entretiens avec Irène Lichstenstein-Fall*, Geneva, Métropolis, 1992, p. 97.
    'The world is constantly polyphonic whereas our reading of it, through neglect or laziness, is monodic.'

86 Alberto Manguel, *A History of Reading*, London, Flamingo, 1997, p. 276.

87 Bouvier, *Routes et Déroutes*, p. 153.
    'For my part, travel and writing have something in common that is very important. Both are an exercise in disappearance, evasion. Because when

you are no longer there, things come. When you are too present, you consume the landscape through a kind of moral corpulence which means it is not possible to see ... And because the whole of existence is an exercise in disappearance, I find that travel and writing are two very good schools.'

88 Magris, *Danube*, p. 52.

3: Making Sense

1 Dervla Murphy, *Muddling Through in Madagascar*, London, Arrow, 1990, p. 132.
2 Murphy, *Muddling*, p. 63.
3 Eva Hoffman, *Exit into History: A Journey through the New Eastern Europe*, London, Minerva, 1994.
4 Miles Smith, 'Preface to *Authorized Version* of Bible', Douglas Robinson, ed., *Western Translation Theory from Herodotus to Nietzsche*, Manchester, St Jerome, 1997, p. 139.
5 Dervla Murphy, *The Ukimwi Road: From Kenya to Zimbabwe*, London, John Murray, 1993, p. 204.
6 Murphy, *Ukimwi Road*, p. 14.
7 ibid., p. 42.
8 Hoffman, *Exit into History*, p. 169.
9 Joseph Brodsky, 'A Place as Good as Any', in *On Grief and Reason*, London, Hamish Hamilton, 1995, pp. 42–3.
10 'Letter of Pedro Vaz de Caminha', Charles David Ley, ed., *Portugese Voyages 1493–1663*, London, J.M. Dent, 1947, p. 47.
11 Redmond O'Hanlon, *Into the Heart of Borneo*, London, Penguin, 1985, p. 62.
12 David Denby, *Sentimental Narrative and the Social Order in France, 1760–1820*, Cambridge University Press, 1994.
13 Étienne Bonnot de Condillac, *Essai sur l'origine des connaissances humaines*, 1746, Galilée, Paris, 1973, pp. 93–5; Jean-Jacques Rousseau, *Essai sur l'origine des langues*, Paris, Hatier, 1983.
14 Denby, *Sentimental Narrative*, p. 85.
15 Marshall Sahlins, *Islands of History*, London, Tavistock, 1987, p. 41.
16 Gillian Beer, *Open Fields: Science in Cultural Encounter*, Oxford, Clarendon Press, 1996, p. 63.
17 'Letter of Pedro Vaz de Caminha', p. 57.
18 V.S. Naipaul, 'After the Revolution', *The New Yorker*, 26 May 1997, p. 46.
19 Naipaul, 'After the Revolution', p. 64.
20 R. Bruce W. Anderson, 'Perspectives on the Role of the Interpeter', Richard W. Brislin, ed., *Translation: Applications and Research*, New York, Gardner Press, 1976, p. 218.
21 Hoffman, *Exit into History*, p. 209.
22 Naipaul, 'After the Revolution', p. 58.
23 Hoffman, p. 254.
24 Jean-Claude Guillebaud, *Sur la route des croisades*, Paris, Arléa, 1993, p. 135. 'Sometimes Ayberk refuses to translate questions that I would like to ask the village notables.'
25 Naipaul, 'After the Revolution', p. 64.
26 Göran Aijmer, 'Comment on article by P. Steven Sangren', *Current Anthropology*, vol. 33, supplement, 1992, p. 296.
27 Hoffman, *Exit into History*, p. 347.
28 Murphy, *The Ukimwi Road*, p. 75.

29 ibid., pp. 28–9.

30 O'Hanlon, *Into the Heart*, p. 148.

31 Murphy, *Muddling*, p. 219.

32 Raymonde Carroll, *Cultural Misunderstandings: The French-American Experience*, University of Chicago Press, 1988.

33 Peter Stallybrass and Allon White, *The Politics and Poetics of Transgression*, London, Methuen, 1986.

34 Mary-Louise Pratt, *Imperial Eyes: Travel Writing and Transculturation*, London, Routledge, 1992, p. 216.

35 George Steiner, 'Two Suppers', *No Passion Spent: Essays 1978–1996*, London, Faber & Faber, p. 390.

36 Julia Kristeva, *Étrangers à nous-mêmes*, Paris, Gallimard, 1988, pp. 22–3.
'Miracle of flesh and thought, the dinner of hospitality is the utopia of foreigners: a momentary cosmopolitanism, the fraternity of the guests who tone down and forget their differences, dinner is outside time. The intoxication of others makes him/her [the foreigner] feel eternal even if they know how temporary it is.'

37 Nicolas Bouvier, *L'usage du monde*, Paris, Payot, 1992, p. 209.

38 Murphy, *Muddling*, p. 36.

39 Hoffman, *Exit into History*, p. 176.

40 Bouvier, *L'usage du monde*, p. 70.
'Here, as in Serbia, music is a passion. It is also an "open sesame" for the foreigner: if he likes music he will have friends. If he records music, everybody, even the police will try to drag up some musicians for him.'

41 Even here, however, the benefits of understanding are sometimes dubious. The true meaning of the lyrics of an Italian opera or of an English pop song can turn out to be dispiritingly banal once you have cracked the code of language.

42 Nicolas Bouvier, 'Voyage, Écriture, Alterité', *L'Échappée belle: Éloge de quelques pérégrins*, Geneva, Métropolis, 1996, p. 59.
'I think that music and laughter, other universal values, often go further in communicating with the "Other."'

43 Nicolas Bouvier, *Routes et Déroutes: Entretiens avec Irène Lichstenstein-Fall*, Geneva, Métropolis, 1992, p. 179.

44 Patrick Süskind, *Das Parfum: Die Geschicte eines Mörders*, Zurich, Diogenes, 1985.

45 Chris Rojek and John Urry, 'Transformations of Travel and Theory', *Touring Cultures: Transformations of Travel and Theory*, London, Routledge, 1997, p. 8.

46 Zygmunt Bauman, *Postmodern Ethics*, Oxford, Blackwell, 1993, p. 24.

47 Alexandra David-Neel, *Voyage d'une parisienne à Lhassa*, 1927, Paris, Plon, 1982, p. 160.
'Phew! . . . a terrible smell suddenly filled the room, the stench of the charnel house.'

48 David-Neel, *Voyage d'une parisienne*, p. 158.
'what was most tiresome and sometimes almost intolerable was the role that I had to continually play in order to maintain my disguise.'

49 Adam Phillips, 'On Risk and Solitude', *On Kissing, Tickling and Being Bored: Psychoanalytic Essays on the Unexamined Life*, London, Faber & Faber, 1993, p. 26.

50 Eamonn Slater, 'Becoming an Irish *Flâneur*', Eamonn Slater and Michel Peillon, eds., *Encounters with Modern Ireland*, Dublin, Institute of Public Administration, 1998, p. 4.

51 Martin Heidegger, *The Question Concerning Technology and Other Essays*, New York, Harper, 1977, p. 134.

52 John Urry, *The Tourist Gaze: Leisure and Travel in Contemporary Societies*, London, Sage, 1990.

53 Mary Louise Pratt, *Imperial Eyes*, pp. 78–80.

54 See Richard Rorty, *Philosophy and the Mirror of Nature*, Oxford, Blackwell, 1980.

55 See Walter J. Ong, *Orality and Literacy: The Technologizing of the Word*, London, Routledge, 1989.

56 Michel Foucault, *Madness and Civilization*, London, Tavistock, 1967; *The Birth of the Clinic*, London, Tavistock, 1976; *Discipline and Punish: The Birth of the Prison*, tr. Alan Sheridan, Harmondsworth, Penguin, 1979.

57 Sara Mills, *Discourses of Difference: An Analysis of Women's Travel Writing and Colonialism*, London, Routledge, 1991, p. 78.

58 Susan Sontag, *On Photography*, Harmondsworth, Penguin, 1979, pp. 9–10.

59 Bouvier, *L'usage du monde*, p. 63.
    'At least as far as the impossible is concerned, a way can always be found to understand one another.'

60 Brian Mossop, 'The Image of Translation in Science Fiction and Astronomy', *The Translator*, vol. 2, no. 1, 1996, pp. 13–15.

61 Jonathan Culler, 'Semiotics of Tourism', *American Journal of Semiotics*, vol. 1, 1981, p. 127.

62 Charles Musser, 'The Travel Genre in 1903-1904: Moving Towards Fictional Narrative', Thomas Elsaesser, ed., *Early Cinema: Space – Frame – Narrative*, London, British Film Institute, 1990, p. 127. See also Wolfgang Schivelbusch, *The Railway Journey: Trains and Travel in the Nineteenth Century*, New York, Urizen Books, 1980.

63 Kate O'Brien, *My Ireland*, London, Batsford, 1962, p. 111.

64 See Urry, *The Tourist Gaze*, pp. 40–65.

65 Mike Featherstone, 'Postmodernism and the Aestheticization of Everyday Life', Scott Lash and Jonathan Friedman, eds., *Modernity and Identity*, Oxford, Blackwell, 1992, pp. 265–90.

66 George Steiner, 'The Retreat from the Word', *Language and Silence: Essays 1958-1966*, London, Peregrine, 1979, p. 33.

67 Beer, *Open Fields*, pp. 321–2.

68 Michael Guillen, *Five Equations that Changed the World*, London, Little Brown, 1995, p. 2.

69 Carol Crashaw and John Urry, 'Tourism and the Photographic Eye', Chris Rojek and John Urry, *Touring Cultures*, p. 178.

70 Reproduced in Ali Behdad, *Belated Travellers: Orientalism in the Age of Colonial Dissolution*, Cork University Press, 1994, p. 51.

71 Quoted in Edward Mendelson, 'Baedeker's Universe', *Yale Review*, Spring 1985, pp. 387–8.

72 James Buzard, *The Beaten Track: European Tourism, Literature and the Ways to 'Culture' 1800-1918*, Oxford, Clarendon Press, 1993, pp. 65–79.

73 Murphy, *The Ukimwi Road*, p. 78.

74 Lisa St Aubin de Terán, *Off the Rails: Memoirs of a Train Addict*, London, Sceptre, 1990, p. 99.

75 Hoffman, *Exit into History*, p. 343.

76 Murphy, *The Ukimwi Road*, p. 55.

77 ibid., p. 88, p. 132.

78 Cited in François Bénichou, 'François Maspero: le passeur de mots', *Magazine littéraire*, no. 351, février 1997, p. 102.

'After spending a week in China you write a book, after three weeks, an article and after a year, nothing.'

79 Hoffman, *Exit into History*, p. 164.
80 François Furet, *Le passé d'une illusion: Essai sur l'idée communiste au XXè siècle*, Paris, Robert Laffont/Calmann-Lévy, 1995.
81 Gillian Rose, *The Broken Middle: Out of our Ancient Society*, Oxford, Blackwell, 1992.
82 Dinesh D'Souza, *The End of Racism: Principles for a Multiracial Society*, New York, Free Press, 1995, p. 122.
83 Flann O'Brien, *The Poor Mouth*, trans. Patrick C. Power, London, Picador, 1973, p. 54.
84 Joep Leerssen, *Mere Irish and Fíor-Ghael*, Cork University Press, 1996, p. 288.
85 See Lawrence Venuti, ed., *Rethinking Translation: Discourse, Subjectivity, Ideology*, London, Routledge, 1992; Lawrence Venuti, *The Translator's Invisibility*, London, Routledge, 1995; Tejaswini Niranjana, *Siting Translation: History, Post-Structuralism and the Colonial Context*, Berkeley, University of California Press, 1992.
86 Hans Erich Nossack, 'Translating and Being Translated', in Rainer Schulte and John Biguenet, *Theories of Translation: An Anthology of Essays from Dryden to Derrida*, University of Chicago Press, 1992, p. 235.
87 For further comments on the necessary incompleteness of translation see my 'Shoring Up the Fragments of the Translator's Discourse: Complexity, Incompleteness and Integration', *META*, vol. 40, no. 3, septembre 1995, pp. 359–66.
88 Murphy, *The Ukimwi Road*, p. 148.
89 Joseph Dunne, 'Culture, Citizenship and the Global Market: Challenges to the "New Europe"', F. Crawley, P. Smeyers and P. Standish, eds., *Universities and the Identity of Europe*, Oxford and Providence, Berghahn, (forthcoming).
90 Dunne, 'Culture, Citizenship and the Global Market'; Paul Ricoeur, 'Quel ethos nouveau pour l'Europe', Peter Koslowski, ed., *Imaginer l'Europe*, Paris, Éditions du Cerf, 1992, pp. 107–19.
91 Magris, *Danube*, p. 225.
92 Hans Erich Nossack, 'Translating and Being Translated', p. 232.
93 Bouvier, *Routes et Déroutes: Entretiens avec Irène Lichstenstein-Fall*, Geneva, Métropolis, 1992, pp. 88–9.
    'Whatever you are able to do, in the end you only have your shortcomings and foolishness to set against the fabulous inventiveness of the world.'
94 Bouvier, p. 87.
    'The writer will find the right word for a thing or the right thing for a word, and these pairs may equally well be light years away from each other as next-door neighbours who are complete strangers.'
95 Hoffman, *Exit into History*, p. 1.
96 Magris, *Danube*, p. 156.
97 Bouvier, *Routes et Déroutes*, pp. 87–8.
    'that s/he has a much richer inner life and is more intelligent than s/he thought'.
98 Dean MacCannell, *The Tourist: A New Theory of the Leisure Class*, 2nd ed., New York, Schocken Books, 1989.
99 See Philip Crang, 'Performing the Tourist Product', Chris Rojek and John Urry, *Touring Cultures*, pp. 137–54.
100 Laurent Lamy, 'Pas de deux: le mésocosme de la traduction comme matrice d'une sémantique frontalière', *Meta*, vol. 40, no. 3, 1995, p. 465.
    'the impossibility of translation makes it possible.'

101 Hoffman, *Exit into History*, p. 263.

102 Hoffman, p. 361.

103 Angelo Ara and Claudio Magris, *Trieste: Un'identità di frontiera*, Turin, Einaudi, 1987.

104 For a discussion of the implications of heteroglossic development for English see Tony Crowley, *Language in History: Theories and Texts*, London, Routledge, 1996.

105 See Jean Delisle and Judith Woodsworth, eds., *Translators through History*, Amsterdam, Unesco/John Benjamins, 1995, pp. 67–98.

106 Paul Fussell, *Abroad: British Literary Traveling Between the Wars*, New York, Oxford University Press, 1980, p. 214.

4: Babel Express

1 Eugène Jolas, *Sur Joyce*, Paris, Plon, 1990, p. 66.

2 James Joyce, *Finnegans Wake*, 1939, London, Faber and Faber, 1980, p. 419. For a recent discussion of language and translation questions in Joyce's work see Ginette Michaud and Sherry Simon, *Joyce*, Ville La Salle, Hurtubise HMH, 1996.

3 Burgundio of Pisa, 'The Risk of Altering So Great an Original', Douglas Robinson, ed., *Western Translation Theory from Herodotus to Nietzsche*, Manchester, St Jerome, 1997, p. 41.

4 Jerome, 'Letter to Pammachius no. 57', Douglas Robinson, ed., *Western Translation Theory*, p. 26.

5 Rajendra Singh, 'On Translation: Some Unfinished Thoughts', *Meta*, vol. 40, no. 3, p. 354.

6 Andreï Makine, *Le testament français*, Paris, Mercure de France, 1995, p. 224.
   'I wanted her to explain, justify herself because she it was who had passed on this (her) French sensibility to me, condemning me to live in this difficult state-between-worlds.'

7 Daniel Simeoni, Translating and Studying Translation: The View from the Agent, *Meta*, vol. 40, no. 3, p. 453.

8 René Descartes, *Discours de la méthode*, 1637, Paris, 10/18, 1977, pp. 28–9.
   'when you spend too much time travelling, in the end you become a foreigner in your own country.'

9 Gregory Bateson, 'Double Bind', in *Steps to an Ecology of Mind*, London, Paladin, 1978, pp. 242–9.

10 Daniel Sibony, *Entre-Deux: l'origine en partage*, Paris, Seuil, 1991, p. 166.
   'As a crossing over, it consists of preventing a language from clinging to its origin, its claim to be The language-origin. It involves freeing ourselves from that which makes the language in which we are immersed set itself up as the Origin of language. Therefore, we must be able to translate it, betray it to other languages that "distort" it. Only then can we move on to other languages; other languages become viable and are called upon to "live". The speaking origin erupts then in the space between-two-languages which it nourishes without invading. Failing this, the subject cannot speak or invent in other languages; the first language is the only origin that exists for her.'

11 Sibony, *Entre-Deux*, p. 301.

12 ibid., p. 302.
   'through which we can escape the horror of the self, satisfy our hunger for the other, for something else, and yet strengthen the self to some extent'.

13 ibid., p. 315.
   'the inability to travel, that is to say, to integrate new, unrecognisable

"places", to integrate the unknown, the unknowable even, is also the inability to form alliances and to share, or to tolerate a multiple origin. It is not a question of going towards the origin but of travelling with the idea of origin, of *making the origin travel*.'

14   John Edwards, *Multilingualism*, London, Penguin, 1995, p. 5.

15   Antoinetta and Gérard Haddad, *Freud en Italie: Psychanalyse du voyage*, Paris, Albin Michel, 1995, p. 25.
      'This leads us to posit the existence of a fifth drive, more basic than the others because it is a precondition of their existence, the *viatorial* drive, the drive of walking and travel. What would be the parameters of this drive? The impetus comes from the enigmatic call of the Elsewhere, of the Unknown, of the Other, which man perceives because he is constantly spurred on by the signifier and the word.'

16   Jean-Michel Rey, *La Naissance de la poésie*, Paris, Métaillié, 1991, p. 16.
      'a way of returning to the self by way of the other, through the ordeal of the foreign.'

17   Marc-Alain Ouaknin, *Bibliothérapie: Lire, c'est guérir*, Paris, Seuil, 1994, pp. 162–3.
      'the cure is passage, voyage, metaphor, a going outside of the self, a dynamic way of being, which turns us into a human being, in this way different from the ontological passivity of the animal or object.'

18   Ouaknin, *Bibliothérapie*, p. 164.
      'The trans-duction of the between-two-languages opens the human being up to her "capacity to be other", to her project of being.'

19   James Clifford, *Routes: Travel and Translation in the Late Twentieth Century*, Cambridge (Mass.), Harvard University Press, 1997, p. 39.

20   Mona Baker, ed., *Routledge Encyclopedia of Translation Studies*, London, Routledge, 1998.

21   Clifford, *Routes*, p. 22.

22   Kate Sturge has written an excellent article detailing the neglect of translation strategies in earlier ethnographic studies: Kate Sturge, 'Translation Strategies in Ethnography', *The Translator*, vol. 3, no. 1, 1997, pp. 21–38.

23   For a discussion of some of the issues involved see: Tejaswini Niranjana, *Siting Translation: History, Post-Structuralism and the Colonial Context*, Berkeley, University of California Press, 1992; Eric Cheyfitz, *The Poetics of Imperialism: Translation and Colonization from* The Tempest to Tarzan, Oxford University Press, 1991.

24   Clifford, *Routes*, p. 60.

25   Eric Wolf, *Anthropology*, New York, Norton, 1964, p. x.

26   Clifford, *Routes*, p. 60.

27   Lynne Bowker, Michael Cronin, Dorothy Kenny and Jennifer Pearson, *Unity in Diversity? Current Trends in Translation Studies*, Manchester, St Jerome, 1998.

28   James Clifford, 'Traveling Cultures', Lawrence Grossberg, Cary Nelson and Paula Treichler, eds., *Cultural Studies*, London, Routledge, 1992, pp. 96–112; Edward Said, 'Reflections on Exile', *Granta*, no. 13, 1984, pp. 159–72.

29   The neglect of nomadism in accounts of world history is repeatedly stressed in Felipe Fernández-Armesto, *Millennium*, London, Black Swan, 1996.

30   Rosa Braidotti, *Nomadic Subjects: Embodiment and Sexual Difference in Contemporary Feminist Theory*, New York, Columbia University Press, 1994, p. 15.

31   Bruce Chatwin, 'Nomad Invasions', *What Am I Doing Here?*, London, Picador, 1990, p. 219.

32 Braidotti, *Nomadic Subjects*, p. 31.

33 Gideon Toury, *In Search of a Theory of Translation*, Tel Aviv, Porter Institute, 1980; Gideon Toury, *Descriptive Translation Studies and Beyond*, Amsterdam and Philadelphia, John Benjamins, 1995.

34 Braidotti, *Nomadic Subjects*, p. 14.

35 Michel Le Bris, *Fragments du royaume: conversations avec Yvon Le Men*, Vénissieux, Éditions de l'Aube, 1995, p. 10.
> 'That face before you ceases to be simply a mass of human flesh, becomes truly human when you realise that behind those eyes there are worlds you will never enter. And this transcendence of the Other which reveals your own in turn, this, in short, is the "thou" that makes me "I". We become part of humanity through being wrenched away from the enclosed world of the Same. It is this gap, which we always try to close, which enables us to live with others – and to live in the same place without it becoming a prison. Because it is in this gap that the powers of the imagination can develop.'

36 For a discussion of digital and analog communication see Anthony Wilden, *System and Structure: Essays in Communication and Exchange*, London, Tavistock, 2nd. ed., 1980, pp. 155–201.

37 Caren Kaplan, *Questions of Travel: Postmodern Discourses of Displacement*, Durham and London, Duke University Press, 1996, pp. 81–2. The quote is taken from Douglas Kellner, *Jean Baudrillard: From Marxism to Postmodernism*, Stanford University Press, 1989, p. 171.

38 For an illuminating discussion of the relationship between translation and theocratic censure which predates monotheism see Douglas Robinson, *Translation and Taboo*, Northern Illinois University Press, 1996.

39 James Clarence Mangan, 'Anthologia Germanica', *Dublin University Magazine*, vol. 7, no. 39, March 1836, pp. 278–302.

40 Jean-René Ladmiral, 'Traduire, c'est-à-dire . . . Phénoménologies d'un concept pluriel', *Meta*, vol. 40, no. 3, 1995, p. 418.
> 'It saves us from having to read the original text.'

41 George Steiner, 'The Pythagorean Genre', *Language and Silence*, Harmondsworth, Peregrine, 1979, p. 102.

42 Oscar Wilde, 'The Decay of Lying', *De Profundis and Other Writings*, Harmondsworth, Penguin, 1977, p. 61.

43 Susan Bassnett, 'The Meek or the Mighty: Reappraising the Role of the Translator', Román Álvarez and M. Carmen-África Vidal, eds., *Translation, Power, Subversion*, Clevedon, Multilingual Matters, 1996, p. 12.

44 Vladimir Nabokov, 'Problems of Translation: *Onegin* in English', Rainer Schulte and John Biguenet, eds., *Theories of Translation: An Anthology of Essays from Dryden to Derrida*, University of Chicago Press, 1992, p. 134.

45 See in particular, Scott Lash and John Urry, *Economies of Signs & Space*, London, Sage, 1994; David Harvey, *The Condition of Postmodernity*, Oxford, Blackwell, 1989.

46 Caren Kaplan and Inderpal Grewal, eds., *Scattered Hegemonies: Postmodernity and Transnational Feminist Practices*, Minneapolis, University of Minnesota Press, 1994.

47 Stuart Hall, 'The Local and the Global: Globalization and Ethnicity', Anthony D. King, ed., *Culture, Globalization and the World System*, London, Macmillan, 1991, p. 20.

48 Georg Simmel, 'The Stranger', in *On Individuality and Social Forms*, University of Chicago Press, 1971, p. 143.

49 Simmel, 'The Stranger', p. 144.

50 Johann Wolfgang von Goethe, 'On Carlyle's German Romances', tr. Ellen von Nardroff and Ernest H. von Nardroff, Douglas Robinson, ed., *Western Translation Theory from Herodotus to Nietzsche*, Manchester, St Jerome, 1997, p. 224.

51 August Wilhelm von Schlegel, 'Dante: On the Divine Comedy', tr. Douglas Robinson, Douglas Robinson, ed., *Western Translation Theory from Herodotus to Nietzsche*, Manchester, St Jerome, 1997, p. 214.

52 Charles Batteux, 'Principles of Translation', tr. John Miller, Douglas Robinson, ed., *Western Translation Theory from Herodotus to Nietzsche*, p. 198.

53 David Harvey, *The Condition of Postmodernity*.

54 Georg Simmel, 'On the Psychology of Money', David Frisby and Mike Featherstone, eds., *Simmel on Culture*, London, Sage, 1997, p. 233.

55 Marshall Berman, *All That Is Solid Melts Into Air: The Experience of Modernity*, London, Verso, 1983, pp. 87–129.

56 Simmel, 'On the Psychology of Money', p. 234.

57 Reinhard Schäler, 'The Problem with Machine Translation', Lynne Bowker, Michael Cronin, Dorothy Kenny and Jennifer Pearson, eds., *Unity in Diversity? Current Trends in Translation Studies*, p. 154.

58 Sharon O'Brien, 'CAT Tools in the Localization Industry', Lynne Bowker, Michael Cronin, Dorothy Kenny and Jennifer Pearson, eds., *Unity in Diversity?*, p. 120.

59 Glen Poor, 'Localising *Windows* and *Office '95*': A Sim-Ship Strategy', *Software Localisation*, vol. 1, no. 1, 1996, p. 1.

60 Wolfgang Sachs, 'Speed Limits', Jeremy Millar and Michiel Schwarz, eds., *Speed – Visions of an Accelerated Age*, London, Whitechapel Art Gallery, 1998, p. 123.

61 Peter Sloterdijk, 'Modernity as Mobilisation', Jeremy Millar and Michiel Schwarz, eds., *Speed – Visions of an Accelerated Age*, p. 43.

62 David Crystal, *English as a Global Language*, Cambridge University Press, 1997, p. 22.

63 Crystal, *English as a Global Language*, p. 10.

64 Schäler, 'The Problem with Machine Translation', p. 154.

65 Schäler, p. 153.

66 Paul Virilio has written widely on the topic of speed but a key early work is Paul Virilio, *Vitesse et politique; essai de dromologie*, Paris, Galilée, 1977.

67 Susan George, 'Fast Castes', Jeremy Millar and Michiel Schwarz, eds., *Speed – Visions of an Accelerated Age*, pp. 115–18.

68 For a discussion of two of these problems, see Jorma Tommola and Marketta Halevä, 'Language Direction and Source Text Complexity: Effects on Trainee Performance in Simultaneous Interpreting', Lynne Bowker, Michael Cronin, Dorothy Kenny and Jennifer Pearson, *Unity in Diversity?*, pp. 177–86.

69 Edward Dimendberg, 'The Will to Motorisation – Cinema and the Autobahn', Jeremy Millar and Michiel Schwarz, eds., *Speed – Visions of an Accelerated Age*, p. 60.

70 Sachs, 'Speed Limits', p. 129.

71 Sachs, p. 132.

72 ibid., p. 132.

73 Karl Marx, *Grundrisse: Foundations of the Critique of Political Economy*, tr. M. Nicolaus, London, Allen Lane/NLR, 1973, p. 539.

74 Sibony, *Entre-Deux*, p. 311.
   'Seeing your mother give birth to you; generation overcome; to be the *first* to arrive in the New World, the world's first born child, arriving in America, the journey's destination, to observe that everything was virgin territory and if needs be to kill everyone to make sure that it was virgin.'

75   Cited in Scott McQuire, 'Pure Speed – From Transport to Teleport', Jeremy Millar and Michiel Schwarz, eds., *Speed – Visions of an Accelerated Age*, p. 30.
76   Kaplan, *Questions of Travel*, p. 142.
77   Ouaknin, *La Bibliothérapie*, p. 408.
        'Creation from empty space makes alterity possible on the basis of separation. Separation, distancing, differentiation, which make fusion impossible. Only bridges can be flung over the abyss to try to cross it without ever really succeeding.'
78   Ouaknin, p. 411.
79   David Homel and Sherry Simon, eds., *Mapping Literature: The Art and Politics of Translation*, Montreal, Véhicule Press, 1988, pp. 15, 19.
80   Paul Fussell, *Abroad: British Literary Travelling between the Wars*, New York, Oxford University Press, 1982, p. 41.
81   Michel Serres, *Le Tiers-Instruit*, Paris, Gallimard, 1992, p. 28.
        'Whoever stays put learns nothing.'
        'All apprenticeship involves travel. Led by a guide, education pushes you outside.'
82   Jennifer Craik, 'The Culture of Tourism', Chris Rojek and John Urry, *Touring Cultures: Transformations of Travel and Theory*, London, Routledge, 1997, p. 119; see also J. Adler, 'Origins of sightseeing', *Annals of Tourism Research*, vol. 16, 1989, pp. 7–29.
83   Stephen A. Wurm, *Atlas of the World's Languages in Danger of Disappearing*, Paris, Unesco Publishing/Pacific Linguistics, 1996.
84   Edwards, *Multilingualism*, p. 116.
85   Edwards, p. 110.
86   Sibony, *Entre-Deux*, p. 280.
        'to have an origin, it is necessary to be able to move way from it and, to return to it, to establish an in-between space that you are able to *cross*.'
87   Stuart Hall, 'The Local and the Global: Globalization and Ethnicity', Anthony D. King, ed., Culture, Globalization and the World System, p. 28.
88   Tony Crowley, *Language in History*, London, Routledge, 1996.
89   Seamus Heaney, 'The Interesting Case of John Alphonsus Mulrennan', *Planet*, no. 41, 1978, pp. 34–40.
90   Crowley, *Language in History*, p. 199.
91   George Steiner, *Errata: An Examined Life*, London, Phoenix, 1998, p. 89.
92   Anthony Giddens, *Modernity and Self-Identity*, Cambridge, Polity, 1991, p. 209.
93   Scott Lash and John Urry, *Economies of Signs & Space*, London, Sage, 1994, p. 254; see also the influential work on the subject of risk, U. Beck, *Risk Society: Towards a New Modernity*, tr. M. Ritter, London, Sage, 1992.
94   George Ritzer, *The McDonaldization of Society*, Thousand Oaks (Cal.), Pine Forge Press, 1993.
95   George Ritzer and Allan Liska, '"McDisneyization" and "Post-Tourism"', Chris Rojek and John Urry, *Touring Cultures: Transformations of Travel and Theory*, London, Routledge, 1997, pp. 99–100.
96   Cited in Ritsker and Liska, p. 99.
97   Crystal, *English as a Global Language*, pp. 95–7.
98   See John Urry on working under the tourist gaze, John Urry, *The Tourist Gaze: Leisure and Travel in Contemporary Societies*, London, Sage, 1990, pp. 66–81.
99   Dean MacCannell, 'Staged Authenticity: Arrangements of Social Space in Tourism Settings', *American Sociological Review*, no. 79, 1973, pp. 589–603; Dean MacCannell, *The Tourist*, 2nd ed., London, Macmillan, 1989.

100 Philip Crang, 'Performing the Tourist Product', Chris Rojek and John Urry, *Touring Cultures: Transformations of Travel and Theory*, pp. 137–54.

101 Ludwig Wittgenstein, *Tractatus Logico-Philosophicus*, London, Routledge & Kegan Paul, 1974, p. 50; Edwards, *Multilingualism*, p. 47.

102 Crystal, *English as a Global Language*, p. 96.

103 Geraldine Pratt and Susan Hanson, 'Geography and the Construction of Difference', *Gender, Place, Culture*, vol. 1, no. 1, 1994, pp. 10–11.

104 Sachs, *Speed Limits*, p. 126.

105 Edwards, *Multilingualism*, pp. 56–7.

106 Eva Hoffman, *Exit into History: A Journey through the New Eastern Europe*, London, Minerva, 1994, p. 69.

107 Dorinne Kondo, 'Dissolution and Reconstitution of Self: Implications for Anthropological Epistemology', *Cultural Anthropology*, vol. 1, no. 1, 1986, p. 74.

108 Le Bris, *Fragments du royaume*, p. 198.
   'you need to lose yourself once to be able to live with others. And that is what is best about the desire to travel. You only become a part of humanity through the experience of going over to the other. This does not mean that you cannot feel yourself at the same time to be profoundly Breton, for example, to cite my own case.'

109 Clifford, *Routes*, p. 36.

5: Final Frontiers

1 Samuel R. Delaney, *Babel-17*, London, Gollancz, 1987.

2 Arthur C. Clarke and Gentry Lee, *Rama Revealed*, London, Orbit, 1994, p. 207.

3 For a survey of English-language science fiction writing dealing with the question of language see Walter Meyers, *Aliens and Linguists*, Athens (Georgia), University of Georgia Press, 1980; see also Marina Yaguello, *Les fous du langage: des langues imaginaires et de leurs inventeurs*, Paris, Seuil, 1984, pp. 79–87; John Kreuger, 'Language and Techniques of Communication as Theme or Tool in Science Fiction', *Linguistics*, vol. 39, 1968, pp. 68–86; Brian Mossop, 'The Image of Translation in Science Fiction & Astronomy', *The Translator*, vol. 2, no. 1, 1996, pp. 1–26.

4 In the case of C-3P0, the hybridity lies in the obvious mix of human and non-human characteristics, a general feature of droids and cyborgs.

5 Clarke and Lee, *Rama Revealed*, p. 225.

6 Delaney, *Babel-17*, p. 75.

7 Delaney, p. 60.

8 See Umberto Eco, *The Search for the Perfect Language*, tr. James Fentress, Oxford, Blackwell, 1995, pp. 7–24.

9 Clarke and Lee, *Rama Revealed*, p. 204.

10 Clarke and Lee, p. 261.

11 Eco, *The Search for the Perfect Language*, pp. 269–92.

12 Clarke and Lee, *Rama Revealed*, p. 263.

13 Douglas Adams, *The Hitch-Hiker's Guide to the Galaxy*, London, Pan, 1979, pp. 49–50.

14 David Crystal, *English as a Global Language*, Cambridge University Press, 1997, p. 13.

15 For an analysis of language and translation questions in *Henry V* see my, 'Rug-Headed Kerns Speaking Tongues: Shakespeare, Translation and the Irish Language', Mark Thornton Burnett and Ramona Wray, *Shakespeare and Ireland: History, Politics, Culture*, London, Macmillan, 1997, pp. 193–212.

16   Aleida Assmann, 'The Curse and Blessing of Babel; or, Looking Back on Univer-salisms', Sanford Budick and Wolgang Iser, eds., *The Translatability of Cultures: Figurations of the Space Between*, Stanford University Press, 1996, p. 87.

17   Assmann, 'The Curse and Blessing of Babel', p. 89.

18   ibid., p. 89.

19   Cited in ibid., p. 100.

20   Rosa Braidotti, *Nomadic Subjects: Embodiment and Sexual Difference in Contempo-rary Feminist Theory*, New York, Columbia University Press, 1994, p. 77.

21   Nicolas Bouvier, *Routes et Déroutes: Entretiens avec Irène Lichstenstein-Fall*, Geneva, Métropolis, 1992, p. 55.

'There must be a balance between the physical and the intellectual world which in my case happened early because every time I could, I left. That was the physical, carnal, musical, vocal discovery of the world. It is what I call learning through the sole of your feet.'

22   Jean-Claude Guillebaud, *Un voyage en Océanie*, Paris, Seuil, 1980.

23   As we argued in Chapter 3 these sensory impressions are likely to be heightened in the absence of a common language as other forms of non-verbal communica-tion are foregrounded. However, no one speaks all the time and even when the traveller does speak the language of the host s/he is susceptible to different expe-riences of the other senses.

24   Edwin Gentzler, 'Translation, Counter-Culture, and *The Fifties* in the USA', Román Álvarez and M. Carmen-África Vidal, eds., *Translation, Power, Subversion*, Cleve-don, Multilingual Matters, 1996, p. 122; see also Daniel Simeoni, 'Translating and Studying Translation: The View from the Agent', *Meta*, vol. 40, no. 3, 1995, pp. 445–60; Luise von Flotow, 'Dis-unity and Diversity: Feminist Approaches to Translation Studies', Lynne Bowker, Michael Cronin, Dorothy Kenny and Jennifer Pearson, eds., *Unity in Diversity? Current Trends in Translation Studies*, Manchester, St Jerome, 1998, pp. 3–13.

25   Pym, *Method in Translation History*, pp. 180–1.

26   Caren Kaplan, *Questions of Travel: Postmodern Discourses of Displacement*, Durham and London, Duke University Press, 1996, p. 172.

27   Nancy Hartsock, 'Rethinking Modernism', *Cultural Critique*, no. 7, autumn 1987, pp. 187–206.

28   Frances E. Mascia-Lees, Patricia Sharpe, and Colleen Ballerino Cohen, 'The Post-modernist Turn in Anthropology: Cautions from a Feminist Perspective', *Signs: Journal of Women in Culture and Society*, vol. 15, no. 1, 1989, p. 29.

29   Mascia-Lees, Sharpe and Cohen, 'The Postmodernist Turn in Anthropology', p. 29.

30   For an examination of the different domains in which translators are subject to marginalisation and/or exclusion see Lawrence Venuti, *The Scandals of Transla-tion: Towards an Ethics of Difference*, London, Routledge, 1998.

31   See my 'The Empire Talks Back: Orality, Heteronomy and the Cultural Turn in Interpreting Studies', in Maria Tymoczko and Edwin Gentzler, *Translation and Power* (forthcoming).

32   Michel Maffesoli, *Du nomadisme: vagabondages initiatiques*, Paris, Librairie Générale Française, 1997, p. 75.

33   Maffesoli, *Du nomadisme*, p. 75.

'a kind of moral prison, a kind of reassuring little institution, a fortress in which you are permanently shut away by your education, career and stereo-typical identity'.

34   Pascal Bruckner, *Le Vertige de Babel: cosmopolitisme et mondialisme*, Paris, Arléa, 1994, p. 47.
      'Contrary to a commonly held assumption, it is not the deification of borders but their uncertainty that has been the misfortune of different peoples, particularly those of Eastern Europe, shunted about through the vagaries of war from one administration to another. The major attraction of borders, once they are recognised and protected, is that you can cross them, play around on the margins, a much more exhilarating exercise than simply getting rid of them. Only conquerors dream of removing borders, particularly those of others.'

35   Bruckner, *Le Vertige de Babel*, p. 31.
      'Making the transition from one civilisation to another is the equivalent of moulting, a metamorphosis that is difficult and laborious and bears no relationship to the discreet movement of the jet connecting the four corners of the globe.'

36   Bruckner, p. 43.
      'Therefore, a movement towards others implies having a homeland, a memory that must be cherished (even if in a relativistic way): I can only extend hospitality to a foreigner if I have a place in which to welcome her.'

37   Michael Keogh, 'Professional Membership', *Translation Ireland*, vol. 10, no. 1, March 1996, pp. 1–2.

38   For an account of the activities of both these groups, see my *Translating Ireland: Translation, Languages, Cultures*, Cork University Press, 1996.

39   James Clifford, *Routes: Travel and Translation in the Late Twentieth Century*, Cambridge (Mass.), Harvard University Press, 1997, p. 269.

40   Paul Gilroy, *The Black Atlantic: Double Consciousness and Modernity*, Cambridge (Mass.), Harvard University Press, 1993, p. 268.

41   Maffesoli, *Du nomadisme*, p. 65.
      'when the wanderer transgresses borders, s/he calls for, perhaps unconsciously, a kind of "heteronomy": law comes from the other, we only exist in relation to the other, which restores concrete meaning and substance to the social body.'

42   Pym, *Method in Translation History*, p. 180.

43   Georg Simmel, 'On the Psychology of Money', David Frisby and Mike Featherstone, eds., *Simmel on Culture*, London, Sage, 1997, p. 238.

44   Karlheinz Stierle, 'Translatio Studii and Renaissance: From Vertical to Horizontal Translation', Sanford Budick and Wolgang Iser, eds., *The Translatability of Cultures: Figurations of the Space Between*, Stanford University Press, 1996, p. 66.

45   Michel de Certeau, *L'invention du quotidien*, I: *Arts de faire*, Paris, Union générale d'éditions, 1980, p. 205.

46   Christine Montalbetti, *Le Voyage, le monde et la bibliothèque*, Paris, Presses Universitaires de France, 1997, p. 115.
      'the notion of *transport*, on which the Aristotelian definition of metaphor is based, affects the reading of metaphor: as the figure effects a *displacement*, the reader finds herself *transported* from one field to the next, according to the same dynamic that informs the reading of fiction, based similarly on the substitution of spaces, on the notion of *breakaway*.'

47   James Carse, *Finite and Infinite Games*, Harmondsworth, Penguin, 1987, p. 102.

48   Arthur Koestler, 'Association and Bisociation', Jerome S. Bruner, Alison Jolly and Kathy Sylva, eds., *Play: Its Role in Development and Evolution*, Harmondsworth,

Penguin, 1976, p. 644. For a full account of Koestler's theory of creativity see Arthur Koestler, *The Act of Creation*, London, Arkana, 1989.

49 Pym, *Method in Translation History*, pp. 186–7.

50 Eamonn Slater, 'Becoming an Irish *Flâneur*', Michel Peillon and Eamonn Slater, *Encounters with Modern Ireland: A Sociological Chronicle 1995–1996*, Dublin, Institute of Public Administration, 1998, p. 2.

51 Adam Phillips, *The Beast in the Nursery*, London, Faber and Faber, 1998, p. 11.

52 Adam Phillips, 'A Stab at Hinting', *The Beast in the Nursery*, p. 84.

53 Adam Phillips, 'The Interested Party', *The Beast in the Nursery*, p. 31.

54 Cited in Phillips, p. 55.

55 Adam Phillips, 'The Beast in the Nursery', *The Beast in the Nursery*, p. 57.

56 Adam Phillips, 'A Stab at Hinting', p. 86.

57 Jean Delisle, *La traduction raisonnée: Manuel d'initiation à la traduction professionnelle de l'anglais vers le français*, Ottawa, Presses de l'université d'Ottawa, 1993; Mona Baker, *In Other Words: A Coursebook on Translation*, London, Routledge, 1992.

58 Eeva Jokinen and Soile Veijola, 'The Disoriented Tourist: The Figuration of the Tourist in Contemporary Cultural Critique', Chris Rojek and John Urry, *Touring Cultures: Transformations of Travel and Theory*, London, Routledge, 1997, p. 29; see also J. Wolff, 'The Invisible Flâneuse: Women and the Literature of Modernity', *Theory, Culture and Society*, vol. 2, 1985, pp. 37–46.

59 P. Parkhurst Ferguson, 'The Flâneur on and off the Streets of Paris', K. Tester, ed., *The Flâneur*, London, Routledge, 1994, p. 35.

60 The four figures are described in Zygmunt Bauman, 'Från Pilgrim till Turist', *Moderna Tilder*, September 1994, pp. 20–34.

61 Jokinen and Veijola, 'The Disoriented Tourist', p. 37.

62 Jokinen and Veijola, p. 38.

63 ibid., p. 44.

64 John Carroll, ed., *Language, Thought and Reality: Selected Writings of Benjamin Lee Whorf*, Cambridge (Mass.), MIT Press, 1972.

65 Geoffrey Pullum, *The Great Eskimo Vocabulary Hoax and Other Irreverent Essays on the Study of Language*, University of Chicago Press, 1991.

66 John Edwards, *Multilingualism*, London, Penguin, 1995, p. 92.

67 Clifford, *Routes*, p. 175.

68 Pym, *Method in Translation History*, pp. 140–1.

69 Tony Crowley, *Language in History*, London, Routledge, 1996, p. 110.

70 Charles Handy, *The Hungry Spirit: Beyond Capitalism – A Quest for Purpose in the Modern World*, London, Arrow, 1998, p. 38.

71 This does not mean, of course, that the absence of knowledge of a language automatically disqualifies a person from making observations on or experiencing another culture as we clearly saw in Chapter 3. The real human limits to language competence are themselves sufficient checks on any excessive idealism in the area and this indeed is one of the reasons why translation exists in the first place. It is, however, possible to argue that a genuine sense of reciprocity involves an explicit acknowledgement of the partial, bounded nature of cultural knowledge that is acquired either without any notion of the language or through the good offices of translation. The temptation too often, alas, is to try to marginalise the fact of language difference and kick over the traces of translation.

72 Cited in John Brockman, *The Third Culture: Beyond the Scientific Revolution*, New York, Simon and Schuster, 1995, p. 22.

73 Jamie James, *The Music of the Spheres: Music, Science and the Natural Order of the Universe*, London, Abacus, 1995, p. xiv.

74 Bouvier, *Routes et Déroutes*, p. 55.
   'Since earliest childhood, I have had a craving for different and somewhat gypsy-like bits of knowledge. I cherish what is called general knowledge and I cobble together bits of knowledge the way you would put back together the pieces of a broken mosaic, wherever I can, unsystematically. And I see these things fit mysteriously into place as if inside a sphere where everything would conspire to create a kind of harmonious, polyphonic whole.'

75 Handy, *The Hungry Spirit*, p. 53.

76 Daniel Simeoni, 'The Pivotal Status of the Translator's Habitus', vol. 10, no. 1, 1998, pp. 1–39.

77 Needless to say late modernity may be a flexible utopia for some and an unstable, exploitative nightmare for others. Translators through cost-cutting, impossible deadlines (see Chapter 4 on speed) and lack of adequate health care and pension schemes are often as exposed to the negative impact of postmodern, free-market logic as any other service provider.

78 Joris-Karl Huysmans, *À rebours*, Paris, Flammarion, 1983, p. 198.

79 Xavier de Maistre, *Voyage autour de ma chambre*, Paris, José Corti, 1991, p. 31.
   'it is both useful and pleasurable to have the soul freed from matter.'

80 William J. Mitchell, *City of Bits: Space, Place and the Infobahn*, Cambridge (Mass.), MIT Press, 1995, p. 7.

81 Cited in Mitchell, *City of Bits*, p. 110.

82 Mitchell, p. 98.

83 Alain Borer, 'L'ère de Colomb et l'ère d'Armstrong', *Pour une littérature voyageuse*, Bruxelles, Éditions Complexe, 1992, p. 36.
   'Henceforth, the figure of the traveller is one of immobility.'

84 Paul Virilio, 'The Last Vehicle', Jeremy Millar and Michiel Schwarz, eds., *Speed – Visions of an Accelerated Age*, London, Whitechapel Art Gallery, 1998, p. 34.

85 Virilio, 'The Last Vehicle', p. 48.

86 Allucquère Roseanne Stone, *The War of Desire and Technology at the Close of the Mechanical Age*, Cambridge (Mass.), MIT Press, 1995, p. 17.

87 Stone, *The War of Desire and Technology*, p. 43.

88 Stone, p. 61.

89 Mary Louise Pratt, *Imperial Eyes: Travel writing and Transculturation*, London, Routledge, 1992, pp. 15–68.

90 Mitchell, *City of Bits*, p. 19.

91 Scott London, 'Postmodern Tourism: An Interview with Pico Iyer', http://www.west.net/~insight/iyer.htm, 12 of 14.

92 Mitchell, *City of Bits*, p. 167.

93 Steve G. Weinberg, 'Get Ready for Web Objects', *Wired*, February 1996, p. 52.

94 Mitchell, *City of Bits*, p. 14.

95 For a survey of the impact of new technology on translation see Minako O'Hagan, *The Coming Industry of Teletranslation*, Clevedon, Multilingual Matters, 1996.

96 Mitchell, *City of Bits*, p. 24.

97 Richard Sennett, *The Conscience of the Eye: The Design and Social Life of Cities*, New York, Norton, 1990, p. xiii.

BIBLIOGRAPHY

Adams, Douglas, *The Hitch-Hiker's Guide to the Galaxy*, London, Pan, 1979.

Adler, J., 'Origins of sightseeing', *Annals of Tourism Research*, vol. 16, 1989, pp. 7–29.

Aijmer, Göran, 'Comment on Article by P. Steven Sangren', *Current Anthropology*, vol. 33, supplement, 1992, pp. 296–7.

Aixelá, Javier Franco, 'Culture-Specific Items in Translation', Román Álvarez and M. Carmen-África Vidal, eds., *Translation, Power, Subversion*, Clevedon, Multilingual Matters, 1996, pp. 52–78.

Allsop, Kenneth, *Hard Travellin': The Story of the Migrant Worker*, London, Pimlico, 1993.

Amati Mehler, Jacqueline, Simona Argentieri and Jorge Canestri, *La Babel de l'inconscient: Langue maternelle, langues étrangères et psychanalyse*, tr. Maya Garboua, Paris, Presses Universitaires de France, 1994.

Anderson, R.B.W. 'Perspectives on the Role of the Interpeter', Richard W. Brislin, ed., *Translation: Applications and Research*, New York, Gardner Press, 1976, pp. 208–28.

Ara, Angelo, and Claudio Magris, *Trieste: Un'identità di frontiera*, Turin, Einaudi, 1987.

Assmann, Aleida, 'The Curse and Blessing of Babel; or, Looking Back on Universalisms', Sanford Budick and Wolgang Iser, eds., *The Translatability of Cultures: Figurations of the Space Between*, Stanford University Press, 1996, pp. 85–100.

Augé, Marc, *La Traversée du Luxembourg*, Paris, Hachette, 1985.

Augé, Marc, *Un ethnologue dans le métro*, Paris, Hachette, 1986.

Bakhtin, Mikhail, *The Dialogical Imagination*, Austin, University of Texas Press, 1981.

Baker, Mona, *In Other Words: A Coursebook on Translation*, London, Routledge, 1992.

Baker, Mona, ed., *Routledge Encyclopedia of Translation Studies*, London, Routledge, 1998.

Bassnett, Susan, 'The Meek or the Mighty: Reappraising the Role of the Translator', Román Álvarez and M. Carmen-África Vidal, eds., *Translation, Power, Subversion*, Clevedon, Multilingual Matters, 1996, pp. 10–24.

Bateson, Gregory, *Steps to an Ecology of Mind*, London, Paladin, 1978.

Bauman, Zygmunt, *Postmodern Ethics*, Oxford, Blackwell, 1993.

Bauman, Zygmunt, 'Från Pilgrim till Turist', *Moderna Tilder*, September 1994, pp. 20–34.

Bauman, Zygmunt, *Globalization: The Human Consequences*, Cambridge, Polity, 1998,

Beck, Ulrich, *Risk Society: Towards a New Modernity*, tr. M. Ritter, London, Sage, 1992.

Beer, Gillian, *Open Fields: Science in Cultural Encounter*, Oxford, Clarendon Press, 1996.

Behdad, Ali, *Belated Travellers: Orientalism in the Age of Colonial Dissolution*, Cork University Press, 1994.

Bénichou, François, 'François Maspero: le passeur de mots', *Magazine littéraire*, no. 351, février 1997, pp. 96–102.

Bennett, Alan, 'What I Did in 1998', *London Review of Books*, vol. 20, no. 2, 21 January 1999, pp. 3–8.

Benveniste, Émile, *Indo-European Language and Society*, tr. Elizabeth Palmer, London, Faber and Faber, 1973.

Berman, Marshall, *All That Is Solid Melts Into Air: The Experience of Modernity*, London, Verso, 1983.

Birkett, Dea, and Sara Wheeler, eds., *Amazonians: The Penguin Book of Women's New Travel Writing*, London, Penguin, 1998.

Boland, Rosita, *Sea Legs: Hitch-Hiking the Coast of Ireland Alone*, Dublin, New Island Books, 1992.

Borer, Alain, 'L'ère de Colomb et l'ère d'Armstrong', *Pour une littérature voyageuse*, Bruxelles, Éditions Complexe, 1992, pp. 17–40.

Bouvier, Nicolas, *L'usage du monde*, 1963; Paris, Payot, 1992.

Bouvier, Nicolas, *Routes et Déroutes: Entretiens avec Irène Lichstenstein-Fall*, Geneva, Métropolis, 1992.

Bouvier, Nicolas, *L'Échappée belle: Éloge de quelques pérégrins*, Geneva, Métropolis, 1996.

Bowker, Lynne, Michael Cronin, Dorothy Kenny and Jennifer Pearson (eds.), *Unity in Diversity? Current Trends in Translation Studies*, Manchester, St Jerome, 1998.

Braidotti, Rosa, *Nomadic Subjects: Embodiment and Sexual Difference in Contemporary Feminist Theory*, New York, Columbia University Press, 1994.

Brockman, John, *The Third Culture: Beyond the Scientific Revolution*, New York, Simon and Schuster, 1995.

Brodsky, Joseph, *On Grief and Reason*, London, Hamish Hamilton, 1995.

Bruckner, Pascal, *Le Vertige de Babel: cosmopolitisme et mondialisme*, Paris, Arléa, 1994.

Bryson, Bill, *Mother Tongue: The English Language*, London, Penguin, 1991.

Bryson, Bill, *Made in America*, London, Secker and Warburg, 1994.

Bryson, Bill, *Notes from a Small Island*, London, Black Swan, 1996.

Buzard, James, *The Beaten Track: European Tourism, Literature and the Ways to 'Culture' 1800–1918*, Oxford, Clarendon Press, 1993.

Byron, Robert, *The Road to Oxiana*, 1937; London, Pan, 1981.

Campbell, Joseph, *The Masks of God: Primitive Mythology*, vol. 1, London, Souvenir Press, 1973.

Carroll, Raymonde, *Cultural Misunderstandings: The French-American Experience*, University of Chicago Press, 1988.

Carroll, John, ed., *Language, Thought and Reality: Selected Writings of Benjamin Lee Whorf*, Cambridge (Mass.), MIT Press, 1972.

Carse, James, *Finite and Infinite Games*, Harmondsworth, Penguin, 1987.

Chatwin, Bruce, *In Patagonia*, London, Picador, 1979.

Chatwin, Bruce, *What Am I Doing Here*, London, Picador, 1990.

Cheyfitz, Eric, *The Poetics of Imperialism: Translation and Colonization from* The Tempest *to* Tarzan, Oxford University Press, 1991.

Clarke, Arthur C., and Gentry Lee, *Rama Revealed*, London, Orbit, 1994.

Clifford, James, 'Traveling Cultures', Lawrence Grossberg, Cary Nelson and Paula Treichler, eds., *Cultural Studies*, London, Routledge, 1992, pp. 96–112.

Clifford, James, *Routes: Travel and Translation in the Late Twentieth Century*, London and Cambridge (Mass.), Harvard University Press, 1997.

Craik, Jennifer, 'The Culture of Tourism', Chris Rojek and John Urry, *Touring Cultures: Transformations of Travel and Theory*, London, Routledge, 1997, pp. 113–36.

Crang, Philip, 'Performing the Tourist Product', Chris Rojek and John Urry, eds., *Touring Cultures: Transformations of Travel and Theory*, London, Routledge, 1997, pp. 137–54.

Crashaw, Carol, and John Urry, 'Tourism and the Photographic Eye', Chris Rojek and John Urry, eds., *Touring Cultures: Transformations of Travel and Theory*, London, Routledge, 1997, pp. 176–95.

Cronin, Michael, 'Marvellous Travelling: Kate O'Brien's Travel Accounts', in Eibhear Walshe, ed., *Ordinary People Dancing: Essays on Kate O'Brien*, Cork University Press, 1993, pp. 137–49.

Cronin, Michael, 'Altered States: Translation and Minority Languages', *TTR*, vol. 8, no. 1, 1995, pp. 85–103.

Cronin, Michael, 'Keeping One's Distance: Translation and the Play of Possibility', *TTR*, vol. 8, no. 2, 1995, pp. 227–43.

Cronin, Michael, 'Shoring Up the Fragments of the Translator's Discourse: Complexity, Incompleteness and Integration', *META*, vol. 40, no. 3, septembre 1995, pp. 359–66.

Cronin, Michael, 'Andere Stimmen: Reiseliteratur und das Problem der Sprachbarrieren', Anne Fuchs and Theo Harden, eds., *Reisen im Diskurs: Modelle der literarischen Fremdenfahrung von den Pilgerberichten bis zur Postmoderne*, Heidelberg, C. Winter Universitätsverlag, 1995, pp. 19–34.

Cronin, Michael, *Translating Ireland: Translation, Languages, Cultures*, Cork University Press, 1996.

Cronin, Michael, 'Rug-Headed Kerns Speaking Tongues: Shakespeare, Translation and the Irish Language', Mark Thornton Burnett and Ramona Wray eds., *Shakespeare and Ireland: History, Politics, Culture*, London, Macmillan, 1997, pp. 193–212.

Cronin, Michael, 'The Cracked Looking Glass of Servants: Translation and Minority Languages in a Global Age', *The Translator*, vol. 4, no. 2, 1998, pp. 145–62.

Cronin, Michael, 'The Empire Talks Back: Orality, Heteronomy and the Cultural Turn in Interpreting Studies', Maria Tymoczko and Edwin Gentzler eds., *Translation and Power* (forthcoming).

Crowley, Tony, *Language in History*, London, Routledge, 1996.

Crystal, David, *English as a Global Language*, Cambridge University Press, 1997.

Culler, Jonathan, 'Semiotics of Tourism', *American Journal of Semiotics*, vol. 1, 1981, pp. 127–40.

D'Souza, Dinesh, *The End of Racism: Principles for a Multiracial Society*, New York, Free Press, 1995.

de Certeau, Michel, *L'invention du quotidien*, I: *Arts de faire*, Paris, Union générale d'éditions, 1980.

de Condillac, Étienne Bonnot, *Essai sur l'origine des connaissances humaines*, 1746, Galilée, Paris, 1973.

de Maistre, Xavier, *Voyage autour de ma chambre*, 1794, Paris, José Corti, 1991.

Delaney, Samuel R., *Babel-17*, London, Gollancz, 1987.

Deleuze, Gilles, and Félix Guattari, *Kafka: Pour une littérature mineure*, Paris, Minuit, 1975.

Delisle, Jean, and Judith Woodsworth, eds., *Translators through History*, Amsterdam, Unesco/John Benjamins, 1995.

Delisle, Jean, *La traduction raisonnée: Manuel d'initiation à la traduction professionnelle de l'anglais vers le français*, Ottawa, Presses de l'université d'Ottawa, 1993.

Denby, David, *Sentimental Narrative and the Social Order in France, 1760–1820*, Cambridge University Press, 1994.

Derrida, Jacques, *Le monolinguisme de l'autre*, Paris, Galilée, 1996.

Descartes, René, *Discours de la méthode*, 1637, Paris, 10/18, 1977.

Dimendberg, Edward, 'The Will to Motorisation – Cinema and the Autobahn', Jeremy Millar and Michiel Schwarz, eds., *Speed – Visions of an Accelerated Age*, London, Whitechapel Art Gallery, 1998, pp. 56–72.

Dunne, Joseph, 'Culture, Citizenship and the Global Market: Challenges to the "New Europe"', F. Crawley, P. Smeyers and P. Standish, eds., *Universities and the Identity of Europe*, Oxford and Providence, Berghahn, (forthcoming).

Eco, Umberto, *The Search for the Perfect Language*, tr. James Fentress, Oxford, Blackwell, 1995.

Edwards, John, *Multilingualism*, London, Penguin, 1995.

Fabian, Johannes, *Time and the Other: How Anthropology Makes its Object*, New York, Columbia University Press, 1983.

Fabian, Johannes, *Language and Colonial Power*, New York, Cambridge University Press, 1986.

Featherstone, Mike, 'Postmodernism and the Aestheticization of Everyday Life', Scott Lash and Jonathan Friedman, eds., *Modernity and Identity*, Oxford, Blackwell, 1992, pp. 265–90.

Fernández-Armesto, Felipe, *Millennium*, London, Black Swan, 1996.

Foucault, Michel, *Madness and Civilization*, London, Tavistock, 1967.

Foucault, Michel, *The Birth of the Clinic*, London, Tavistock, 1976.

Foucault, Michel, *Discipline and Punish: The Birth of the Prison*, tr. Alan Sheridan, Harmondsworth, Penguin, 1979.

Friel, Brian, *Translations*, London, Faber & Faber, 1971.

Fuchs, Anne, and Theo Harden, eds., *Reisen im Diskurs: Modelle der literarischen Fremdenfahrung von den Pilgerberichten bis zur Postmoderne*, Heidelberg, C. Winter Universitätsverlag, 1995.

Furet, François, *Le passé d'une illusion: Essai sur l'idée communiste au XXè siècle*, Paris, Robert Laffont/Calmann-Lévy, 1995.

Fussell, Paul, *Abroad: British Literary Traveling Between the Wars*, New York, Oxford University Press, 1980.

Gentzler, Edwin, 'Translation, Counter-Culture, and *The Fifties* in the USA', Román Álvarez and M. Carmen-África Vidal, eds., *Translation, Power, Subversion*, Clevedon, Multilingual Matters, 1996, pp. 116–37.

George, Susan, 'Fast Castes', Jeremy Millar and Michiel Schwarz, eds., *Speed – Visions of an Accelerated Age*, London, Whitechapel Art Gallery, 1998, pp. 115–18.

Gibbons, John, *Tramping through Ireland*, London, Methuen, 1930.

Giddens, Anthony, *Modernity and Self-Identity*, Cambridge, Polity, 1991.

Gilroy, Paul, *The Black Atlantic: Double Consciousness and Modernity*, Cambridge (Mass.), Harvard University Press, 1993.

Gleick, James, *Chaos: Making a New Science*, London, Cardinal, 1987.

Graves, Charles, *Ireland Revisited*, London, Hutchinson, 1949.

Guillebaud, Jean-Claude, *Un voyage en Océanie*, Paris, Seuil, 1980.

Guillebaud, Jean-Claude, *Sur la route des croisades*, Paris, Arléa, 1993.

Guillen, Michael, *Five Equations that Changed the World*, London, Little Brown, 1995.

Haddad, Antoinetta and Gérard, *Freud en Italie: Psychanalyse du voyage*, Paris, Albin Michel, 1995.

Hall, Stuart, 'The Local and the Global: Globalization and Ethnicity', Anthony D. King, ed., *Culture, Globalization and the World System*, London, Macmillan, 1991, pp. 19–39.

Harvey, David, *The Condition of Postmodernity*, Oxford, Blackwell, 1989.

Handy, Charles, *The Hungry Spirit: Beyond Capitalism – A Quest for Purpose in the Modern World*, London, Arrow, 1998.

Hartsock, Nancy, 'Rethinking Modernism', *Cultural Critique*, no. 7, autumn 1987, pp. 187–206.

Heaney, Seamus, 'The Interesting Case of John Alphonsus Mulrennan', *Planet*, no. 41, 1978, pp. 34–40.

Heaney, Seamus, *Station Island*, London, Faber and Faber, 1984.

Heidegger, Martin, *The Question Concerning Technology and Other Essays*, New York, Harper, 1977.

Hoffman, Eva, *Lost in Translation*, London, Minerva, 1991.

Hoffman, Eva, *Exit into History: A Journey through the New Eastern Europe*, London, Minerva, 1994.

Homel, David, and Sherry Simon, eds., *Mapping Literature: The Art and Politics of Translation*, Montreal, Véhicule Press, 1988.

Huysmans, Joris-Karl, *A rebours*, Paris, Flammarion, 1983.

Ingram, Susan, 'Translation, Autobiography, Bilingualism', in Lynne Bowker, Michael Cronin, Dorothy Kenny and Jennifer Pearson, eds., *Unity in Diversity? Current Trends in Translation Studies*, Manchester, St Jerome, 1998, pp. 15–22.

Jakobson, Roman, 'On Linguistic Aspects of Translation', Rainer Schulte and John Biguenet, *Theories of Translation: An Anthology of Essays from Dryden to Derrida*, University of Chicago Press, 1992, pp. 144–51.

James, Henry, *Italian Hours*, New York, Houghton Mifflin, 1909.

James, Jamie, *The Music of the Spheres: Music, Science and the Natural Order of the Universe*, London, Abacus, 1995.

Jokinen, Eeva, and Soile Veijola, 'The Disoriented Tourist: The Figuration of the Tourist in Contemporary Cultural Critique', Chris Rojek and John Urry, *Touring Cultures: Transformations of Travel and Theory*, London, Routledge, 1997, pp. 23–51.

Jolas, Eugène, *Sur Joyce*, Paris, Plon, 1990.

Joyce, James, *Finnegans Wake*, 1939, London, Faber and Faber, 1980.

Kaplan, Alice, *French Lessons: A Memoir*, University of Chicago Press, 1993.

Kaplan, Caren, *Questions of Travel: Postmodern Discourses of Displacement*, Durham and London, Duke University Press, 1996.

Kaplan, Caren, and Inderpal Grewal, eds., *Scattered Hegemonies: Postmodernity and Transnational Feminist Practices*, Minneapolis, University of Minnesota Press, 1994.

Kellner, Douglas, *Jean Baudrillard: From Marxism to Postmodernism*, Stanford University Press, 1989.

Keogh, Michael, 'Professional Membership', *Translation Ireland*, vol. 10, no. 1, March 1996, pp. 1–2.

Kerridge, Roy, *Jaunting through Ireland*, London, Michael Joseph, 1991, p. 315.

King, Russell, John Connell and Paul White, eds., *Writing across Worlds: Literature and Migration*, London, Routledge, 1995.

Koestler, Arthur, 'Association and Bisociation', Jerome S. Bruner, Alison Jolly and Kathy Sylva, eds., *Play: Its role in Development and Evolution*, Harmondsworth, Penguin, 1976, pp. 643–9.

Koestler, Arthur, *The Act of Creation*, London, Arkana, 1989.

Kondo, Dorinne, 'Dissolution and Reconstitution of Self: Implications for Anthropological Epistemology', *Cultural Anthropology*, vol. 1, no. 1, 1986, p. 74–88.

Kreuger, John, 'Language and Techniques of Communication as Theme or Tool in Science Fiction', *Linguistics*, vol. 39, 1968, pp. 68–86.

Kristeva, Julia, *Étrangers à nous-mêmes*, Paris, Gallimard, 1988.

Lacarrière, Jacques, *Chemin Faisant: Mille kilomètres à pied à travers la France*, Paris, Fayard, 1977.

Ladmiral, Jean-René, 'Traduire, c'est-à-dire...Phénoménologies d'un concept pluriel', *Meta*, vol. 40, no. 3, 1995, pp.409–20.

Lamy, Laurent, 'Pas de deux: le mésocosme de la traduction comme matrice d'une sémantique frontalière', *Meta*, vol. 40, no. 3, 1995, pp. 461–77.

Lash, Scott, and John Urry, *Economies of Signs & Space*, London, Sage, 1994.

Le Bris, Michel, *Fragments du royaume: conversations avec Yvon Le Men*, Vénissieux, Éditions de l'Aube, 1995.

Leader, Darian, *Why Do Women Write More Letters Than They Post?*, London, Faber and Faber, 1996.

Leerssen, Joep, *Mere Irish and Fíor-Ghael*, Cork University Press, 1996.

Lepenies, Wolf, 'Translation's Role in National Identity', *Times Higher Education Supplement*, 2 October 1992.

Ley, Charles David, ed., *Portugese Voyages 1493–1663*, London, J.M. Dent, 1947.

London, Scott, 'Postmodern Tourism: An Interview with Pico Iyer', http://www.west.net/~insight/iyer.htm.

MacCannell, Dean, 'Staged Authenticity: Arrangements of Social Space in Tourism Settings', *American Sociological Review*, no. 79, 1973, pp. 589–603.

MacCannell, Dean, *The Tourist: A New Theory of the Leisure Class*, 2nd ed., New York, Schocken Books, 1989.

Maffesoli, Michel, *Du nomadisme: vagabondages initiatiques*, Paris, Librairie Générale Française, 1997.

Magris, Claudio, *Danube: A Sentimental Journey from the Source to the Black Sea*, tr. Patrick Creagh, London, Collins Harvill, 1989.

Makine, Andreï, *Le testament français*, Paris, Mercure de France, 1995.

Mallarmé, Stéphane, *Oeuvres complètes*, Paris, Gallimard, 1975.

Mandelbrot, Benoît, *The Fractal Geometry of Nature*, New York, Freeman, 1977.

Mangan, James Clarence, 'Anthologia Germanica', *Dublin University Magazine*, vol. 7, no. 39, March 1836, pp. 278–302.

Manguel, Alberto, *A History of Reading*, London, Flamingo, 1997.

Marx, Karl, *Grundrisse: Foundations of the Critique of Political Economy*, tr. M. Nicolaus, London, Allen Lane/NLR, 1973.

Mascia-Lees, Frances E., Patricia Sharpe, and Colleen Ballerino Cohen, 'The Postmodernist Turn in Anthropology: Cautions from a Feminist Perspective', *Signs: Journal of Women in Culture and Society*, vol. 15, no. 1, 1989, pp. 7–33.

Mendelson, Edward, 'Baedeker's Universe', *Yale Review*, Spring 1985, pp. 386–403.

Meyers, Walter, *Aliens and Linguists*, Athens (Georgia), University of Georgia Press, 1980.

Mezciems, Jenny, '"Tis Not to Divert the Reader": Moral and Literary Determinants in Some Early Travel Narratives', Philip Dodd, ed., *The Art of Travel: Essays on Travel Writing*, London, Frank Cass, 1982, pp. 2–16.

Michaud, Ginette and Sherry Simon, *Joyce*, Ville La Salle, Hurtubise HMH, 1996.

Mills, Sara, *Discourses of Difference: An Analysis of Women's Travel Writing and Colonialism*, London, Routledge, 1991.

Mitchell, William J., *City of Bits: Space, Place and the Infobahn*, Cambridge (Mass.), MIT Press, 1995.

Montalbetti, Christine, *Le Voyage, le monde et la bibliothèque*, Paris, Presses Universitaires de France, 1997.

Morin, Edgar, *Penser l'Europe*, Paris, Gallimard, 1990.

Mossop, Brian, 'The Image of Translation in Science Fiction & Astronomy', *The Translator*, vol. 2, no. 1, 1996, pp. 1–26.

Murphy, Dervla, *Muddling Through in Madagascar*, London, Century, 1986.

Murphy, Dervla, *The Ukimwi Road: From Kenya to Zimbabwe*, London, John Murray, 1993.

Musser, Charles, 'The Travel Genre in 1903–1904: Moving Towards Fictional Narrative', Thomas Elsaesser, ed., *Early Cinema: Space – Frame – Narrative*, London, British Film Institute, 1990, pp. 123–32.

Nabokov, Vladimir, 'Problems of Translation: *Onegin* in English', Rainer Schulte and John Biguenet, eds., *Theories of Translation: An Anthology of Essays from Dryden to Derrida*, University of Chicago Press, 1992, pp. 127–43.

Naipaul, V.S., 'After the Revolution', *The New Yorker*, 26 May 1997, pp. 46–69.

Newby, Eric, *Round Ireland in Low Gear*, London, Viking, 1987.

Ní Mhaoileoin, Úna, *Turas go Túinis*, Dublin, Sáirséal agus Dill, 1969.

Nic Eoin, Máirín, and Liam Mac Mathúna, *Ar Thóir an Fhocail Chruinn: Iriseoirí, Téarmeolaithe agus Fadhbanna an Aistriúcháin*, Dublin, Coiscéim, 1997.

Niranjana, Tejaswini, *Siting Translation: History, Post-Structuralism and the Colonial Context*, Berkeley, University of California Press, 1992.

Nossack, Hans Erich, 'Translating and Being Translated', Rainer Schulte and John Biguenet, *Theories of Translation: An Anthology of Essays from Dryden to Derrida*, University of Chicago Press, 1992, pp. 228–38.

Nussbaum, Martha C., *Love's Knowledge: Essays on Philosophy and Literature*, Oxford University Press, 1990.

Ó Catháin, Diarmuid, 'Ramblings', *Lixnaw 1995*, Lixnaw, Ceolann, 1995, pp. 9–13.

Ó Searcaigh, Cathal, *Out in the Open*, tr. Frank Sewell, Indreabhán, Cló Iar-Chonnachta, 1997.

Ó Rinn, Liam, *Turus go Páras*, Dublin, Oifig Díolta Foilseacháin Rialtais, 1931.

O'Brien, Kate, *Farewell Spain*, 1937; rpt. London, Virago, 1985.

O'Brien, Kate, *My Ireland*, London, Batsford, 1962.

O'Brien, Flann, *The Poor Mouth*, tr. Patrick C. Power, London, Picador, 1973.

O'Brien, Sharon, 'CAT Tools in the Localization Industry', Lynne Bowker, Michael Cronin, Dorothy Kenny and Jennifer Pearson, eds., *Unity in Diversity? Current Trends in Translation Studies*, Manchester, St Jerome, 1998, pp. 115–22.

O'Hagan, Minako, *The Coming Industry of Teletranslation*, Clevedon, Multilingual Matters, 1996.

O'Hanlon, Redmond, *Into the Heart of Borneo*, London, Penguin, 1985.

Ong, Walter J., *Orality and Literacy: The Technologizing of the Word*, London, Routledge, 1989.

Ouaknin, Marc-Alain, *Bibliothérapie: Lire, c'est guérir*, Paris, Seuil, 1994.

Parkhurst Ferguson, P., 'The Flâneur on and off the Streets of Paris', K. Tester, ed., *The Flâneur*, London, Routledge, 1994.

Phillips, Adam, *On Kissing, Tickling and Being Bored: Psychoanalytic Essays on the Unexamined Life*, London, Faber and Faber, 1993.

Phillips, Adam, *The Beast in the Nursery*, London, Faber and Faber, 1998.

Poor, Glen, 'Localising *Windows* and *Office '95*': A Sim-Ship Strategy', *Software Localisation*, vol. 1, no. 1, 1996, p. 1.

Pratt, Mary-Louise, *Imperial Eyes: Travel Writing and Transculturation*, London, Routledge, 1992.

Pratt, Geraldine, and Susan Hanson, 'Geography and the Construction of Difference', *Gender, Place, Culture*, vol. 1, no. 1, 1994, pp. 5–29.

Pullum, Geoffrey, *The Great Eskimo Vocabulary Hoax and Other Irreverent Essays on the Study of Language*, University of Chicago Press, 1991.

Pym, Anthony, *Method in Translation History*, Manchester, St Jerome, 1998.

Raban, Jonathan, *Old Glory: An American Voyage*, London, Picador, 1986.

Raban, Jonathan, *Coasting*, London, Picador, 1987.

Raban, Jonathan, *Hunting Mister Heartbreak*, London, Picador, 1990.

Rey, Jean-Michel, *La Naissance de la poésie*, Paris, Métaillié, 1991.

Ricoeur, Paul, 'Quel ethos nouveau pour l'Europe', Peter Koslowski, ed., *Imaginer l'Europe*, Paris, Éditions du Cerf, 1992, pp. 107–19.

Ritzer, George, *The McDonaldization of Society*, Thousand Oaks (Cal.), Pine Forge Press, 1993.

Ritzer, George, and Allan Liska, '"McDisneyization" and "Post-Tourism"', Chris Rojek and John Urry, *Touring Cultures: Transformations of Travel and Theory*, London, Routledge, 1997, pp. 96–109.

Robinson, Jane, *Wayward Women: A Guide to Women Travellers*, Oxford University Press, 1990.

Robinson, Douglas, *Translation and Taboo*, Northern Illinois University Press, 1996.

Robinson, Douglas, ed., *Western Translation Theory from Herodotus to Nietzsche*, Manchester, St Jerome, 1997.

Robinson, Tim, *Stones of Aran: Labyrinth*, Dublin, Lilliput Press, 1995.

Rojek, Chris, and John Urry, 'Transformations of Travel and Theory', Chris Rojek and John Urry, eds., *Touring Cultures: Transformations of Travel and Theory*, London, Routledge, 1997, pp. 1–19.

Rorty, Richard, *Philosophy and the Mirror of Nature*, Oxford, Blackwell, 1980.

Rose, Gillian, *The Broken Middle: Out of our Ancient Society*, Oxford, Blackwell, 1992.

Rousseau, Jean-Jacques, *Essai sur l'origine des langues*, Paris, Hatier, 1983.

Russell, Mary, *The Blessings of a Good Thick Skirt: Women Travellers and Their World*, London, Flamingo, 1994.

Sabin, Margaret, 'The Spectacle of Reality in *Sea and Sardinia*', Philip Dodd, ed., *The Art of Travel: Essays on Travel Writing*, London, Frank Cass, 1982, pp. 85–104.

Sachs, Wolfgang, 'Speed Limits', Jeremy Millar and Michiel Schwarz, eds., *Speed – Visions of an Accelerated Age*, London, Whitechapel Art Gallery, 1998, pp. 123–32.

Sahlins, Marshall, *Islands of History*, London, Tavistock, 1987.

Said, Edward, 'Reflections on Exile', *Granta*, no. 13, 1984, pp. 159–72.

Schäler, Reinhard, 'The Problem with Machine Translation', Lynne Bowker, Michael Cronin, Dorothy Kenny and Jennifer Pearson, eds., *Unity in Diversity? Current Trends in Translation Studies*, Manchester, St Jerome, 1998, pp. 151–6.

Schivelbusch, Wolfgang, *The Railway Journey: Trains and Travel in the Nineteenth Century*, New York, Urizen Books, 1980.

Schutz, H., 'The Stranger: An Essay in Social Psychology', A. Brodersen, ed., *Studies in Social Theory, Collected Papers II*, The Hague, Martinus Mjnoff, 1964, pp. 91–105.

Semprun, Jorge, *Adieu, vive clarté . . .*, Paris, Gallimard, 1998.

Sennett, Richard, *The Conscience of the Eye: The Design and Social Life of Cities*, New York, Norton, 1990.

Serres, Michel, *Le Tiers-Instruit*, Paris, Gallimard, 1992.

Sibony, Daniel, *Entre-Deux: L'origine en partage*, Paris, Seuil, 1991.

Simeoni, Daniel, 'Translating and Studying Translation: the View from the Agent', *Meta*, vol. 40, no. 3, 1995, pp. 445–60.

Simeoni, Daniel, 'The Pivotal Status of the Translator's Habitus', *Target*, vol. 10, no. 1, 1998, pp. 1–39.

Simmel, Georg, 'The Stranger', in Donald N. Levine, ed., *On Individuality and Social Forms*, University of Chicago Press, 1971, pp. 143–9.

Simmel, Georg, 'On the Psychology of Money', David Frisby and Mike Featherstone, eds., *Simmel on Culture*, London, Sage, 1997, pp. 233–43.

Simon, Sherry, *Gender in Translation*, London, Routledge, 1996.

Singh, Rajendra, 'On Translation: Some Unfinished Thoughts', *Meta*, vol. 40, no. 3, 1995, pp. 354–5.

Slater, Eamonn, 'Becoming an Irish *Flâneur*', Eamonn Slater and Michel Peillon, eds., *Encounters with Modern Ireland*, Dublin, Insitute of Public Administration, 1998, pp. 1–6.

Sloterdijk, Peter, 'Modernity as Mobilisation', Jeremy Millar and Michiel Schwarz, eds., *Speed – Visions of an Accelerated Age*, London, Whitechapel Art Gallery, 1998, pp. 43–52.

Sontag, Susan, *On Photography*, Harmondsworth, Penguin, 1979.

Spenser, Edmund, *A View of the Present State of Ireland*, ed. W.L. Renwick, Oxford, Clarendon, 1970.

St Aubin de Terán, Lisa, *Off the Rails: Memoirs of a Train Addict*, London, Sceptre, 1990.

Stallybrass, Peter and Allon White, *The Politics and Poetics of Transgression*, London, Methuen, 1986.

Steiner, George, *Language and Silence: Essays 1958–1966*, London, Peregrine, 1979.

Steiner, George, *Real Presences*, London, Faber and Faber, 1989.

Steiner, George, *No Passion Spent: Essays 1978–1996*, London, Faber and Faber, 1996.

Steiner, George, *Errata: An Examined Life*, London, Phoenix, 1998.

Stengel, Erwing, 'On Learning a New Language', *International Journal of Psychoanalysis*, vol. 20, 1939, pp. 45–60.

Stierle, Karlheinz, 'Translatio Studii and Renaissance: From Vertical to Horizontal Translation', Sanford Budick and Wolgang Iser, eds, *The Translatability of Cultures: Figurations of the Space Between*, Stanford University Press, 1996, pp. 55–67.

Stoker, Bram, *Dracula*, 1897, London, Dent; rpt. 1993.

Stone, Allucquère Roseanne, *The War of Desire and Technology at the Close of the Mechanical Age*, Cambridge (Mass.), MIT Press, 1995.

Sturge, Kate, 'Translation Strategies in Ethnography', *The Translator*, vol. 3, no. 1, 1997, pp. 21–38.

Süskind, Patrick, *Das Parfum: Die Geschicte eines Mörders*, Zurich, Diogenes, 1985.

Theroux, Paul, *The Kingdom by the Sea*, London, Penguin, 1984.

Thieme, John, 'Authorial Voice in V.S. Naipaul's *The Middle Passage*', in Philip Dodd, ed., *The Art of Travel: Essays on Travel Writing*, London, Frank Cass, 1982, pp. 139–51.

Thoreau, Henry David, *Walden*, Carl Bode, ed., *The Portable Thoreau*, London, Penguin, 1982.

Todorov, Tzvetan, *L'homme dépaysé*, Paris, Seuil, 1996.

Tommola, Jorma, and Marketta Halevä, 'Language Direction and Source Text Complexity: Effects on Trainee Performance in Simultaneous Interpreting', Lynne Bowker, Michael Cronin, Dorothy Kenny and Jennifer Pearson, eds., *Unity in Diversity? Current Trends in Translation Studies*, Manchester, St Jerome, 1998, pp. 177–86.

Toury, Gideon, *In Search of a Theory of Translation*, Tel Aviv, Porter Institute, 1980.

Toury, Gideon, *Descriptive Translation Studies and Beyond*, Amsterdam and Philadelphia, John Benjamins, 1995.

Tylor, Edward, *Primitive Culture: Researches into the Development of Mythology, Philosophy, Religion, Language, Art and Customs*, London, 1871.

Urbain, Jean-Didier, *L'idiot du voyage: Histoires de touristes*, Paris, Payot, 1993.

Urbain, Jean-Didier, *Sur la plage: Moeurs et coutumes balnéaires*, Paris, Payot, 1994.

Urry, John, *The Tourist Gaze: Leisure and Travel in Contemporary Societies*, London, Sage, 1990.

Venuti, Lawrence, ed., *Rethinking Translation: Discourse, Subjectivity, Ideology*, London, Routledge, 1992.

Venuti, Lawrence, *The Translator's Invisibility: A History of Translation*, London, Routledge, 1995.

Venuti, Lawrence, *The Scandals of Translation: Towards an Ethics of Difference*, London, Routledge, 1998.

Virilio, Paul, *Vitesse et politique; essai de dromologie*, Paris, Galilée, 1977.

Virilio, Paul, 'The Last Vehicle', Jeremy Millar and Michiel Schwarz, eds., *Speed – Visions of an Accelerated Age*, London, Whitechapel Art Gallery, 1998, pp. 32–48.

von Flotow, Luise, *Translation and Gender: Translating in the 'Era of Feminism'*, Manchester, St Jerome, 1997.

von Flotow, Luise, 'Dis-unity and Diversity: Feminist Approaches to Translation Studies', Lynne Bowker, Michael Cronin, Dorothy Kenny and Jennifer Pearson, eds., *Unity in Diversity? Current Trends in Translation Studies*, Manchester, St Jerome, 1998, pp. 3–13.

Weinberg, Steve G., 'Get Ready for Web Objects', *Wired*, February 1996, pp. 52–5.

Wilde, Oscar, 'The Decay of Lying', *De Profundis and Other Writings*, Harmondsworth, Penguin, 1977.

Wilden, Anthony, *System and Structure: Essays in Communication and Exchange*, London, Tavistock, 2nd. ed., 1980.

Wilson, Barbara, *Gaudí Afternoon*, Seattle, Seal Press, 1990.

Wittgenstein, Ludwig, *Tractatus Logico-Philosophicus*, London, Routledge & Kegan Paul, 1974.

Wolf, Eric, *Anthropology*, New York, Norton, 1964.

Wolff, J., 'The Invisible Flâneuse: Women and the Literature of Modernity', *Theory, Culture and Society*, vol. 2, 1985, pp. 37–46.

Wurm, Stephen A., *Atlas of the World's Languages in Danger of Disappearing*, Paris, Unesco Publishing/Pacific Linguistics, 1996.

Yaguello, Marina, *Les fous du langage: des langues imaginaires et de leurs inventeurs*, Paris, Seuil, 1984.

INDEX

accent, 2, 11–14, 18, 28, 34, 36, 46–8, 164–5n
  in *Star Trek*, 131
Adams, Douglas
  Hitch-Hiker's Guide to the Galaxy, 129, 131
Ahmad, Shir, 46
Aijmer, Göran, 74–5
analog mode of translator/traveller, 106–7
Anderson, R. Bruce W., 73
anthropology, 33, 102–4, 124
Ara, Angelo, 96
Argentieri, Simona, 11, 20–1, 37, 43, 61
Artaud, Antonin, 102
Assmann, Aleida, 132
au-pairs and language, 144–5
auto-translation, 146–7
  see also machine translation; science fiction
Ayatollah Montazeri, 74

'Babel fish', 129, 131
Babel myth, 84, 120–1, 132
  signifying breakdown of communication, 89–90
  signifying expulsion from originary state, 120
Baedecker, Karl, 85–6
Baker, Mona, 143
Bakhtin, Mikhail, 35, 120

barbarism, 69
Barlow, John Perry, 151–2
Bateson, Gregory, 100
Batteux, Charles
  Principes de littérature, 110
Baudelaire, Charles, 63
Baudrillard, Jean, 116
  Cool Memories, 106–7
Bauman, Zygmunt, 79–80
Beer, Gillian, 72, 84
Benveniste, Émile, 37–8
Berwanger, Nikolaus, 43
bilingualism, 27, 75, 118–19, 123–4
Bly, Robert, 66
Boland, Rosita, 17, 18, 19, 21, 23, 36
  Sea Legs, 16, 19, 33
Borer, Alain, 152
Bouvier, Nicolas, 40, 52, 54, 57–8, 60, 66–7, 78, 79, 82, 93, 133, 150
Braidotti, Rosa, 105
  Nomadic Subjects, 104–5, 133
Bridges, Thomas, 55
Brodsky, Joseph
  'A Place as Good as Any', 70
Bruckner, Pascal
  Le Vertige de Babel, 136
Bryson, Bill, 14, 15, 18, 19, 21, 33–5, 36, 84, 149
  Notes from a Small Island, 12, 19, 20, 22, 25, 27, 31–2

Burgess, Anthony, 22
Burgundio of Pisa, 98
Buzard, James, 102
  The Beaten Track, 86
Byron, Robert, 41, 42, 45, 53, 54
  The Road to Oxiana, 40, 46, 51, 55, 56, 59, 65

Caeserae's *Chronicle*, 98
Campbell, Joseph, 56
Canestri, Jorge, 11, 20–1, 37, 43, 61
capitalism, 109, 115–16, 182n
Caplan, Karen, 109, 116–17, 134
  Questions of Travel, 106–7
Carroll, Raymonde
  Évidences invisibles, 77
Carse, James, 140
Chatwin, Bruce, 35, 54, 105
  In Patagonia, 40, 41, 51, 55
Clarke, Arthur C.
  and Lee, *Rama Revealed*, 127–8, 129
Clifford, James, 4, 146–7
  Routes, 18, 33, 102–4, 125, 137, 138
  Translation and Fieldwork in the Twentieth Century
Cohen, Colleen B., 135
comedy in language *see* language; mistranslation
Computer-Aided Translation (CAT), 112
  see also machine translation
conference interpreters, 114–15
contact zones, 18, 19, 21
Cook, Thomas and John, 121
'Cook's Tour' of language, 19
Craik, Jennifer, 118
Crang, Philip, 123
Crashaw, Carol, 85
Crowley, Tony
  Language in History, 120
Crystal, David, 118, 123, 131
  English as a Global Language, 113
Culler, Jonathan, 83
cultural difference, 24–6, 40–3, 49, 87–92, 96–7, 126, 145, 157
  effect of translation on, 66

culture and language, 44–7, 52–3, 145–6
cybertravel *see* information technology

Daily Express, 9
Dante's *Divine Comedy*, 110
Darwin, Charles, 55
David-Neel, Alexandra, 46
  Voyage d'une parisienne à Lhassa, 52–3, 80
de Caminha, Pedro Vaz, 70–1, 72
de Certeau, Michel, 139
de Condillac, Étienne Bonnot
  Essai sur l'origine des connaissances humaines, 71
Delaney, Samuel
  Babel-17, 127, 128–9, 130
Delisle, Jean, 143
de Maistre, Xavier, 152
  Voyage autour de ma chambre, 151
Denby, David, 71
Derrida, Jacques, 38, 47
  Le monolinguisme de l'autre, 35
Descartes, René
  Discours de la méthode, 99–100
Dickens, Charles, 24
dictionaries and manuals, 52
Diderot, Denis
  Le Neveu de Rameau, 71
Dimendberg, Edward, 115
Disney World, 121
'displacement' theory, 22, 118
drogman in oriental literature, 85
D'Souza, Dinesh
  The End of Racism, 28, 89
Dunne, Joseph, 92

Edwards, John, 101, 118–19, 123, 146
English language
  in Ireland, 120, 148
  sublanguages of, 2–3, 137
  used in travel industry, 122–3
  as a world language, 5, 28, 49, 50, 85, 89, 111–12, 113, 118, 119–20, 145
Eskimo languages and 'snow', 145–6
esperantosamizdat, 43

estrangement strategies, 16, 17, 26, 31
Eurospeak, 99, 111
exoticism, 3, 9, 11–12, 14–16, 31, 41–3,
    90–1, 107, 157

Fabian, Johannes, 27
'fast castes', 114–16
Featherstone, Mike, 84
feminist analysis, 134–5
Fenton, James, 71, 76
flâneur/flâneuse as translator, 6, 141–5,
    156
Foucault, Michel, 81–2
fractal geometry, 17
    see also travel
Freud, Sigmund, 142
Friel, Brian
    Translations, 28, 60
Fully Automatic High-Quality Transla-
    tion, 113
Furet, François
    Le passé d'une illusion, 89
Fussell, Paul, 17, 52, 102
    Abroad, 97

Gell-Man, Murray, 149
gender
    and the flâneur, 144
    and vocational choice, 60–1
Gentzler, Edwin, 66, 134
George, Susan, 114
Gibbons, John, 9, 23, 25, 36
Gilroy, Paul, 137
Gleick, James, 16
globalisation, 1, 3, 5, 50, 84, 85, 89, 91,
    109, 111, 113, 117, 119–20, 121,
    151
Goethe, 132
Grand Tour, 118, 125
Graves, Charles, 18, 26, 36
    Ireland Revisited, 14–15
Grewal, Inderpal, 109
guide books, 4, 85–7
    in science fiction, 130
Guillain, Robert, 88

Guillebaud, Jean-Claude, 74
    Un voyage en Océanie, 133
Guillen, Michael
    Five Equations that Changed the World,
    84

Haddad, Antonietta and Gérard
    Freud en Italie, 101
Hall, Stuart, 109, 119–20
Handy, Charles, 148
Hanson, Susan, 123
Hartsock, Nancy, 135
Heaney, Seamus, 120
    Station Island, 64
Heidegger, Martin, 81, 116
Herder, Johann, 10
heteronymous translation, 146–7
Hitler, Adolf, 6
Hockett, Charles, 22
Hoffman, Eva, 73, 74, 76
    Exit into History, 68–9, 70, 74, 78, 86–7,
    88, 93, 96, 124
    Lost in Translation, 30, 45, 48, 60
Homel, David, 117
hospitality industry, 51–2
Huysmans, Joris-Karl
    À rebours, 151

identity, 80–1, 100
    cultural identity, 22, 29–32, 58, 80
    and resistance, 94–7
    of the student, 126
    and language, 16, 47, 61–2
    and names, 30–32
    see also polyidentity
idiom, 59
immigrants, 13, 32
    fear of assimilation, 124
    and language learning, 44
imperialism, 21, 30, 32, 107
infantilisation in language learning,
    43–4, 69–70, 71–2
information technology (IT), 111–14,
    117, 150–6
    cybertravel, 5, 153–6

Internet, 133, 151–2, 155
Multiple-User Domains, 153, 154
instantaneous transparency, 112–14
interlingual translation, 2, 3, 4, 10–11,
    17–18, 29–30, 32, 45–6, 58, 65
Internet *see* information technology
interpreters, 3–4, 72–6, 85, 146–7
conference, 114–15
'informants', 54
and virtual travel, 155–6
intersemiotic translation, 2, 4, 58, 70,
    87, 89
intertextuality, 50–2
intralingual translation, 2–3, 4, 13, 16,
    17–19, 20, 26, 29, 31, 32, 33, 35, 37, 58
Irish language, 95
revival movement, 120
Irish theme pubs, 155
Iyer, Pico, 155

Jakobson, Roman, 2, 4
James, Henry
Italian Hours, 45
James, Jamie, 149
Jokinen, Eeva, 144
Jolas, Eugène, 98
Joyce, James, 58, 98, 120

Kaplan, Alice
French Lessons, 61
Kapor, Mitch, 151–2
Kellner, Douglas, 107
Kenny, Dorothy, 164, 172, 174, 177, 182,
    185, 187, 188, 190
Keohane, Robert O., 147
Kerridge, Roy, 14, 18, 36
Jaunting through Ireland, 13, 27
kinetic resistance in translation, 116–17
Koestler, Arthur, 140
Kondo, Dorinne, 124
Kristeva, Julia, 47, 78

Lacarrière, Jacques, 62, 64, 133, 150
Ladmiral, Jean-René, 108
Lamy, Laurent, 95

language
comedy in, 11, 31, 32, 45–7, 51–2
and culture, 44–7, 52–3, 145–6
culture-specific items, 40–3
fragmented origin of, 28, 120–1
and humanity, 14
and identity, 16, 47–8
and immigration, 13, 32
and nationalism, 10, 49, 58–9, 103
and nationality, 48–50
plurality of, 6, 16
purism, 34–5
see also sublanguages
language difference, 15–16, 58, 157
and immigration, 13
resistance of, 123
language learning, 11, 35, 50, 52–5
adult resistance to, 43–4
dwelling-in-travelling, 125–6
infantilisation in, 43–4, 69–70, 71–2
kinetic resistance, 116–17
modern language departments, 125–6
and risk, 123–4
of translators, 65
Lash, Scott, 121, 150
Leader, Darian, 61–2
Le Bris, Michel, 106
Lee, Gentry, 127–8, 129
Leerssen, Joep
Mere Irish and Fíor-Ghael, 90
Lepenies, Wolf, 25
Lévinas, Emmanuel, 37, 117
Liska, Allan, 121–3

MacCannell, Dean, 94, 122
machine translation, 5, 113–14, 155
see also auto-translation; science fiction
McKinsey (consulting firm), 150
Macpherson, James, 108
Maffesoli, Michel, 135–6, 137–8
Magris, Claudio, 67, 92, 94, 96
Danubio, 43, 49
Makine, Andreï
Le testament français, 99
Mallarmé, Stéphane, 59, 64

Mandelbrot, Benoît, 16–17
Mangan, James Clarence, 108
Manguel, Alberto, 66–7
Mann, Thomas
  Death in Venice, 124
Marshall, Joyce, 117
Marx, Karl
  Grundrisse, 115
Mascia-Lees, Frances E., 135
mathematics as language, 84–5
Maxwell, James Clerk
  Theory of Heat, 111
Mehler, Jacqueline Amati, 11, 20–1, 37,
  43, 61
Mendelssohn, Moses, 134
menu writing, 20
metaphors, 139–41, 164n, 181n
Mills, Sara, 62, 102
  Discourses of Difference, 82
mime *see* sign-language
minority languages, 4, 26–8, 46, 89, 123
  linguistic survival of, 118–21
  and non-mother-tongue translation,
    136–7
  and transaction costs, 147–8
  and translation resistance, 95–7
mistranslation and comedy, 2, 45–6,
  51–2
Mitchell, William J., 153, 154, 155
  City of Bits, 151
money and the teleological chain, 138–9
monoglossia, 10, 14, 28, 120
  Visa vision of, 111–2
monolingualism, 26, 35, 119
Montalbetti, Christine
  Le Voyage, le monde et la bibliothèque, 139
Morin, Edgar, 18
Morris, Jan, 36
Mossop, Brian, 82–3
Mulrennan, John Alphonsus, 120
Multiple-User Domains *see* information
  technology
Murphy, Dervla, 70, 80, 94
  Muddling through in Madagascar, 40,
    49, 51–2, 54, 68, 77, 78

On the Ukimwi Road, 69, 75–6, 86, 87–8,
  91
Murray, John, 86
music as communication, 79, 170n
Musser, Charles, 83

Nabokov, Vladimir, 109
Naipaul, V.S., 32, 72–4
names, 28–32
  and cultural difference, 31–2
  naming and renaming, 29–32
nationalism
  cultural, 145
  and language, 10, 49, 58–9, 103, 148
  in Wales, 27
Newby, Eric, 36, 37
  Round Ireland in Low Gear, 26–7, 31
Ní Mhaoileoin, Úna, 45, 46, 48, 49, 51,
  54, 55, 58–9, 95
nomadism, 2, 4, 6, 36, 96, 98, 104–6,
  110, 124–6, 137–8
  and embodied translator, 134–5
non-verbal sign systems, 2
Nossack, Hans Erich, 90–1, 93
Nussbaum, Martha, 63

O'Brien, Flann
  The Poor Mouth, 89–90
O'Brien, Kate
  Farewell Spain, 56, 62
  My Ireland, 56, 83
O'Brien, Sharon, 112
'octospider' language, 127–30, 133
O'Faoláin, Sean, 36
O'Hanlon, Redmond, 71, 76, 77
O'Neill, Hugh, 146–7
Ong, Walter J., 24
oral tradition, 22–4
  see also storytellers
originary texts, 100–1
Ó Rinn, Liam, 39, 48, 54
Ó Searcaigh, Cathal, 29
Ossianic forgeries, 108
Ouaknin, Marc-Alain, 117
  Bibliothérapie, 102

Park, Mungo, 81
Pentecost, 131–2
Peres, Maruch Komes
  and Rus, *Ta Jlok'ta Chobtik Ta K'u'il*, 103
Phillips, Adam, 56–7, 80
  The Beast in the Nursery, 141–3
placenames, 28–9, 31–2, 60
Plato
  The Symposium, 78
pocket translators, 50
polyidentity, 18–19, 26
Pound, Nigel, 9
Pratt, Geraldine, 123
Pratt, Mary Louise, 18, 77, 82, 102
  Imperial Eyes, 81
proactive translation, 107
proper nouns, 28–32
psychology learning compared to trans-
    lation learning, 141–3
Pullum, Geoffrey, 145–6
Pym, Anthony, 134, 135, 141, 147

Raban, Jonathan, 19–20, 21, 23, 36,
    43–4, 53
  Coasting, 16, 33
  Hunting Mister Heartbreak, 12, 13, 15,
    19, 22, 26, 29–30, 33
  Old Glory, 12, 18, 20
racism, 107
  of Irish language movement, 120
'rambling houses', 23–4, 65
Reagan, Ronald, 12, 23
reciprocity and translation, 146–7,
    182n
resistance to translation, 94–6
  kinetic, 116–17
Return of the Jedi, 128
Rey, Jean-Michel, 102
Ricoeur, Paul, 91–2, 96
Ritzer, George
  and Liska, *The McDonaldization of
    Society*, 121
Robinson, Douglas, 102
Robinson, Tim
  Labyrinth, 17

Rojek, Chris
  and Urry, *Touring Cultures*, 21–2, 79, 138
Roosevelt, Theodore, 13
Rose, Gillian, 89
Rosler, Martha, 115
Rousseau, Jean-Jacques
  Essai sur l'origine des langues, 71
*Routledge Encyclopedia of Translation
    Studies*, 102
Rus, Diane L., 103

Sabin, Margaret, 36
Sachs, Wolfgang, 112, 115
Sahlin, Marshall
  Islands of History, 72
Said, Edward, 104
St Aubin de Terán, Lisa, 52, 53, 59, 60
  Off the Rails, 44, 45, 54, 58, 86
St John Chrysostom's *Homilies on the
    Gospel of John*, 98
St Jerome, 98
Sapir-Whorf hypothesis, 145–6
Schäler, Reinhard, 113–14
Schutz, H., 44–5
science fiction, 5, 129–33
  automatic translation in, 129–30, 131,
    132
  semiotics of, 82–3
  translation themes, 127–31
  travel guides in, 130
semiotics
  of science fiction, 82–3
  and tourism, 83
Semprun, Jorge, 48
  Adieu, vive clarté, 46–7
Sennett, Richard, 156
Serres, Michel, 117
  Le Tiers-Instruit, 148
Sewell, Frank, 29
Shakespeare, William
  Henry V, 131
Sharpe, Patricia, 135
Sibony, Daniel, 11, 26, 47, 119
  Entre-Deux, 100, 116
sign-language, 68, 70–2, 76

Simeoni, Daniel, 151
  'Translating and Studying Translation',
    99
Simmel, Georg, 16, 21, 109–10, 138–9, 154
Simon, Sherry, 117
simultaneous translation, 115
Singh, Rajendra, 99
Slater, Eamonn, 81, 84, 141
Sloterdijk, Peter, 113
Smith, Miles, 69
Sontag, Susan, 82
sourcier/cibliste controversy, 107
Spenser, Edmund, 32
  A View of the Present State of Ireland, 30
Stallybrass, Peter, 77
Star Trek, 129, 131
Star Wars, 128
Steiner, George, 108
  'The Exact Art', 29
  Real Presences, 64
  'The Retreat from the Word', 84, 85
  'Two Suppers', 78
Stendhal, 93
Stengel, Erwing, 43
stereotyping, 4, 58–9, 88, 107
  of tourists, 44
Stierle, Karlheinz, 139
Stoker, Bram
  Dracula, 1, 7
Stone, Allucquère Roseanne, 153
storytellers, 23–4, 65
sublanguages, 2–3, 19–20, 137
Süskind, Patrick
  Perfume, 79
Sykes, Christopher, 54
Systran system, 114

tachocracy, 113–14
Tannen, Deborah, 61
territorialism, 6, 135–8
Theroux, Paul, 15, 16, 18, 19, 21, 32, 33,
    36, 37
  The Kingdom by the Sea, 10, 12, 14, 17,
    22, 23, 25–6, 27–8, 34
  linguistic displacement, 22

Thieme, John, 32
'third' culture and translation, 148–50
Thoreau, Henry David, 57
Todorov, Tzvetan, 65–6
tourism, 1, 3, 5, 6, 9–10, 17, 19, 21–2,
    43, 44, 80, 81, 82, 84, 117–18, 152
  the 'anti-tourist', 36, 52
  in Kenya, 69, 82
  language and, 122–3
  McDisneyisation of, 121–3
  as semiotics, 83
  staged authenticity, 94
  see also guide books; travel
trader, translator as, 109–12
transaction costs and translation, 147–8
transcendence and travel writing, 63–5,
    88
  linguistic, 88–9
  semiotic, 89
translatability, 26, 29, 55, 84
  and accent, 13–14
  culture-specific items, 40–3
  and lexical exoticism, 14–16
  and names, 31
  of prestigious literary texts, 95, 100
translation
  and anonymity, 103
  as betrayal, 101
  as cure, 102
  diaspora, 137
  discretion in, 66–7
  fidelity of, 38
  as forgery, 108–9
  see also interpreters
Translation Service, 114
translation studies, 104–9, 150
  compared to learning psychology,
    141–3
  'hinting', 144
transport, 121
travel
  and age, 80–1
  displacement, 65–6, 87, 100
  film as, 83
  food, 77–8, 80, 81

fractal, 16–19, 26, 37, 88
horizontal, 19, 54, 88
loneliness of, 54–5, 68–9
and modernity, 1, 4, 5, 27
risks associated with, 80–1
role of language in, 1–2, 21–3
sensory experience, 70, 76–81, 87, 154–5
visual, 81–5
vertical, 19, 88, 161n
see also guide books; tourism
travel writing, 2, 68–9, 133–4
and accent, 12–14, 18
construction of national cultures, 22–3
and disguise, 52–3, 153–4
epistemic, 37
and fantasy, 39–40, 87, 108
and hospitality, 37–8, 78
and language, 9–11, 14–16
and language acquisition, 52–3, 76
metaphor in, 139–41
ocular, 37
orality in, 24
Renaissance, 40
sense of 'home', 32–5
third culture, 149–50
and translation, 17–21, 36–8, 41–3, 54–9, 92–4
triangulation in, 59–60
women travellers, 60–2
see also interpreters
travel industry *see* tourism
triangulation
in translation, 59–60, 89
travel writing, 59–60
Tupi Indians, 71
Twain, Mark, 36
Tylor, Edward
Primitive Culture, 14

Uganda, 87–8
UNESCO *Atlas of the World's Languages in Danger of Disappearing*, 118
United Nations, 84
universalism, 4, 89–92, 95, 97, 132
Urbain, Jean-Didier, 102
Urry, John, 9, 82, 102, 121, 150
and Rojek, *Touring Cultures*, 21–2, 79, 85, 138
The Tourist Gaze, 81
US National Air Intelligence Center (NAIC), 114

Veijola, Soile, 144
Vernet, Thierry, 54, 79, 82
viatorial drive, 101–6
Virilio, Paul, 114, 152
visual imagery, 81–5
film, 83
photography, 82
von Schlegel, August Wilhelm, 110

Weinberg, Steve G., 155
White, Allon, 77
White, Kenneth, 157
Wilde, Oscar
'The Decay of Lying', 108
Wilson, Barbara
Gaudí Afternoon, 6–7
Winnicott, D.W., 142, 143
Wittgenstein, Ludwig
Tractatus, 123
Wolf, Eric, 103–4
women
as dweller-in-travelling, 144–5
translators, 60–2
as embodied subjects, 134–5
travel writers, 60–2

Yaghan language, 55
Yámana people, 55